Theorising Transnational Migration

Routledge Research in Transnationalism

1 **New Transnational Social Spaces**
International Migration and
Transnational Companies in the
Early 21st Century
Edited by Ludger Pries

2 **Transnational Muslim Politics**
Reimagining the Umma
Peter G. Mandaville

3 **New Approaches to Migration?**
Transnational Communities and
the Transformation of Home
*Edited by Nadje Al-Ali
and Khalid Koser*

4 **Work and Migration**
Life and Livelihoods in a
Globalizing World
*Edited by Ninna Nyberg Sorensen
and Karen Fog Olwig*

5 **Communities across Borders**
New Immigrants and
Transnational Cultures
*Edited by Paul Kennedy
and Victor Roudometof*

6 **Transnational Spaces**
*Edited by Peter Jackson,
Phil Crang and Claire Dwyer*

7 **The Media of Diaspora**
Edited by Karim H. Karim

8 **Transnational Politics**
Turks and Kurds in Germany
Eva Østergaard-Nielsen

9 **Culture and Economy in the
Indian Diaspora**
*Edited by Bhikhu Parekh,
Gurharpal Singh and Steven Vertovec*

10 **International Migration and
the Globalization of Domestic
Politics**
Edited by Rey Koslowski

11 **Gender in Transnationalism**
Home, Longing and Belonging
among Moroccan Migrant Women
Ruba Salih

12 **State/Nation/Transnation**
Perspectives on Transnationalism
in the Asia-Pacific
*Edited by Brenda S. A. Yeoh
and Katie Willis*

13 **Transnational Activism in Asia**
Problems of Power and
Democracy
*Edited by Nicola Piper
and Anders Uhlin*

14 **Diaspora, Identity and Religion**
New Directions in Theory and
Research
*Edited by Waltraud Kokot,
Khachig Tölölyan
and Carolin Alfonso*

15 **Cross-Border Governance in the
European Union**
*Edited by Olivier Thomas
Kramsch and Barbara Hooper*

16 **Transnational Connections and the Arab Gulf**
Edited by Madawi Al-Rasheed

17 **Central Asia and the Caucasus**
Transnationalism and Diaspora
Edited by Touraj Atabaki and Sanjyot Mehendale

18 **International Migration and Security**
Opportunities and Challenges
Edited by Elspeth Guild and Joanne van Selm

19 **Transnational European Union**
Towards a Common Political Space
Edited by Wolfram Kaiser with Peter Starie

20 **Geopolitics of European Union Enlargement**
The Fortress Empire
Edited by Warwick Armstrong and James Anderson

21 **Rethinking Transnationalism**
The Meso-link of Organisations
Edited by Ludger Pries

22 **Theorising Transnational Migration**
The Status Paradox of Migration
Boris Nieswand

Theorising Transnational Migration
The Status Paradox of Migration

Boris Nieswand

NEW YORK   LONDON

First published 2011
by Routledge
711 Third Avenue, New York, NY 10017

Simultaneously published in the UK
by Routledge
2 Park Square, Milton Park, Abingdon, Oxon OX14 4RN

*Routledge is an imprint of the Taylor & Francis Group,
an informa business*

© 2011 Boris Nieswand

The right of Boris Nieswand to be identified as author of this work has been asserted in accordance with sections 77 and 78 of the Copyright, Designs and Patents Act 1988.

Typeset in Sabon by IBT Global.

All rights reserved. No part of this book may be reprinted or reproduced or utilised in any form or by any electronic, mechanical, or other means, now known or hereafter invented, including photocopying and recording, or in any information storage or retrieval system, without permission in writing from the publishers.

Trademark Notice: Product or corporate names may be trademarks or registered trademarks, and are used only for identification and explanation without intent to infringe.

Library of Congress Cataloging-in-Publication Data
Nieswand, Boris.
  Theorising transnational migration : the status paradox of migration / by Boris Nieswand.
    p. cm. — (Routledge research in transnationalism ; 22)
  Includes bibliographical references and index.
  1. Immigrants—Cultural assimilation. 2. Immigrants—Social conditions. 3. Transnationalism. 4. Emigration and immigration—Social aspects. I. Title.
  JV6342.N54 2011
  304.8—dc22
  2010053378

ISBN13: 978-0-415-58455-5 (hbk)
ISBN13: 978-0-203-81043-9 (ebk)

Contents

List of Figures, Tables and Maps   ix
Acknowledgments   xi

Introduction   1

1   Migration and Society   14

2   Ghana and its Migrants   37

3   Processes of Localisation   68

4   Processes of Transnationalisation   95

5   The Status Paradox of Migration   124

Conclusion   151

Notes   167
References   175
Index   195

Figures, Tables and Maps

FIGURES

3.1	Ghanaians in Germany (1967–2008).	69
3.2	Ghanaians in Berlin (1973–2008).	74
3.3	Ghanaians in Berlin by age group, 1982 and 2008.	76
4.1	Kinship diagram Family 1 *Kojo Yeboah*.	107
4.2	Kinship diagram Family 2 *Yaw Asare*.	111
4.3	Kinship diagram Family 3 *Afua Konadu*.	114

TABLES

2.1	Ghanaians in Western Europe (2008)	54
2.2	Persons by Place of Residence	59
2.3	Receiving Countries in Europe	62
2.4	Educational Status of Transcontinental Migrants	64
3.1	Cities with Large Ghanaian Populations in Germany (2008)	72

MAPS

2.1	Research region in Ghana	56

Acknowledgments

First, I would like to express my special gratitude to Günther Schlee, who had the initial project idea and supervised the Ph.D. thesis out of which this book has developed. The department of *Integration and Conflict* at the Max Planck Institute for Social Anthropology in Halle provided a vibrant intellectual environment for my work. Moreover, I would like to thank Nina Glick Schiller, Stephen Reyna, Steven Vertovec, Richard Rottenburg, Dereje Feyissa, Jörn Eichler, Andrea Riester, Olaf Zenker, Markus Höhne, Christiane Falge and Heike Drotbohm for their intellectual contributions, their help and their encouragement. Without them and their inspiration this book would not be the same. Moreover, I feel deeply indebted to the generosity and kindness of my Ghanaian informants and friends, who gave me insight into their lives and helped me to conduct my research in Ghana and Germany. Among many who supported my work I would like to single out Isaac Appiah Kubi, Victor Boadum, Gideon Alabami Kayar and Stephen Kofi Owusu, who contributed most substantively to the success of this study.

Furthermore, I would like to acknowledge the institutions that have supported my doctoral thesis. First of all, I want to thank the Max Planck Society and the Max Planck Institute for Social Anthropology in Halle/Saale for their generous financial and logistical support of my research. In addition, I would like to thank the Graduate School Asia and Africa in World Reference Systems at the Martin Luther University Halle-Wittenberg for providing me with a six-month writing-up scholarship and the Max Planck Institute for the Study of Religious and Ethnic Diversity which supported me in reworking my Ph.D. thesis into a book. In this context, special thanks go to Astrid Finke, Jutta Turner, Christiane Kofri, Fanny Hocker, Birgitt Sippel and Diana Aurisch, who helped me edit the manuscript at different stages of the work.

And last but not least, I want to thank my daughter Judith and my family for helping me to keep one foot on the ground.

Introduction

Integration is a major political idiom in the discussion about migration and its consequences for Western Europe. Societal transformations like the 'ageing' of Western societies, the demand for qualified labour, migration-related ethnic and cultural diversification of national populations, growing internal inequalities, the crisis of multiculturalism and last but not least the imagined threat of Islamist terror attacks have initiated new political debates and policies on how migrants and minorities should be incorporated. In this context integration is first and foremost understood as a relationship of migrants with the receiving society and its institutions. The migrants' connections to their countries of origin or other cross-border relationships are rarely conceptualised as relevant aspects of migrants' integration into society.

In contrast to this dominant view of integration, transnational migration studies, which became a well-established field of research within the last one or two decades, have empirically shown that migrants' cross-border relationships are a self-evident element of many migrants' daily lives and that they are in themselves neither more nor less beneficial or threatening than other social activities. The problematic or exceptional character that is ascribed to them is not so much a result of their societal impact but rather reflects that they deviate from the presumption that people should have one clear focus in their lives, which should be located in one nation-state only.

Although migrants' pathways of *simultaneous incorporation* (Levitt and Glick Schiller 2004) into different nation-states are in many ways an everyday phenomenon, they long remained underresearched. According to some students of transnational migration this was related to the *methodological nationalism* (Wimmer and Glick Schiller 2002a; Beck 2008) of the social sciences. Methodological nationalism refers to the assumption, which became objectified in the form of research agendas and habitual academic perspectives on the social world, that nation-states are quasi-natural units of describing and theorising the social world.

Building on the conceptual work done by students of transnational migration, the study presented here aims to demonstrate the empirical and theoretical usefulness of an alternative paradigm which can be characterised as *methodological transnationalism* (Khagram and Levitt 2008; Nieswand 2008a). In this framework it is asked how migrants' different modes of inclusion, within and across national borders, interact with each other in relation to a social phenomenon under examination and a theoretical problem. The empirical and theoretical question at the centre of interest is to develop a methodologically transnationalist perspective on migrants' social status. In doing so, this study hopes to make an empirically grounded contribution to the understanding of social stratification and its representations in the context of the world society. If the concept of world society is used in the following it does not imply an imaginary of a homogenous and integrated whole or a political community as was typical for the imaginaries of national societies. Rather it is a label signifying a conceptual framework in which the interaction of multiple polities and social relations can be examined. The idea of world society insists on the point that society and polity have to be distinguished as units of analysis (Stichweh 2000) and that under the conditions of globalisation the former is *not* spatially limited in a *theoretical* sense, which self-evidently could be presumed, but only in a *practical* sense that should be empirically explored. In this sense, the notion of the world society, above all, is a conceptual reaction to the fact that technologically and politically induced transgressions of space as an *absolute* limitation of social spheres of communication challenge spatially defined notions of society (Luhmann 1987 [1984]). Although the scale of the world society itself will be the empirical unit of reference at only a few points, for instance with regard to the description of global social inequalities, it is nevertheless important as an underlying societal epistemology that guides the study. It will be more extensively argued in Chapter 1 that there is a close link between notions of society and the way migration is conceptualised. The theoretical reflections presented here shall in the first place contribute to explaining recent shifts in the perspective on migration-related phenomena and to developing a better understanding of the societal epistemology of migration studies.

THE STATUS PARADOX OF MIGRATION

Although transnational migration studies have documented many different forms of cross-border activities, until now there have been few empirically grounded efforts to theorise them in the framework of integration and status theory. This study aims to contribute to closing this gap. In the study's course the theorem of the *status paradox of migration* will be developed. It focuses on a situation that is characteristic for a larger class of labour migrants from the global south to the countries of the global north whose members are neither highly qualified according to the standards of the receiving country nor unskilled according to the standards of their countries of origin. This class of persons often migrates under difficult legal conditions; their qualifications are devalued in the destination countries and, as a result, they are forced to accept positions in the low-income segments of the labour market including the informal sector, although this does not fit the status to which they legitimately could aspire in their countries of origin with reference to their education, their family background and/or their professional experiences. Consequently, migration is often accompanied by the experience of loss of social status in the receiving areas. However, economic marginalisation, racialisation and subjection to an unfavourable legal situation in the destination countries are only parts of a larger picture. At the same time, many migrants actively strive for—and often are partially successful in achieving—social and economic inclusion in their country or region of origin. Global economic inequalities and improved facilities for communication and transfer of resources, such as cheap calls, bank transactions, flights and transport facilities for goods (Vertovec 2009), provide them with opportunities to build up symbolic representations of a middle class status in their countries of origin and, thereby, to overtake larger parts of the local population. In this sense, migrants gain status in the sending countries. The transnational dynamic of losing social status and gaining it at the same time, which occurs along with mutually conditioned forms of *status inconsistency*, is theorised as the status paradox of migration.

In particular the well-documented increase in migrant remittances between the immigration areas in the global north and the emigration areas in the global south (e.g. World Bank 2001; Munzele Maimbo and Ratha 2005; Vertovec 2009: 103–19) indicated that transnational forms of resource management are important for understanding migration-related globalisation processes. Several emigration countries, including such varied ones as the Philippines, Morocco, Haiti, Albania, Mexico and Ghana, became heavily economically dependent on migrants' remittances. The existing aggregations and analyses of the figures and, related to it, the considerations regarding to what extent remittances are beneficial for the development of the respective countries, were important to prove the significance of transnational relations. Nevertheless, they do not go very far in engaging with the sociocultural impact of these processes. Viewed through the lens of status theory it is obvious that although not all remittances directly affect local and national status arenas, many do so. Migrants' investments in houses, in local businesses, in consumer goods, in family rituals and status symbols are well observed by local populations in the emigration areas. Their social visibility has an impact on local ideas of how a good and satisfying life can be achieved and the respect of others can be earned. These sociocultural consequences of migrant remittances are much less examined than their economic dynamics.

To describe the focussed transnational status dynamics as a paradox, above all, has rhetorical reasons. As Luhmann (1993: 292–94) has pointed out, the notion of the paradox was used by classical Greek rhetoricians far

4 Theorising Transnational Migration

more than by logicians. The rhetoricians primarily considered it a linguistic form to create an 'irritation' of dominant self-evidence by speaking *against* (Greek: *para*) the *dominant opinion* (Greek: *doxa*). The self-evident knowledge which is 'irritated' by the concept of the status paradox of migration is the dominant sociological discourse on social status, based on the implicit presumption that persons normally have a more or less consistent overall status or class membership related to one national society (cf. Bourdieu 1979; Vester, von Oertzen, Geiling, Hermann and Müller 2001)—which is maintained even in cases in which globalisation is taken into account (Wallerstein 1975; Goldthorpe 2002). Beside the sociological literature on national status groups and classes, there exist numerous often ethnographic accounts of migrants' status-relevant activities in their respective countries or regions of origin (e.g. Mitchell 1959: 28; Diko and Tipple 1992; Twum-Baah, Nabila and Aryee 1995a: 221; Thomas 1998; Riccio 2001; Hahn 2004; Newell 2005; Nyamnjoh 2005). Although these practices contribute, according to the authors, to the migrants' social prestige in the locality of origin, they often are not set in relation to the migrants' status in the receiving areas.

The question of why migration-related paradoxes of social status are a mere side note in the context of migration studies is connected to academic traditions. While political science and sociological perspectives on social inequality have long been dominated by methodological nationalism (Beck 2008; Kreckel 2008), anthropologists who documented status-related migrants' activities did not feel responsible for theorising their observations in the framework of a broader status theory. In this sense, transnational forms of status production were not invisible but remained underrepresented and undertheorised because of institutional 'reception barriers' (Kreckel 2008: 30), which are engrained in the respective disciplinary traditions (Beck 2008: 22).

It was above all students of transnational migration who pointed to multiple and incongruent forms of social status among migrants. It was highlighted that resources earned in the country of residence were transferred to the country of origin in order to improve or consolidate the migrants' class position 'back home' (Basch, Glick Schiller and Szanton Blanc 1994: 279–80; Glick Schiller and Fouron 2001b). In this framework, the likelihood was highlighted that migrants occupy disparate class positions in both contexts (Goldring 1996: 76; Levitt and Glick Schiller 2004: 1015; Beck 2008: 32) and that this contradicts conventional conceptions of social class (Glick Schiller and Fouron 2001a: 152–53). Some authors underlined the compensatory psychological function of migrants' status-related activities during 'home visits' for the harsh working-class lives in the receiving areas (Elwert 1984: 67; Pries 1996: 463). Anja Weiß (2002, 2005, 2006) emphasised the significance of formal and informal regimes of convertibility of economic, social and cultural resources from one context to another for understanding the migration-related transnationalisation of social inequality. She argues that national borders do not inhibit transnational forms of status attainment but create specific configurations of opportunities and limitations by which these are shaped and filtered. In particular, the legal access to high-wage labour markets, mediated through the possibilities of legally entering a country and through the recognition of educational and professional qualifications, constitutes an important dimension of social inequality which divides citizens of rich and poor countries, on the one hand, and between more and less privileged classes within the countries of the global south, on the other.

From a historical perspective the migratory movements from the countries of the global south to the global north are linked to long-term processes of increasing differences in wealth and buying power between countries and world regions (Bronschier 2002) and of improving possibilities of communicating them even to formally peripheral regions of the globe.[1] In this context, some aspects, such as the efficiency of (anti-)migration policies or the disparities between rich and poor countries, document the power of nation-states to influence individuals' opportunities and life courses. At the same time, the way migrants circumvent legislations and border regimes and the way they manage their resources within and across national borders also demonstrate the limits of the nation-state's power in controlling mobility and its consequences.

In this sense, the migration of Africans to Western Europe is part and parcel of a 'globalisation from below' (Guarnizo and Smith 1998b; Schlee 2001b; Mohan and Zack-Williams 2002), which is not to be understood in opposition to economic globalisation 'from above' but as an intrinsic part of it. Historically, the increase in the migration from Africa to Europe is situated within a period of qualitative transition from the political post-World War II order—which was ideologically and politically shaped by the Cold War, postcolonialism and the hegemony of the nation-state—to a more complex situation in which the relations of power, ideology and socio-spatial organisation of society become reconfigured.

Following a methodologically transnationalist perspective, the case study connects different ends of the migrants' reality of simultaneous incorporation and puts them in relation to each other. Thereby the status paradox transcends simplistic representations of labour migrants as either fully self-determined entrepreneurs who strategically circumvent legal and economic obstacles to 'hedge their bets' (e.g. Elwert 2002), or as mere victims of anti-migration policies, racialisation and exploitation in the receiving countries (e.g. Bukow 1992). Furthermore, it overcomes dichotomised views of migrants as either integrated in the respective receiving society or being part of segregated island-like ethnic communities. The daily struggle of transnational migrants to make something good out of their situation in the sending as well as the receiving countries under difficult social conditions demonstrates the complexities of agency and determination in the context of transnational migration.

Since the empirical phenomena which constitute the status paradox might appear familiar to many migrants as well as to students of migration, the study might raise the question whether there is anything new about it in the first place. I argue in the following that the salience of some of the empirical phenomena which are theorised as a status paradox does not devalue this study but rather underlines its contribution to the field of migration studies. Observed with an adequate conceptual apparatus, more complicated and influential social processes appear behind a superficial banality of the phenomena. This is not only empirically insightful in the context of transnational migration studies but affects the general understanding of the link between integration, society and social status.

PROMISES OF EDUCATION AND IMAGINARIES OF MODERNITY

Nowadays, children learn at school in most places in the world that those among them who perform well will get a respectable and well-paid job in the future, which simultaneously contributes to the development of 'the nation' and the wellbeing of the individual (Meyer, Kamens and Benavot 1992). In this sense, formal education not only conveys a particular corpus of knowledge to young people but also changes their symbolic relationship to the social world. Having a better education than others is supposed to make a significant difference in the social positioning of a person, which in countries with a generally lower standard of education appears even more pronounced than it is in countries with a relatively high standard of education. The history of Ghana and other African countries shows that in cases in which general living conditions do not allow for the realisation of status aspirations that are encouraged by the attendance at educational institutions, the disappointment of these expectations might have profound societal effects. Obviously, the idea that education is the silver bullet to individual and societal progress cannot easily be adapted to deviating socio-economic conditions. One reason for its relative stability is the crucial importance to Western 'social imaginaries' of modernity (Taylor 2002), which have diffused along with other institutions of the modern nation-state to large parts of the globe in the course of the last centuries. Besides their promises of individual and collective prosperity, imaginaries of modernity also imply a utopia of statehood. They evoke hope that the world can be made a better place by the provision of schooling facilities, rational organisation of the state, an increase in white collar jobs, public infrastructure, public health care institutions and the redistribution of wealth by a fair welfare-state. The imaginaries of modernity and the attached narratives of societal progress thereby provide politically and scientifically authorised visions of a better future 'for the masses', which are even more vivid in these countries which obviously lack (some of) these 'benefits of modernity' than in those countries which are supposed to have achieved them. Despite a long tradition of critique of modernisation as an academic theory (e.g. Englund and Leach 2000; Stichweh 2000: 207–19), its persistence seems to be closely connected to a practical question: if the poor countries are not meant to 'develop', what alternative promises can they make to their citizens? In this sense, a rejection of the political project of modernisation includes an element of giving up hope that some states of the global south will be able to significantly improve the social, economic and political living conditions of their citizens (Ferguson 2001: 145).

In several parts of Africa, imaginaries of modernity implicate a bitter-ironical element of nostalgia. The (perhaps temporary) failures and difficulties of several nation-state projects of modernisation after independence left many of those who lived through the time of transition from the colonial to the postcolonial part of their histories with a memory of a past in which the door to modernity had been open but was then closed by later developments (cf. Ferguson 1999). As a consequence, in those parts of Africa where the state was not able to keep its promises of development, modernity often changed from being a vision for the future of a country to a geographical elsewhere.

For the case of Ghana I want to focus on the link between the expansion of formal education, imaginaries of modern status and transcontinental migration (cf. Chapter 5). It will be argued that in particular during the 1970s and 1980s experiences of status inconsistency played an important role among Ghanaians with some degree of formal education. It contributed to initiate, first, transnational and, later, transcontinental migration in larger numbers. Thereby migration became an attempt to achieve individually what was not delivered collectively.

AFRICA AND EUROPE

While African migrants to Europe had long been of relatively marginal academic interest, more recently a larger number of studies have emerged of several sub-Saharan African groups in different European countries. Among them are Zimbabwean (Pasura 2008) and Ghanaian migrants (Mohan 2006) in Great Britain; Eritreans (Schröder 1992; Conrad 2005), Sudanese (Weißköppel 2005b), Ghanaians and Cameroonians in Germany (Fleischer 2007); Ghanaians in the Netherlands (Ter Haar 1998b; Mazzucato 2006); Nigerians in Spain (Kastner 2010); Somali migrants in Europe (Schlee 2001a, 2004a; Kleist 2008); Sudanese and Somali migrants in Norway (Assal 2004); Ivorian (Newell 2005), Senegalese (Salzbrunn 2001), Malian (Timera 1997) and Congolese migrants (MacGaffey and Bazenguissa-Ganga 2000) in France; and Senegalese (Zinn 1994; Carter 1995 [1992], 1997; Riccio 2001; Grillo and Riccio 2004) and Ghanaian (Riccio 2008) migrants in Italy.[2]

The intensification of the attention that is paid to sub-Saharan Africans in Europe is connected to several factors, among them a general increase in their numbers since the late 1970s; a diversification of migration destinations of African migrants, now also including former emigration countries like Italy and Spain; an academic interest in globalisation and transnationalisation processes 'from below'; and a revived concern with the link between migration and development (Faist and Reisenauer 2009). Not least, the significance of African migration to Europe was demonstrated to a larger public by dramatic television images showing desperate Africans trying to illegally enter the European Union in small boats or—as in the case of the Spanish enclaves of Ceuta and Melilla—by climbing the fences to the European Union. Although these patchy media representations are only a small part of a much larger and more complex situation, they demonstrated to a European public that global social inequalities and south–north migration are issues of broader political concern. At the same time, their disturbing ambivalence between being requests for humanitarian support and solidarity, on the one hand, and being iconic visualisations of the imagined threats of undocumented migration, on the other hand, created a selective and distorted perception of migration from Africa to Europe. Although empirical research has increased, it still requires ethnographic studies that help to contextualise the fragments of existing information and to create a more adequate understanding of these processes. In this context, it is essential to engage with the history of migration in Africa (e.g. Manchuelle 1997). What is rarely referred to in the public representations of sub-Saharan African migration to Europe is the fact that recent forms of migration of Ghanaians, Senegalese, Malians, Congolese or Nigerians, to name only some of the more important groups, build on previous forms of labour migration that were first shaped by colonialism and, later, by the postcolonial nation-states. Although these interconnections are empirically complex and fragmented, the increase in and diversification of migration from Africa to Europe and America is a new chapter in the unequal and power-loaded history that has connected these three continents for centuries.

Ghana is an important example in the context of Africa because in its relatively young history it was often one step ahead of other countries on the continent. It was the first colony in sub-Saharan Africa to become independent in 1957; it was the first country south of the Sahara whose policy of state-induced development ended in a serious debt crisis; it was one of the countries which submitted to the structural adjustment programmes of the IMF (International Monetary Fund) earlier and more consistently than others; it more recently became an example for the success of liberalisation and democratisation policy in Africa; and, last but not least, Ghanaians were among the forerunners of the new type of labour migration from Africa to the global north, which is the focus of this study.

Of course, (more or less) voluntary migration of Gold Coasters[3] to Europe is not a new phenomenon but has been documented since the eighteenth century (Brentjes 1976; Jenkins 1985). However, the last emigration wave from Ghana, which started in the last quarter of the twentieth century, differs in terms of quality and quantity from earlier forms. Much more than the migration of a few students, businesspersons, sailors and soldiers from the colonial Gold Coast to Europe, it resembles—in respect to its extent, the migrants' motivations and its social effects—the labour migration within Africa during the first half of the twentieth century. Nevertheless, it is different in one important respect. Instead of being encouraged by the receiving areas, the increase in the number of Ghanaians in Western Europe took place despite a growing selectivity and rigidification of migration regimes which were meant to prevent (most) African and other migrants from the global south from entering and settling.[4] For many of them the risky illegal circumvention of the borders of the EU (European Union) countries has become the only possibility for entering the global north.

Due to its vicissitudinous past, Ghana is an instructive case for showing how historical changes affect patterns of migration. As the labour demand of the colonial economy could not be satisfied by local supply in the early twentieth century, the British colonial government took intense efforts, including force, to promote mobility among the population in the colonial Gold Coast. The undersupply of labour was not least related to the fact that the whole region of West Africa had demographically suffered under the consequences of the transatlantic slave trade for centuries. Subsequently, the south of Ghana became one of the major destinations for labour migrants from all over West Africa. Starting in the 1960s, Ghana gradually changed from a country of immigration to a country of emigration. Today, an estimated 5 to 15 per cent of the Ghanaian population live outside their country of birth and their remittances have become one of the major national sources of foreign exchange (IMF 2005: 7).

The migrants' social relationships to Ghana and the inflow of resources have initiated a far-reaching process of transnationalisation to which the Ghanaian political system also reacted. The last decade witnessed an incisive change in Ghanaian politics of inclusion. It became a politically dominant representation that migrants' remittances and their loyalty to the Ghanaian nation-state are a resource for the development of the country. This tendency became most explicit under the NPP (New Patriotic Party) government led by President J. A. Kufuor that was in power between 2001 and 2009 (Owusu 2003: 406). It introduced double citizenship in order to give Ghanaians the possibility to acquire the citizenship of the receiving country without losing their Ghanaian one. A Non-Resident Ghanaian Secretariat was established in 2003, which was to coordinate diaspora activities. In February 2006, the so-called Representation of the People Amendment Act was passed by the Ghanaian parliament granting Ghanaian citizens who live outside the country the right to vote.

By employing the concept of diaspora and creating state institutions for migrant inclusion, Ghana has adapted its discourse of national belonging to the conditions of mass migration. This process included an adjustment to the political definition of citizenship. While in the 1950s the government's central undertaking was to nationalise the ethnically diverse population living in the territory of Ghana, at the turn of the millennium it became important to maintain the loyalty and flows of resources within a population that is geographically dispersed but perceived as being connected by 'blood' and 'culture'. Beyond Ghana, this paradigm shift in the evaluation of migration and the understanding of citizenship can also be observed in different forms and degrees in several other African countries, including Senegal, Ethiopia, Eritrea, Sierra Leone, Cameroon and Nigeria (Nieswand 2011). However, the new diaspora policies not only affect institutions in Africa but also in the receiving countries. They create opportunities for Ghanaians and other Africans abroad to represent themselves as a group that acts as a benevolent patron for their compatriots 'at home' (Nieswand 2009).

Parallel to their increased political recognition, the transnational activities of Ghanaian migrants also became a focus of academic study. In this context, transnational migrants' remittances (Van Hear 2002; Kabki, Mazzucato and Appiah 2004; Mazzucato, van den Boom and Nsowah-Nuamah 2008), home visits, development activities of migrant associations (Mazzucato 2006; Sieveking, Fauser and Faist 2008; Nieswand 2009; Schmelz 2009), business investments (Black, King and Tiemiko 2003; Asiedu 2005; Decker 2005), political activism (Owusu 2003), house building in Ghana (Diko and Tipple 1992; Owusu 2003) and the funding and organisation of family rituals (Mazzucato, Kabki and Smith 2006) were documented. It was argued that these practices affect Ghanaian society in many ways.

Additionally in the case of Germany, a growing interest in smaller migrant groups like Africans can be noticed, which is related to the diversification of the migrant population in Germany since the 1980s (e.g. Dettmar 1989; Englert 1995; Lentz 2003; Weißköppel 2005b; Baraulina, Kreienbrink and Riester 2011). Specific studies on Ghanaian migrants in Germany are relatively rare and did not exist before the late 1980s. The existing ones cover diverse aspects like return migration (Haferkamp 1989; Roos 1996; Martin 2005), motivations and economic strategies of Ghanaian labour migrants (Loeffelholz von Collberg 1987), church foundation and transnational religious activities (Jach 2005) and development activities (Schmelz 2009).

Summarising the diverse literature for the purposes of this study, three broad, basic orientations toward Ghanaian and other African transcontinental migrants in Europe can be distinguished. One body of literature focuses on migrants' inclusion in the receiving area, another corpus predominantly describes transnational social activities of migrants and a third type of literature (Riccio 2001; Jach 2005; Glick Schiller, et al. 2005; Mazzucato 2007) connects both perspectives with each other and thereby points in the direction which this study aims to follow.

METHODS AND RESEARCH DESIGN

The study presented here cuts across classical disciplinary responsibilities of anthropology and sociology. Although it is in some respects transdisciplinary, with regard to the applied methodology and its self-reflexive elements, it has a particular anthropological character. The study aims to explore and to explicate partly self-evident sociocultural knowledge that underlies and frames the everyday life of transcontinental Ghanaian migrants. Characteristically for an anthropological study, the description of the often implicit webs of meaning in which the actors navigate becomes entangled with those of the scientific observers (Rottenburg 2001: 44). The reflection of the linkage between the content of the study and the analytical stance from which it is being observed is one of the threads that is pursued throughout the study.

Empirically, the study is based on 15 months of multi-sited ethnography (Marcus 1995) at different locations in Germany and Ghana between 2001 and 2007.[5] Factually, the tracing of social relationships and investigating them from different geographically separated but socially connected sites had a creative effect on the outcomes. The experience of the different ways migration was perceived and represented in Ghana and Germany, respectively, shifted my attention almost necessarily to the paradoxes and contradictions of transnational migration.

In the course of my field study, I applied a method mix that included participant observation, different types of interviewing, archive work, media analysis, genealogical methods and a micro-census on migration in a Ghanaian village. In the first phase of the research project, which lasted from June 2001 to September 2001, I established first contacts with Ghanaians in Germany and conducted explorative interviews and participant observations in different German cities. In the second phase, which lasted from October 2001 to December 2001, I continued the explorative research strategy in Accra and Kumasi in Ghana. In this phase, I also gathered information about general perceptions and assessments of migration in Ghana, the effects of German and European anti-immigration policies and how returnees experienced their situation. Afterwards, my networks from Ghana led me to Berlin, where the second largest Ghanaian population in Germany is located. From February to August 2002, I conducted fieldwork in Berlin, which included, among many other activities, extensive participant observation in churches, afro shops, bars and migrant organisations. Generally, informal interaction, for instance after church or in the back rooms of afro shops, was important for requiring a more intimate knowledge of different experiences of being a Ghanaian migrant in Germany. This was of particular importance because many Ghanaian migrants were—partly because of the experiences they had had with German state representatives—careful and suspicious of participating in a research project and exposing themselves to documentary methods, such as recorded interviewing.

Again, following personal networks from Berlin, I decided to go to Dormaa Ahenkro, a middle-scale town in Ghana's mid-west, where I stayed from July to October 2003. In particular, my stay in a house of an extended family out of which several persons had migrated to Europe and the social relations I could trace with their help gave me valuable and intimate insights into how family members in Ghana interact with their relatives abroad and how they perceive the situation.

In total, I classified 158 talks as interviews. They included 59 biographical, 39 issue-centred, mostly so-called expert interviews with representatives of institutions and 60 semi-standardised group interviews on kinship relationships and migration in a village in the Dormaa District of the Brong Ahafo Region. Many other informal talks and short interviews, in particular with informants whom I regularly met as well as observational data on social situations, were documented in the form of field notes.

The multi-sited ethnographic strategy which I applied in my research soon took me to the limits of my capacity to trace the interlocking and multilayered networks of which the migrants and their institutions were part (Weißköppel 2005a: 63). Therefore, practices of limiting the research focus to certain localities, persons, networks and institutions gained an increasing importance in the course of the research process. Thereby the ethnographic study of transnational migrants pushes the anthropological notion of 'the field' with its localist connotation beyond itself. The field is no longer a particular locality, although it includes several of them, but an intrinsically hybrid analytical horizon against which the empirical data becomes contextualised. At some points it becomes impossible to determine to what extent the field reflects meaningful forms of self-structuration of the examined people or is an artificial construct of an academic observer, respectively. However, the constructedness of 'the field' does not contradict its empirical reality. Only by engaging in the active and conscious processes of constructing and limiting the field of observation can researchers observe the empirical phenomena in which they are interested in the context of mobile populations (cf. Marcus 1995: 106). Without the factual existence of social networks to be traced, no localities to do research in would have been identified, and without making decisions as to where and what is to be observed, no observations would have been possible. In the dilemma of methodological rigidification, on the one hand, and explorative openness, on the other hand, the applied strategy of following networks and spending a longer period of time at a limited number of field sites accentuated the exploratory character of the study.

STRUCTURE OF THE BOOK

The book is divided into five chapters. In Chapter 1, it is argued that social scientific migration theories, implicitly or explicitly, presume a notion of society as a social unit across whose borders migration is considered as most relevant. Altogether, three pairs of concepts of society and methodological perspectives on migration are identified: the immigrant in the nation-state, the 'tribesman' in the city and the migrant in the world society. Against this theoretical background, *methodological transnationalism* is presented as the analytical framework applied in this study. Chapter 2 focuses on the historical changes in the patterns of migration to and from Ghana during the last century. Moreover, a case study on migration patterns from the Dormaa District in Ghana's Brong Ahafo Region is presented. In this context a particular accent is placed on the link between formal education and labour market opportunities. Chapter 3 examines the localisation processes of Ghanaians in Germany with special attention paid to the situation in Berlin. The focus will be on demographic processes, institution-building and configurations of identity. In Chapter 4, the corresponding process of transnationalisation of Ghanaian migrants' life-worlds is analysed. In this respect, global economic disparities will be described that create incentives for transfers of resources from high-wage and strong currency countries to low-wage and weak currency countries. These gains in buying power are an economic base of the relative status increase many migrants can achieve by transferring resources from the immigration country to the country of origin. In addition, social obligations and expectations of reciprocity within families are identified as an important factor that contributes to the relative temporal stability of transnational relationships. In this respect it is important to note that redistribution of resources among kin in Ghana, where state welfare institutions are only weakly developed, is crucial for securing the livelihoods of individuals. Transnational migrants remain included in a system of kin obligations and delayed reciprocity. They often bear, as relatively wealthy members of their families, a high responsibility that requires them to engage themselves transnationally on a regular basis. As an effect, these practices also contribute to an increase of the migrants' status as affluent patrons of their extended families.

In Chapter 5, the transnational status paradox of migration will be portrayed. First, the implicit foundation of modern imaginaries of education and social status will be examined theoretically and historically. Subsequently, it is argued that from the local perspective in Ghana transcontinental migration offered a way of overcoming experienced forms of status inconsistencies, which were caused by the predicaments of the Ghanaian nation-state. However, transcontinental migration did not solve the problem but often caused the status paradox of migration. The paradox's practical consequences are described using the ethnographical example of the Burger, an ideal type of labour migrant for whom the status paradox applies.

1 Migration and Society

Scientific approaches to migration in many cases include implicit assumptions about the character of a given society within which or across whose borders migration occurs. I will argue that the way the relationship between a society, its members and their culture is imagined has a significant impact on how migration is conceptualised, and vice versa. The connection between the employed notion of society and the theorisation of migration will be examined for a selection of sociological and anthropological approaches. Moreover, transnational migration studies, which are the paradigm this study feels affiliated with, will be contextualised within the broader field of migration studies in order to work out its specificity. The explication and the comparison of different methodological frameworks for the study of migration contribute to a clearer understanding and, perhaps, a relativisation of some of the antagonisms in the field of migration studies. This concerns in particular the relationship between the approaches which argue within the nation-state paradigm of society, and those which employ a world societal framework.

Niklas Luhmann in a encyclopedia article defined society as 'the most comprehensive system of human coexistence' (in Fuchs-Heinritz, et al. 1994: 235). Referring to the numerous controversies which have emerged about society's more specific qualities he added, 'There is no agreement on further qualifying characteristics'.[1] Luhmann's quotation reflects that the concept of society is an important background assumption which shapes social scientific research agendas rather than a clearly distinct object that could be empirically described or theoretically defined in a simple way.

However, despite these difficulties in defining and delimiting society, it appears complicated (if not impossible) to conceptualise social phenomena, in particular migration, without referring to society and affirming some implicit assumptions about its character. The importance of 'society' for migration studies is connected to the fact that social theory regards the members of a society as its constituting parts.[2] As migration changes the composition of 'the personnel' of a society, it also changes the society.

The nation-state had developed into the dominant political form of statehood during the late eighteenth and through the nineteenth centuries and consequently became the paradigmatic imaginary of society in the social sciences. Therefore, students of migration in Europe and North America normally examined the effects of migration on national societies.

In Africa the situation was different. Since most sub-Saharan African states became independent only after the late 1950s and the nation-state was and is in several regions not very strongly developed, it was much more the binary of modernity and tradition which influenced the study and representation of migration. In particular those migrants received academic attention who crossed the border between 'traditional society' and 'modern society'.

However, within both analytical frameworks, it was primarily intersocietal migration which was studied. In Western Europe and North America, intersocietal migration referred to citizens of one nation-state who had migrated to another. Consequently, the 'foreigner' became 'the prototype of the stranger'[3] (Hahn 1997: 155), and migration research became to a large extent 'foreigner research'. Since the major social differentiations in Africa were expected to separate 'modern' from 'traditional' societies, it was the migrant from the rural 'traditional societies' living and working in the enclaves of the 'modern society', such as the big cities and the centres of the export economy, who coined the dominant image of the stranger. In both cases society was methodologically conceptualised as a relatively unitary and integrated whole, in which the respective type of migrant—the 'foreigner in the nation-state' or 'the tribesman in the city'—appeared as an alien object, whose behaviour and relationship to the receiving society attracted academic attention.

As I will elaborate in more detail below, transnational migration studies and other approaches which have emerged within the globalisation discourse deviate from these notions of society and argue for less territorialised concepts of society. Giving up the clear methodological inside/outside differentiation, which had instructed the selection of paradigmatic cases of migrants in the two mentioned approaches, affects the general conceptualisation of migration and integration.

MIGRATION AND THE NATION-STATE

For several decades, in particular U.S. American migration studies were dominated by assimilationism. Its foundation as a scientific theory goes back to the sociologists of the Chicago School, who started to study immigrants in urban settings in the 1920s. Robert E. Park developed the so-called *race relation circle* in which he described successive stages of immigrants' social and cultural adjustment to the 'racial' groups of the receiving society (cf. Park and Burgess 1969 [1921]). The race relation circle aimed at a general social theory of cultural contact and ethnic relations beyond the more narrow focus of immigration to the United States (Park 1950).[4] The stages, which ethnic groups that encounter each other were expected to go through within the race relation circle, were social contact, competition, conflict, accommodation and, finally, assimilation (Park 1950 [1926]; Park and Burgess 1969 [1921]).

While accommodation referred to the establishment of peaceful intergroup relations, assimilation implied the adoption of the majority's collective memories and identities by the minority. The race relation circle was considered a slow and gradual process of which the migrants themselves were only partly aware. Whether the social and cultural adaptation was considered to be symmetric, i.e. affecting both groups, or asymmetric, i.e. primarily affecting the minority, was left open by Park and his colleagues (Park and Burgess 1969 [1921]: 360). Moreover, they did not indicate how probable a finalisation of the assimilation process was in their view. In his article *Our Racial Frontier on the Pacific*, Park (1950 [1926]: 151) spoke of a tendency towards assimilation. In a later writing (Park 1950 [1937]: 194), he stated that assimilation was one of three possible outcomes of the contact between racially distinct groups.[5]

Although assimilation was considered functional for enhancing the internal cohesion of a society, pressure exerted on the minority by the majority to adapt to the standards of the dominant 'race' was considered dysfunctional. It was expected to disturb the gradual and unconscious dynamic of assimilation (Park and Burgess 1969 [1921]: 364–65).

After Park, the rise of the theory of assimilation was corroborated by the U.S. American experience of immigration until the 1960s. According to the dominant representation of the U.S. migration history the country was depicted as a 'melting pot of nations'. In fact, many of the European migrants who came to the United States between the 1880s and the 1920s were assimilated to the American mainstream during the two World Wars, when home ties often had been cut and pressure had increased for siding with the 'new home country'. Moreover, political changes of the U.S. immigration regime led to a reduction of the influx of new immigrants who could reactivate transnational social ties (Alba and Nee 2003: 126–27).

In this framework, the assimilation approach aimed at examining and predicting the adaptation of immigrants to the mainstream of U.S. society. At the core of this view was the idea that the integration of a national society increased if its members were culturally and ethnically more or less homogeneous. Migrants, as members of another society, were perceived as 'foreign elements' whose behaviour could possibly affect the cohesion of the receiving society as a whole.

From the very beginning, the theory of assimilation had to deal with empirical counterevidence. Certain kinds of religious and racial differences, in particular those between white Anglo-Saxon Protestants (WASPs), Afro-Americans, Catholics and Jews remained persistent. One way of dealing with the problem within the discourse of assimilationism was to temporalise the dissolution of difference within a cross-generational model according to which only the third generation of immigrants was expected to be socially and culturally assimilated (Galitzi 1929; Hitti 1924; Duncan 1933).

Additionally, the idea was developed that multiple melting pots existed, which were differentiated by religion and 'race' (Kennedy 1944, 1952; Herberg 1956). According to this view, immigrants were expected to assimilate to one of several ethno-cultural segments of the U.S. American population. This way, the idea of assimilation was adapted to the model of a plural society with stable ethnic, cultural and religious differentiations.

A refined version of assimilation theory was presented by Milton Gordon in his book *Assimilation in American Life* (1964). He developed a multidimensional concept of assimilation around the two theoretical key variables of structural assimilation and cultural assimilation (acculturation).[6]

Structural assimilation referred to a process of social integration in the primary groups of the dominant segment of society, indicated, for instance, by friendship relations with members of the core society or residence in a 'white middle class' living quarter. Structural assimilation was central for Gordon and entailed other forms of assimilation, like identification with the society, intermarriage and acculturation (Gordon 1964: 80–81). Under cultural assimilation or acculturation Gordon understood the process of adapting to the cultural standards of the receiving country. While he perceived (partial) acculturation as an inevitable effect of the exposure to the receiving society, he considered structural assimilation as contingent. In his view, prejudices and discrimination against immigrants and their descendants by members of the core society were particularly obstructive to structural assimilation.

Despite the factual existence of ethno-economic segmentation, so-called 'eth-classes', for Gordon, white Anglo-Saxon Protestants formed the core of the society, at which the other groups converged culturally and socially. Although he was sceptical about the success of the dissolution of the 'eth-classes', assimilation nevertheless remained the standard by which he evaluated empirical deviation (Gordon 1975: 85).

Different from the expectations of the 1950s, the 1960s and 1970s witnessed a global increase in the number of so-called ethnic and 'racial' conflicts. In this situation it appeared more problematic to conceptualise ethnic and cultural difference as a mere residue, which was destined to die away (cf. Gordon 1975: 85). Instead, ethnicity became increasingly interpreted as a relatively persistent pattern of internal differentiation of 'modern societies'. In this context, some of the core assumptions of assimilationism became criticised. It was questioned, on the one hand, whether assimilationism provided an empirically adequate description of group relations and, on the other hand, whether it was legitimate to declare the assimilation of ethnic others a politically desirable goal.

Critical authors objected that the normative ideal of assimilation was an ideology which legitimated the economic, social and cultural dominance of the WASP segment over less privileged groups of the society (Kymlicka 2003 [1995]: 62). In particular, representatives of the civil rights movements of the 1960s in the United States depicted the demand for conformity with the white mainstream population as an illegitimate means of political oppression.

One of the most prominent contributions to migration studies of this period, which questioned the empirical adequacy of the model of assimilation, was Glazer and Moynihan's *Beyond the Melting Pot* (1963). They argued for the case of New York that factually no single core culture existed to which immigrants could adapt, because the U.S. American urban society had become polycentric and pluralistic. Therefore, the idea of the United States as a melting pot had to be adapted to a more complex empirical situation. As we have seen above, the more sophisticated models of assimilation, which were developed by Kennedy, Gordon and others, took into consideration that the U.S. American society was in actual fact culturally and socially not homogenous. Nevertheless, the crucial point was that social homogeneity remained the normative benchmark of assimilationism. Moreover, assimilationists, as Gordon (1975) himself later admitted, did not develop a notion of power by which existing asymmetries and patterns of segmentation could be described in critical terms.

On a more theoretical level, the critique of assimilationism reflected the fact that the discourse on society shifted from an emphasis on homogeneity, equality, consensus and functional equilibrium to an emphasis on internal diversity, power differentials and conflict during the 1960s and the 1970s (Dahrendorf 1959; Rex 1961). As a result, the concept of ethnicity, which became a major idiom in which to speak about heterogeneity, power and conflict in complex societies, moved from the margins of the theory of modern society to its centre (Hannerz 1974; Esman 1977; Gans 1979; Portes and Manning 1986) and the concept of assimilation became discredited as ideological and simplistic.

During the 1980s and 1990s, the pluralist discourse on society culminated in the political model of multiculturalism (Chicago Cultural Studies Group 1992; Cohn-Bendit and Schmid 1992; Taylor 1994; Kymlicka 2003 [1995]). Charles Taylor's *The Politics of Recognition* (1994) gave this discourse a philosophical underpinning. Although it is not representative for multiculturalist discourses in a statistical sense, in his work some of the theoretical particularities of multiculturalism are more developed and clearly formulated than in other works.

Taylor points out that political liberalism is based on a norm of indifference towards the culture of a person or a group. In order to avoid discrimination and to guarantee the equal treatment of all citizens, culture was considered legitimate as a private affair but not as something that should make a difference in terms of how individuals and groups are treated by the state. As a consequence, as Taylor argues, liberal states face difficulties to find adequate ways of dealing with the internal cultural diversity of plural societies, in particular in cases in which questions of cultural self-determination cause conflicts between the majority and a minority. According to Taylor (1994: 27–29) these problems are deeply rooted in the modern notion of the individual. Modern persons are not any longer defined by an objectified and externally ascribed position within a stratified society, as they were in Europe for a long time, but perceive, above all, their 'authentic inner selves' as a central referent of the determination of their identity. In order to develop an unproblematic relationship to their selves, individuals depend on the public recognition of these aspects of their person, which they perceive as central for determining their identity. Persons who are not recognised in these respects by others are not able to develop a consistent self-image. Therefore, according to Taylor, the political control of the recognition of identity claims has become a crucial power resource and field of political struggle in 'modern societies': 'Non-recognition or misrecognition [of identity] can inflect harm, can be a form of oppression, imprisoning someone in a false, distorted, and reduced mode of being' (Taylor 1994: 25).

Since recognition affects the core of personhood, Taylor emphasised that cultural minorities face problems of a special nature, which also require a special treatment by the state (Taylor 1994: 39). Although the legitimacy of modern statehood is based to a great extent on its strong equality norm, it is, according to him, incapable of protecting minorities' rights adequately against the power of the majority. In order to allow cultural minorities a limited form of collective self-determination, the state must, as Taylor argues, at some points break with the liberal principle of difference-blindness (Taylor 1994: 51–60). In this sense, multiculturalism is a political theory that stresses the legitimacy of culturally founded minority rights and offers an alternative to liberalism for organising the coexistence of ethnic groups in a society.[7]

Taylor's paradigmatic example was the francophone minority in Canada, whose collective identity claims are particularly linked to the public use of French. The linguistic hegemony of the English-speaking majority would have implied the risk that French as a communication language died out and the collective identity of the Francophone minority suffered substantial damage. He argued that the right of the minority to maintain their culture could only be guaranteed if the rights of the majority, in respect to the public use of the English language, were limited to some extent, as was done in the Canadian province of Quebec. Therefore, the collective rights of the minority to recognition of their particularity could only be protected by restricting the majority's rights in a locally limited area.

The core idea of multiculturalism is that equality and justice between cultural groups can be increased by recognising collective cultural differences[8] and by providing societal institutions for their protection. Thereby, multiculturalism can be understood as a political model of anti-assimilationism.[9] The peaceful coexistence of culturally and ethnically distinct groups is not only perceived as an empirical reality, as in the case of Gordon's understanding of assimilationism, but also as a desirable goal. Nevertheless, both models of assimilationism and multiculturalism perceive the nation-state as the self-evident unit in which cultural and ethnic difference between populations is recognised and processed.

In critical terms the role of ethnicity in modern societies was examined within the framework of 'racialisation' (Rex 1970; Bukow and Llaryora 1988; Balibar and Wallerstein 1990; Bukow 1992; Miles 1993a, 1993b, 1998; Rex and Mason 1994 [1986]; Solomos 1994 [1986]); Hall 1996 [1980]; Barot and Bird 2001). A classical text in this tradition is Oliver C. Cox's book *Class, Caste and Race* (1948), in which he explained the significance of the category of 'race' by its functionality for organising and disguising exploitation in capitalist societies. The authors of the 1970s and 1980s who referred to Cox tried in different ways to soften Cox's rather orthodox Marxist argument (Gabriel and Ben-Tovim 1978; Solomos 1994 [1986]; Hall 1996 [1980]). One of the most important authors within this debate was Robert Miles, who coined the concept of 'racialisation'. He combined social constructivist and Marxist ideas in order to demonstrate how the category of 'race' was created in an interplay of political, scientific and economic factors. Although Miles generally emphasised (1993a: 40) that 'race' should not be reduced to class, he identified a link between the development of capitalism and the modern idea of 'race'. According to him, racialisation was part and parcel of the emergence of modern class structures in Europe. The dominant classes distinguished themselves socially from the dominated classes by sophisticating their manners. The resulting behavioural differences between the upper and working classes were attributed to the physical inferiority of the latter. In this sense, political and economic forms of domination became reinterpreted and naturalised as manifestations of biological difference. As Miles argued, Africans and other 'racial others' became victims of racialisation only after the working classes in Great Britain had been affected by this process (Miles 1993a: 46–47; 1998). Despite all contextual and historical changes of the notion of 'race', the core of racialisation was for Miles the projection of power relations within capitalist national societies on the bodies of the dominated classes. Since 'race' aimed at legitimating internal inequalities between different classes and external inequalities between colonising and the colonised people within the context of capitalism, according to Miles, it is an intrinsically modern idea.[10]

In the field of migration studies the approach of racialisation was dominantly applied to 'foreigners' and minorities within a nation-state. In this context, some authors highlighted, as Miles, the modern character of racist ideologies and emphasised the close link between these ideologies and nationalism (Balibar 1990; Bauman 1990; Bukow 1992).[11] Although the racialisation approach criticised self-representations of Western nation-states as universalist difference-blind political systems, it methodologically affirmed them as units of their analysis.

The sociologist Hoffmann-Nowotny (1973) presented a theoretical approach to ethnic difference in modern societies which combined liberal and critical views on the subject. He described how migrants, mostly from Italy, took over the bottom position of the Swiss status hierarchy (*Unterschichtung*) during the 1960s and 1970s. This process provided the 'native Swiss' lower and working classes with the opportunity of upward mobility. Nevertheless, because their increase in social status was threatened by the potential status mobility of the immigrants, they reacted defensively and tended to support policies of ethnic closure and of keeping the immigrants back from attaining citizenship rights. Hoffmann-Nowotny concluded that these exclusionist strategies were neo-feudal[12] (ibid: 302) because they violated basic liberal equality norms of modern societies. Ultimately, he argued, they also weakened the economic position of Switzerland in the world economy because they facilitated an underexploitation of human resources. Although Hoffmann-Nowotny did not use the term racialisation, his analysis focussed on similar empirical phenomena. The most significant difference between the two approaches is that Hoffmann-Nowotny generally highlighted the rational features of modern society, which were counteracted by 'neo-feudal' politics of exclusion, while Miles considered the legitimation of exploitation through biological pseudo-facts a characteristic feature of capitalist economies. Hoffmann-Nowotny took over an agnostic position in relation to the empirical stability of ethnic differentiation in 'modern' nation-states. According to him, it was due to open and uncertain political processes whether 'neo-feudal' tendencies or equality norms of modern societies would prevail in the end.

As a more affirmative reaction to the critique of assimilationism, the concept of integration was introduced to migration studies in the 1970s. While in the framework of assimilationism the relationship between ethnic groups was of main interest, integration primarily focuses on the effects of unequal distribution of central societal resources, in particular money, power, education and office, between 'natives' and 'foreigners' for the cohesion of a society. The major differentiation is not ethnic homogenisation vs. diversification, as in assimilationism, but integration vs. conflict.[13] Although culture and ethnicity are considered, in accordance with liberal state theory, private affairs, they become political issues if they contribute to the socio-economic marginalisation of entire groups. If cultural difference leads to collective economic disparities, it increases the conflict potential of societies and is according to integration theory, therefore, negative for the social integration of a society (Esser 2001: 97; Heckmann 2005). Accordingly, Esser (2001: 103) emphasised that, ultimately, any stabilisation of ethnic difference in modern societies leads to ethnic stratification and, consequently, to conflict.

However, integration theoreticians did not argue that cultural assimilation should be an end in itself, but emphasised that ethnicity only matters because relative homogeneity is functional for the integration of a society. Nevertheless, since unequal power relations make it improbable that the majority will adapt to the standards of the minority (Heckmann 2005: 274), integration of migrants into the society factually means that the members of ethnic minorities adapt to the cultural standards of the majority.[14] The more the cultural difference of migrants is seen as a cause for their marginalisation, the less the integrationist approach can be practically differentiated from assimilationism, despite its different methodological and theoretical starting point. Both approaches under these conditions refer to a closely interlinked complex of socio-economic inequality and ethnic difference, the dissolution of which is considered a main concern for national policy-makers and researchers (Esser 1999, 2001; Heckmann 2005: 279).

On a general level, it became clear that the role of ethnic and cultural differences was a key issue in the history of the social-scientific debate on migration in Western societies. Despite the profound dissensions in regard to the evaluation of (migration-related) ethnic difference, all approaches presented above—assimilation, racialisation, multiculturalism, re-feudalisation and integration—refer to the nation-state as a self-evident unit within which ethnic difference is described, analysed and evaluated.

RURAL–URBAN MIGRATION AND SOCIETY

For several decades, rural–urban migration used to be the major focus of migration studies in Africa. Stimulated by economic growth many people from the rural hinterlands migrated to the urban centres during the late colonial and the early postcolonial period (cf. Chapter 2). In this context, it became a highly relevant question whether migration contributed to the development of the emerging African countries into 'modern' industrialised nation-states.

Cities in particular were perceived as strategic sites for studying the encounters of the members of 'traditional societies' with modernity. Consequently, the 'tribesman in the city' became the paradigmatic type of the stranger in African migration studies.[15] The dominant societal imaginary behind the research on rural–urban migration was the binary distinction between modern and traditional society.

As in the context of the nation-state paradigm of society, also in the framework of migration studies in sub-Saharan Africa the role of ethnicity became a central issue of controversy. According to classical modernisation theory, it was expected that by being integrated into the modern sector the 'tribesmen', who migrated from the rural hinterland to the cities, were gradually transformed into individualised modern wage labourers. Finally, the migrants' adaptation processes to the standards of 'modern society' were expected to culminate in their *detribalisation*. The parallels between the detribalisation hypothesis and the assimilation hypothesis are obvious.

Both perceive ethnic or 'tribal' difference as something alien to modern society and its dissolution as the core of migration processes.

In opposition to the detribalisation hypothesis, several empirical studies of rural–urban migration emphasised the persistence of 'tribal' identities and 'traditional cultures' (Fortes 1936: 50–51; Rouch 1956; Skinner 1960; Velsen 1960). In this context, Rouch (1956: 138–39) introduced the term of *supertribalisation* as a counter-concept to detribalisation. He argued that ethnicity was a means by which migrants could mobilise support in the receiving area and exclude competitors. Therefore, it did not lose but even gained functional significance in the framework of rural–urban migration.

Wallerstein (1960: 130–32) refined Rouch's argument and distinguished between political and territorial units, which he called 'tribes', and segments of the urban population, which he called 'ethnic groups'. On the one hand, the political and territorial units of the hinterland lost, according to Wallerstein, importance in the course of the colonisation and modernisation of the African societies. On the other hand, he argued that ethnic groups, as urban support networks and forms of political organisation of migrants, gained importance. Therefore, detribalisation—as the partial disintegration of the 'traditional societies' of the rural hinterland—entailed supertribalisation in the 'modern segment' of society.

Different from more pessimistic appraisals of the role of ethnicity, according to Wallerstein, the formation of ethnic groups did not endanger but even contributed to the integration of the decolonising nation-states (Wallerstein 1960: 134–137). Being perceived as legitimate forms of political representation by the respective populations themselves, ethnic groups were important institutions for the mediation between individuals and the state. Wallerstein argued that, at the individual as well as at the societal level, ethnicity provided migrants in particular with social means for coping with a situation of rapid economic and social change.

Instead of depicting ethnicity as a traditional residue in the modern world, both Wallerstein and Rouch stressed its functional aspects for the modernisation of African societies. Nevertheless, by describing urban ethnicity as a creative modification of a traditional principle of social organisation to the conditions of the 'modern world', these authors remained entangled in the binary societal epistemology of modernisation theory. They just interpreted the role of ethnicity in an optimistic rather than in a pessimistic way.

The relation between the 'traditional African societies' and the 'modern society' was also one of the key questions of the scholars of the so-called Manchester School (Mitchell 1959 [1956]: 27–28, 44; Gluckman 1961; Epstein 1967: 280). Like Wallerstein, they distinguished the 'traditional' political and cultural units of the rural hinterland, which they called 'tribe' or 'tribal structure', from an urban type of 'tribalism', which they took as a specifically modern phenomenon. On the one hand, the 'tribal structure' was, according to Epstein (1967: 280), 'a particular kind of social regimen in which social relationships are organised within a distinctive structural and cultural framework'. On the other hand,

> urban tribalism was foremost a means of classifying the multitude of Africans of heterogeneous origin who live together in towns, and this classification is the basis on which a number of new African groupings, such as burial and mutual help societies, are formed to meet the demands of urban life.
>
> (Gluckman 1961: 67)

Gluckman argued that rural–urban migrants become modern and remain traditional at the same time. He stressed their ability to switch between two different social roles which are attached to two different socio-spatial orders (Werbner 1984: 161).[16] In this sense, ethnicity was not perceived as an expression of a stable, primordial and collective culture but was seen as rooted in the norms and expectations that are evoked by specific social situations. Because the migrants met with different social orders at different localities, they acted as tribesmen in the rural context and as townsmen in the urban context.

By taking a situationalist stance, the scholars of the Manchester School circumvented Rouch's and Wallerstein's question of whether ethnicity was reinforced or weakened by rural–urban migration. They differentiated between two kinds of ethnicity which refer to two discrete systems of social organisation: the modern city and the tribal entities of the hinterland.

Nevertheless, all cited authors agreed on a general definition of the broader social situation. On the one hand, they affirmed the modernisation theoretical binary of the 'modern urban society' and the 'rural traditional society' as organising framework. On the other hand, they deviated from classical modernisation theory in two respects. Firstly, all of them highlighted the persistence and functionality of ethnicity in the modern urban sector. Secondly, they agreed that the social structures of the 'traditional society' were not simply destroyed by the contact with 'modernity' but that both types of society persisted parallel to each other (Rouch 1956; Skinner 1960; Velsen 1960; Fortes 1971; Hart 1971; Watson 1971 [1958]; Schildkrout 1974).

The emphasis of the distinction between modern and traditional societies invites the question of how the mobility of persons in between them affects it. In this context, the term 'circular migration' was introduced to stress the self-repeating character of the movements back and forth between the modern urban and the traditional rural society (Skinner 1960, 1965; Mitchell 1961, 1969; Epstein 1967: 279; Hart 1971). By transferring resources and by seasonally commuting between the cities and the communities of origin, it was argued, circular migrants reproduced both the 'modern urban society', which was subsidised by cheap labour, and the 'traditional rural society', which materially profited from the migrants remittances. Thereby, migration contributed to the emergence of a meta-system in which both types of society got entangled with each other and their binary structure was reproduced in relation to each other.

In the late 1960s, a critical approach gained significance within the field of rural–urban migration studies (cf. Frank 1967; Galtung 1972 [1971]). According to the so-called dependency theoreticians, incorporation into the capitalist system neither reduced, as modernisation theory presumed, nor stabilised, as the scholars of the Manchester School assumed, but rather widened the gap between the urban centres and the rural periphery. It was emphasised that it was above all capitalist modes of exploitation that turned formerly unconnected and undeveloped regions into impoverished and underdeveloped regions (Ferguson 1999: 140–41). In this framework, migration was seen as a forced reaction to the growing impoverishment and the underdevelopment of the rural areas, which in turn was the result of the violent incorporation into the capitalist system (e.g. Plange 1979: 659).

The mobility of young men was expected to aggravate the situation of rural households, which lost the most physically productive part of their labour force to the capitalist segment of society. In this sense, migration was considered to be part of a self-reinforcing process of impoverishment that resulted in widening structures of inequality, dependency and exploitation between the centre and the periphery (Gregory and Piché 1978: 45).

Although dependency theory changed the terminology from modern society/traditional society to centre/periphery, methodologically the line of division remained the same. However, a major difference between dependency theory and modernisation theory was that the former emphasised more strongly the existence of a meta-system, namely, global capitalism, in which the dualism of traditional society/periphery and modern society/centre was created and structurally cemented. Although the representatives of the Manchester School had already pointed to systematic interconnections of 'tribal society' and 'urban society' (Gluckman 1961: 81), dependency theory conceptualised the coupling of periphery and centre much tighter and emphasised a causal link between the centrality of the centre and the marginality of periphery.

Because of the epistemological dualism which for a long time dominated African migration studies, the 'tribesman in the city' was the paradigmatic type of migrant in all approaches cited. Although the migrants coming from the rural hinterland to the cities 'overstepped' the line of division between the modern and the traditional system, the differentiation itself remained fundamental to the analytical frameworks according to which this type of mobility was selected as most remarkable.

Both the nation-state paradigm of migration studies and rural–urban migration studies affirmed imaginaries of society as a relatively stable, internally homogenous and unitary system from which cross-border movements by definition remained a deviation. In this sense, the binary of traditional and modern society as well as imaginaries of the national society are variations of the same basic idea of society.¹⁷

MIGRATION AND WORLD SOCIETY

Since the 1980s, the social sciences have experienced a general shift towards global perspectives on their subjects, which has also affected the study of migration. This facilitated the development of new concepts or the revival of older concepts, respectively, which emphasised the relevance of cross-border forms of sociality among migrants and their descendants. In the following, I will focus on three concepts which were developed to theorise migration-related forms of transnational and global interconnections: first, diaspora, second, global ethnoscape and, third, transnational social field.

The process of globalisation went through several waves of intensification of global interactions in the past, which were followed by phases of decreasing intensity of global exchange (Harvey 1989; Robertson 1990; Wimmer and Glick Schiller 2002a; Friedman 2004: 64–65). While most of the social science literature deals with the last wave, which started in the 1970s and profited from the end of the Cold War, the period between 1880 and 1925 was often depicted as a 'crucial take-off period of globalisation' (Robertson 1990: 19).

The neglect of global interconnections, which was characteristic for parts of the social sciences after World War II, was attributed by academic observers, on the one hand, to the cyclical character of globalisation waves, and to the methodology of the social sciences, on the other. Since the period following World War II was a golden era of the nation-state, its equation with society appeared more self-evident than it does today. Wimmer and Glick Schiller (2002a) underlined that not least the research agendas of the social sciences contributed to a reification of imaginaries that most relevant social processes occur within the borders of a single nation-state and, thereby, produced a systematic neglect of those social relationships that cross national borders.

Since the 1970s attempts were started to separate the concept of society more clearly from the political form of the nation-state. In this context global concepts of society were developed. They do not any longer understand society as a politically integrated social whole or as an imagined community but as the most comprehensive unit of human coexistence in which the empirical entities of social life, like states, institutions, groups or individuals, potentially or factually interact with each other (Featherstone 1990: 4; Luhmann 2005 [1971]: 64).¹⁸ The two, probably most prominent, approaches in sociology in which the spatial scope of society was expanded to the globe were Niklas Luhmann's theory of the *Weltgesellschaft* (world society; Luhmann 1998: 145–71; Stichweh 2000; Heinz, Münch and

Tyrell 2005; Luhmann 2005 [1971]) and Wallerstein's world system theory (Wallerstein 1974). Additionally, the historian Fernand Braudel (2002 [1979]) and the anthropologist Eric Wolf (1982) developed global perspectives on their respective subjects of studies by which they challenged more spatially limited notions of society.

All of these authors highlighted the fact that 'modern society' or 'modern capitalism', respectively, developed in the course of a historical process which gradually transcended geographical borders and incorporated (large parts of) the globe into a single social system. Dissatisfied with the methodological limitations of the nation-state paradigm of society these authors emphasised the global scope of processes of social integration, interdependencies and exchange.

After this more theoretical starting point, the discourse of globalisation, which went along with an opening up of the concept of society, became prominent in many fields of empirical study in the social sciences during the second half of the 1980s and the 1990s. This could be observed in the field of economic globalisation (e.g. Harvey 1989; Sassen 1991, 1994), the study of culture and ethnicity (e.g. Robertson 1992; Appadurai 1996; Featherstone 1999), the study of organisations (e.g. Meyer, et al. 1997), the study of science and (information) technology (e.g. Castells 1996) and last but not least in migration studies.

In particular in migration studies, which in Europe and North America were probably even more than other fields dominated by the nation-state paradigm, these changes in the understanding of society created a demand for concepts which allowed for a better examination of the cross-border forms of sociality in which migrants and their descendants are involved. In this context at least three concepts became prominent: diaspora, global ethnoscape and transnational social field.

Diaspora

The first conceptual choice to study the transnational social relationships of migrants and their descendants is the concept of diaspora (Hall 1990; Safran 1991; Clifford 1994; Cohen 1996, 1997; Gilroy 1997; Vertovec 1997). The term diaspora equally refers to prenational, national and postnational forms of cross-border interconnections and identities. 'Seen as a form of social organisation diasporas have predated the nation-state, live uneasily within it and now may, in significant respects, transcend and succeed it'(Cohen 1996: 520).

It was in particular the accent on the historical persistence of non-national forms of social relationships which contributed to the theoretical attraction of the concept of diaspora. Although originally referring to Greek colonies in Asia Minor and the Mediterranean, the modern notion was most importantly influenced by its use in the book of Deuteronomy, which referred to the forced dispersal and enslavement of the

Jews after the destruction of the temple in Jerusalem in the sixth century BC (Cohen 1997: 3–5). In the twentieth century, in particular the Shoah and the foundation of the state of Israel left their impact on the semantic connotation of the term.

As an analytical term, diaspora refers to a shared sense of belonging of a geographically scattered population, which is often based on the collective memory of a homeland. Frequently, it combines the motifs of (forced) migration and maintenance of a group consciousness over a longer period of time with a motif of victimhood and oppression in the receiving areas (Gilroy 1994: 209). Apart from the Jewish experiences, the term diaspora was also prominently applied to the case of forced migration of Africans in the context of the slave trade (cf. Hall 1990; Gilroy 1993; Clifford 1994), the emigration of Irishmen during the nineteenth century, and the forced migration of Armenians after their deportation by the Turkish army to Syria and Mesopotamia in 1915 (Cohen 1997: 27–28).

In the course of time, the use of the word diaspora was successively expanded to other ethnic groups. Increasingly, it was applied to all kinds of migrant or minority populations which maintained a certain sense of ethnic difference and a consciousness of originating from 'somewhere else'. Within this process of semantic opening the notion of victimhood, which was particularly dominant in the Jewish and the Afro-American narrative of diaspora, was sometimes supplemented by a notion of resistance against state policies of assimilation (Hall 1990; Clifford 1994), or it was replaced by a more descriptive usage which plainly referred to the maintenance of transnational relationships by migrant populations (Sheffer 1995; Akyeampong 2000; Koser 2003). In the political sciences, the term diaspora was also used to describe groups of migrants which participated actively in the politics of their 'homelands' (Esman 1986; Sheffer 1986).

Altogether, there are at least four reasons that have contributed to the career of the term diaspora:

First, it provides a conceptual framework, which is able to grasp the generation-spanning maintenance of minority identities. The emphasis put on the persistence of diasporic identities offers an alternative to the assimilationist narrative of homogenisation and successive dissolution of cultural and ethnic difference (Clifford 1994: 307). Thereby, the term diaspora resonates with the pluralistic turn in the understanding of society described above.

Second, a crucial difference between cultural pluralism and the diaspora approach is associated with the transnational orientation of the latter. Diasporas are normally social formations which exceed the borders of a single nation-state. Therefore, the discourse of diaspora provides a framework to examine migrants' life-worlds beyond the confinements of methodological nationalism (Clifford 1994: 307). Gilroy (1993), for example, described in his study *The Black Atlantic* an alternative public space that connected different diasporic groups of African origin for centuries and comprises the large geographical area around the Atlantic Ocean including parts of Africa, Europe, the Caribbean and the Americas.

Third, the existence of diasporic groups gives evidence of the fact that cultural patterns and identities could be reproduced over long distances among dispersed populations. In this sense, culture appears as a fluid communicative process. Thereby, the term diaspora resonated with the anthropological criticism of territorialised models of culture (cf. Thornton 1988; Fuchs and Berg 1993; Appadurai 1996).

Fourth, the discourse of diaspora related to the criticism of Western imaginaries of modernity (Foucault 1983; Bauman 1990; Wimmer 2002). On the one hand, the experiences of some diasporic groups exhibited the violent elements of minority–majority relationships and national assimilation policies, which were often neglected in the dominant representations of national history. By revealing the dark and exclusionary sides of the nation-state the concept of diaspora functions as a critical comment on the Western narrative of modernisation and progress. On the other hand, the persistence of diasporic groups also documents a counter-history of resistance against assimilationist pressures.

Some commentators objected to the use of the term diaspora, arguing that its rootedness in the Jewish history made it too specific and too charged with connotations to apply to other cases. In this context it was particularly the notion of victimhood which was identified as a problematic semantic inheritance because it reduced the often complex histories of minorities, including the Jewish, to a single aspect (Cohen 1996, 1997).

Brubaker (2005: 1–2) objected that, in particular, the inflationary use of the concept of diaspora has rendered it meaningless. According to him, the term has lost its analytical focus because it refers to too many different phenomena.

Probably the most fundamental critique was that the concept of diaspora did not distinguish clearly enough between identity discourses and factual groups (Anthias 1998; Brubaker 2005; Wimmer and Glick Schiller 2002a: 324). It was argued that by taking a group's description as diaspora at face value, scientific observers ran into the danger of reifying a holistic, essentialist and ideological imaginary of large populations as communities in a way that tends to downplay internal heterogeneity, to overlook the historicity of different diaspora discourses, and gloss over the political agendas that are put across by them. Some authors (Brubaker 2005: 15; Kleist 2008; Nieswand 2008b) proposed in this context to refrain from using diaspora as an analytical term and instead prefer to make the histories, politics and pragmatics of the use of the concept of diaspora an object of empirical study.

Global Ethnoscape

Another concept, which was developed to theorise social relations of migrants and non-migrants beyond the level of the nation-state is 'global ethnoscape' (Appadurai 1996, 1998, 1999). Appadurai examined in his book *Modernity at Large* (1996) the modes of (re)production of culture, identity and locality under the conditions of globalisation and mass migration. The last globalisation wave marked, according to him, a caesura, which facilitated a profound deterritorialisation of culture and reinforced the significance of imagination for the creation of reality (ibid: 9).

Before, this imagination was limited to certain realms of social life, like myths, dreams or rituals, and was dominated by some groups of actors, like religious experts, rulers or Western academics (ibid: 6). Due to globalisation processes and technological innovations, an increasing number of people participate in global flows of communication that provide individuals with meaningful material to envision themselves and their social environment in multiple ways. Even individuals who live in formerly peripheral regions become aware of the existence of alternative life sketches. As a result, imagination has become, according to Appadurai, a powerful social force in the contemporary world: 'The imagination is now central to all forms of agency, is itself a social fact, and is the key component of the new global order' (ibid: 31).

The term ethnoscape emphasises, in opposition to more essentialist and territorially bounded concepts of culture, the predominance of fluidity, heterogeneity and mobility in the making of selves, groups, cultures and localities in the contemporary world (Appadurai 1996: 60). Parallel to Anderson (1983), who showed the significance of print technology for the constitution of national publics, Appadurai highlighted the importance of electronic mass media and communication technologies for the creation and recreation of global ethnoscapes.

At the same time, the emergence of global ethnoscapes is also closely linked to the mobility of 'tourists, immigrants, refugees, exiles, guest workers and other moving groups or individuals' (ibid: 33). Although mobile populations are of strategic importance for the emergence of global ethnoscapes (Appadurai 1998: 12), within the deterritorialised ethnoscape itself the distinction between 'migrants' and 'natives' is transcended. Because it is of secondary relevance where individuals who participate in an ethnoscape are located and whether they were born at this place, being a migrant ceases to be a primary criterion to distinguish these individuals. In this sense, Appadurai's concept facilitates a perspective on migrants and their social relationships, which is decisively different from those that were presented before.

The emphasis of global communicative flows led Appadurai to speak of a 'post-national world'. It marks the caesura between the epoch of the dominance of a territorialised and territorialising nation-state and the contemporary era of deterritorialisation and globalisation. One consequence is that migrants are no longer exclusively expected to adapt to the conditions of a nation-state, but also that the nation-state has to adjust to the conditions of migration (Appadurai 1996: 158–77).

Despite the general emphasis on deterritorialisation, for Appadurai, 'situations' and 'localities' remained important as sites in which globally floating signs and referents, materiality and imagination, subjectivity and objectivity merge into a concrete given. Appadurai called the empirical project in which the situational interplay and entanglement between the local and the global should be studied 'transnational anthropology' (Appadurai 1996: 48), 'transnational cultural studies', 'cosmopolitan ethnography' or 'macroethnography' (ibid: 50).

However, one problem within Appadurai's conceptual framework is that it remains ambiguous whether he primarily refers to global flows of signs and symbols as units of analysis or to localities in which the work of configuring them is done in the form of face-to-face interaction. As a consequence, there remains a methodological and theoretical gap between the localities, on the one hand, and the global ethnoscapes, on the other hand, that makes it difficult to apply Appadurai's conceptual apparatus in the field of migration studies.[19] This is reinforced by the problem that it is unclear whether his work should be read as a theory of the globalisation of culture, as a conceptual framework for its empirical study, or as a general programmatic appeal for a reorientation of anthropology. What is more, the narrative of an epochal caesura becomes an analytical burden at points at which it might make more sense to stress historical longue durée continuities or slow and gradual changes rather than fast and fundamental rupture. However, Appadurai's core argument, that the global spread of and access to global flows of information has an impact on the possibilities of imagination and on social life in general and migration processes in particular is plausible. Whether this makes imagination-based ethnoscapes 'key component[s] of the new global order' (Appadurai 1996: 31) is another question which is beyond the scope of this study.

Transnational Social Field

'Transnational social field' is the last term to conceptualise migration within a world societal framework that will be presented. In the early 1990s, some scholars (Rouse 1991, 1992; Glick Schiller, Basch and Szanton Blanc 1992; Basch, Glick Schiller and Szanton Blanc 1994) described how migration in many cases did not go along with a radical break of the migrants' social relationships to their country of origin. Instead, many migrants continued to be active participants in their families, localities and countries of origin. It was observed that migrants sent regular remittances, came for visits, participated in family rituals, followed country of origin related media, communicated extensively with relatives and friends in the sending countries, were involved in cross-border businesses or development projects and participated in the political affairs of their countries of origin. In this context, it was argued that an adequate representation and interpretation of migration processes required including the transnational dimension of social life in which migrants invest a lot of money, time and commitment (Glick Schiller, Basch and Szanton Blanc 1992: 1).

In the beginning, it was highlighted that the transnational phenomena were qualitatively new (Glick Schiller, Basch and Szanton Blanc 1992; Pries 1996). But, soon it was shown that transnational social relationships were already important in earlier periods of mass migration (Foner 1997; Gabaccia 1999; Morawska 2001: 178; Waldinger and Fitzgerald 2004: 1187–88). Subsequently, it was emphasised that transnational social relationships had been accompanying the nation-state ever since its institutionalisation in different forms and intensities, but were for a long time overlooked by the social sciences (Wimmer and Glick Schiller 2002a; Levitt and Glick Schiller 2004; Pries 2005: 5; Levitt and Jaworsky 2007).

According to Wimmer and Glick Schiller (2002a), it required a relative decline of the power of the nation-state to shift academic attention to these phenomena.

> Perhaps it is more difficult to see the world in three dimensions when the sun stood at its zenith. In the evening, shadows grow and allow us to perceive the environment in clearer contours. What we discover in this twilight, is how transnational the modern world always has been, even in the high days when the nation-state bounded and bundled most social processes.
> (Wimmer and Glick Schiller 2002b: 218)

To conceptualise cross-border relationships of migrants different terms were employed by different scholars, such as 'transnational social field' (Basch, Glick Schiller and Szanton Blanc 1994; Goldring 1998; Glick Schiller and Fouron 1999; Levitt and Glick Schiller 2004; Glick Schiller 2004; Levitt and Jaworsky 2007), 'transnational social space' (Pries 1996, 1997, 1998, 2001; Salzbrunn 2001; Müller-Mahn 2005) 'transnational social formation' (Guarnizo and Smith 1998a: 27), 'transnational living' (Guarnizo 2003) and 'transnational community' (Goldring 1996; Smith 1998; Vertovec 1999). Although these concepts stressed different nuances, all of them tried to cover the same or, at least, very similar social phenomena. They referred to relatively stable and persistent social relationships, identifications, patterns of communication and transfers of resources, which connect migrants and non-migrants in two or more nation-states, mostly the migrants' country of origin and the country of residence. Briefly, I will compare the three most prominent of them, transnational social field, transnational social space and transnational community, and highlight the comparative advantages of the notion of transnational field.

Generally, the physical metaphor of the 'field' implies an unbounded zone of influence emerging around a given force. In its metaphorical sense, it refers to cross-border forms of sociality as social forces around which situational transnational fields of power and influence emerge. The point that is highlighted by the field metaphor is that social fields are influential unbounded entities created by social practices which affect the social reality in their reach. They exist in so far as they matter in a practical sense.

In the case of the metaphor of transnational 'social space', not force or impact, but space, is the primary referent. Since one of the most characteristic aspects of transnational activities is that they transcend spatial limitations (Bommes 2003: 103–4), it appears more appropriate to use the field metaphor than the space metaphor to address the structural dimension of transnational interactions and relationships. Since the concept of transnational social field allows for describing collective as well as individual activities, it is more abstract than the concept of 'transnational community' and can therefore be applied to a wider range of phenomena. While transnational communities can be described as collective actors in transnational fields, 'transnational field' cannot be reduced to the activities of social groups.

Glick Schiller and her colleagues defined the transnational social field 'as an unbounded terrain of interlocking egocentric networks' (Glick Schiller and Fouron 1999: 344), which exceeds national borders. By highlighting the relevance of networks, this group of researchers distinguished themselves from Appadurai's idea of ethnoscape that presumes the primacy of deterritorialised flows of signs in the process of cultural globalisation, on the one hand, and approaches like diaspora that primarily look at groups. For Glick Schiller and her colleagues the transnationalisation of migrants' life-worlds is deeply embedded in concrete nets of personal relationships.

Different from what some critics argued (Bommes 2003: 102; Waldinger and Fitzgerald 2004: 1178; Fitzgerald 2009), the more matured versions of 'transnationalism' did not aim at a methodological *anti*-nationalism. Much more than denying its relevance, transnationalists have an intrinsically ambiguous relationship to the nation-state (Hannerz 1996: 6; Kearney 1995; Glick Schiller 2004; Pries 2005).

On the one hand, *trans*national relates to aspects of sociality which exceed the borders of a single nation-state and, thereby, transcend methodological nationalism. On the other hand, within the gesture of transgression the nation-state remains the central entity of reference of trans*nationalism* (Faist 2000).[20]

More recently, some authors have suggested that it would be better to understand transnationalism not merely as a framework to study migrants' long-distance relationships but rather to examine multiple pathways of 'simultaneous incorporation' (Levitt and Glick Schiller 2004; Glick Schiller, et al. 2005; Nieswand 2008a) of migrants in different socio-spatial entities within and across national borders. Although migrants, as individuals or groups, play a key role for the constitution of the transnational social fields, they are not the only actors included in them (Glick Schiller 2004: 458; Levitt and Glick Schiller 2004). Additionally, non-migrants (e.g. Drotbohm 2009) and organisations (e.g. Pries 2008) located either in the receiving country or in the country of origin may participate in them.

As I have shown above, the extension of the focus of migration research to non-migrants was also a characteristic of the concepts of diaspora and ethnoscape. More generally, this widening of the analytic optic can be described as a decentring of migration studies. Studying the broader social processes that are entangled with and entailed by spatial mobility means that migrants are no longer the only group of interest, and the fact that they have migrated might assume different meanings in different contexts. This decentring of migration studies is intrinsically related to the shift in the underlying imaginaries of society from national society to world society. Since the expectation that the mobility of goods, persons and communication exceeds smaller political and geographical units, like nation-states, is inscribed in the perspective of the world society itself, the perception of cross-border migration changes accordingly. The 'migrants in the world society' become normalised and lose the methodological salience of the 'foreigners in the nation-state' and the 'tribesmen in the city'. Among other social actors they become participants in transnational social fields, diasporas or ethnoscapes in which present or past mobility may or may not be the most relevant criteria of differentiation. This shift is particularly analytically productive in cases, such as those of transnational families or diverse urban neighbourhoods, in which the emergent social configurations crosscut the distinction between 'locals' and 'migrants'.

Moreover, since the relation between the social fields, diasporas and ethnoscapes in which people act and the world society cannot be imagined in the same way as the relationship between persons and society, within the nation-state paradigm, also the corresponding notion of integration changes. Conventional ideas of integration oscillate between a descriptive notion that aims at measuring to which extent a person is part of a national society and a normative notion that declares integration a desirable goal (Esser 2001). This ambivalence derives from the theoretical framework in which the term was developed. As mentioned above, in classical political theory it is assumed that the persistence of pluralist national societies requires a certain degree of consensus on norms and values among its members that is supposed to counteract the centrifugal forces of differentiation and to overcome potential lines of societal conflict (Rawls 1987; Parsons and Shils 2001 [1951]). In this context, the migrants' adaptation to the socio-cultural standards of the receiving society was expected to increase cohesion and, therefore, to contribute to internal peace. Because peace is generally more desirable than conflict, the term integration is charged with a normative subtext: only integration, and *not* disintegration, of migrants can be considered a societally appreciable goal (Esser 2001: 107). Multiple forms of inclusion in different nation-states, as they were documented by students of transnational migration, were perceived by some theorists as either an obstacle or at least negligible in relation to the politically dominant process of integrating migrants into the receiving country (Esser 1999:

23; Bommes 2003: 107; Heckmann 2005: 279). A world societal epistemology challenges this notion of integration in two ways (Glick Schiller, et al. 2005). First, from this perspective it is not self-evidently given that national forms of inclusion into the receiving country are primary and others are secondary. Second, if social inclusion is generally considered a partial, situational and fragmented process that can involve multiple social entities at different localities within the world society, migrants' cross-border relationships are not any longer an anomaly but a sociological normality.

Therefore, the shift in the underlying society concept entails a more descriptive and agnostic notion of integration/inclusion, which refers simply to the fact of participation in a social context. Its impact and meaning is a matter of empirical study. This non-normative turn is in accordance with some more recent developments in social theory (cf. Luhmann 2005 [1971]: 73–76). The world society, due to its internal diversity and its lack of global institutions of governance, can no longer be perceived as a bounded and unitary system. It is a chiffre for emergent social complexity rather than for a political community based on consensus. In this respect, it differs from older concepts of society.[21]

METHODOLOGICAL TRANSNATIONALISM AND THE EPISTEMOLOGY OF MIGRATION STUDIES

This chapter provided an overview of a selection of different approaches to migration studies. It was argued that there exists a linkage between the methodology of migration studies, the applied concepts of society and the selected paradigmatic type of migrant. Altogether, I identified three pairs of concepts of society and paradigmatic types of migrant—'the foreigner in the nation-state', 'the tribesman in the city' and 'the migrant in the world society'—which each constitutes a specific perspective on human mobility.

In particular, the shift towards world society as underlying concept has, as I argued, profound implications. It entails a more formal and agnostic conceptualisation of the relationship between persons and society.

If one approaches transnationalism itself with the same sceptical attitude, which informed Wimmer and Glick Schiller's analysis of methodological nationalism, it becomes clear that it is not free of methodological assumptions but only has different ones, which might be more or less adequate in relation to an empirical case and an intellectual problem. Observing the world in one way necessarily excludes seeing it in another. Therefore, it is not abstinence from methodological presumptions, but reflexivity, which might distinguish social scientific knowledge from other types of knowledge.

In order to make the methical presumptions of this study transparent I will differentiate between empirical and methodological transnationalism in the following (Khagram and Levitt 2008; Nieswand 2008a).[22]

Empirical transnationalism refers to the description of social phenomena which cross-cut national borders but which are, as compared to global phenomena, more limited in scope (Glick, Schiller and Fouron 2001). In distinction to this, *methodological transnationalism* will denote an analytical framework allowing for the description and analysis of multiple and simultaneous forms of inclusion of migrants and non-migrants in different socio-spatial contexts and institutions within a global society without prejudging the primacy of one of them.

The latter is the methodological framework applied in the present case study. It is particularly the relationship of distinct types of migrant inclusion in different social-spatial contexts that will be of major interest for the presented study. It is assumed that a methodological framework cannot be falsified or verified in the narrow sense of the word but has to demonstrate its *usefulness* in relation to an empirical case and an intellectual problem. In this sense, the following study of transnational Ghanaian migrants is to *demonstrate* what was *said* before; namely, that methodological transnationalism allows for modes of describing and theorising migration which particularly differ from those delivered by the nation-state paradigm of migration study. In this framework special empirical and intellectual attention will be paid to questions of social status.

2 Ghana and its Migrants

The first part of this chapter presents an overview of the political, social and economic processes that affected labour migration to and from Ghana during the last century. In this context, a special emphasis is put on the political economy of the migratory system that is considered important to understand labour migration from a macro-perspective. The second part of the chapter complements the historical account of the first part by presenting a migration case study from the Brong Ahafo Region in Ghana.

THE COLONIAL SYSTEM OF LABOUR MIGRATION

The Gold Coast was one of the centres of the transatlantic slave trade in the seventeenth and eighteenth centuries. The slave trade itself, as well as internal wars connected to slave raids and rivalries over the control of its profits, left a deep imprint on the social, economic and political landscape of the Gold Coast even before it formally became a colony.

Until the late nineteenth century the British, who had prevailed in the competition of different European powers on the coast, were relatively indecisive and hesitant about their role in the hinterland of the Gold Coast. In the course of the escalation of the conflict with the Asante Confederation during the nineteenth century, the British defeated its army decisively in 1874 and destroyed Kumasi. The victory created a power vacuum, which endangered the prospering of trade. Additionally, the colonial rivalry between the European nations became stronger in the late nineteenth century. In its course, British colonialism changed from the 'mid-Victorian stance of balanced budgets, limited intervention and informal coastal control' to a '"new imperialism" of military force, annexation and development' (Dumett 1981: 199).

The establishment and expansion of the colonial states in West Africa during the late nineteenth and early twentieth centuries became the most important political precondition for the emergence of a new system of labour migration (Caldwell 1967: 111). In the Gold Coast, it went along with a period of rapid economic growth, which the country experienced from 1900 to 1913 and which continued from 1922 to 1929 (Hopkins 1973: 179–85). The colonial export economy with its plantations, mines, infrastructure projects and the trade sector relied on a supply of cheap wage labourers, in particular in the southern forest belt and the coastal regions of the Gold Coast.

Parallel to the penetration of colonial rule and the increase of state revenues the transport infrastructure was extended and improved (Rouch 1956: 27–28). Roads, railways and lorry transport facilitated new forms of regional integration, which linked the northern savannahs more closely to the economically prospering south. It allowed seasonal and circular forms of mass migration from the savannah regions.

In terms of labour supply, the period between the 1880s and the 1920s was marked by a substantive lack of workers that was euphemistically called a 'recruitment problem' (Berg 1965). The scarcity of manpower was partly a consequence of the warfare and raids that took place in the framework of the slave trade and which led to a profound decrease in the population of West Africa for centuries (Hopkins 1973: 122). Therefore, the undersupply of labour reflected the fact that there were not enough young men available and the relaxation of the labour market situation was a by-product of the population growth during the twentieth century. Reservations about the working conditions in some fields of the wage labour sector were another reason that aggravated the shortage of labour. Some local farmers rejected the rigidly regimented type of work they were confronted with, particularly in the mines and infrastructure projects of the colonial administration. Changes in the local demand structure played a role in the increasing acceptance of labour conditions. Because of a rise in the purchasing power of those parts of the rural population that were involved in cash cropping or labour migration and the improved accessibility of relatively cheap industrially produced consumer goods, these items became part of the rural status economy. In this context, in particular, a monetarisation and commodification of bride wealth came about in many societies (Berg 1964: 402), which put pressure on young men to leave their villages in order to earn money.

Compared to other colonies, the extent of the forced recruitment of labour was relatively low in the Gold Coast. Neither were poll taxes levied, nor did the colonial government systematically force people to work.[1] Nevertheless, the colonial administration used different positive and negative sanctions to recruit workers, ranging from monetary incentives, head money paid to local authorities, to more or less directly exerted pressure on local authorities (Gregory and Piché 1978: 42–43).

In the course of the first decades of the twentieth century, labour migration had become an increasingly widespread, socially accepted and voluntary activity in the Gold Coast. In 1938/39 the Labour Department of the Gold Coast wrote in its report on the situation at the mines, that had faced labour undersupply for decades: 'Work on various mines is still the most popular immigrant labour and companies had no difficulties in obtaining locally all the labour they have needed' (Annual Labour Department Report 1938/39, cited in Greenstreet 1972: 35). At this time, the colonial labour migration system was fully established.

Besides mining, cash crop production had a profound impact on the migration patterns in the Gold Coast. Until the nineteenth century, activities connected to the slave trade were the most rewarding sources of cash income in the South of the Gold Coast. Those parts of the profits remaining in Africa were controlled by a small political and military elite. In contrast to this, cash crops like oil palm fruits, palm kernels and rubber, which had been exported since the 1830s, provided economic opportunities for broader segments of the population (Hopkins 1973: 125–26).

Cocoa, the most important cash crop, spread throughout the Gold Coast during the last decades of the nineteenth century and dominated Ghana's economic development during the entire twentieth century. Because of the shorter distance to Europe and lower land prices, cocoa from the Gold Coast was cheaper than Latin American cocoa (Schmidt-Kallert 1994: 91). The price advantage and the rapid growth of the world market for cocoa led to a strong demand and entailed a fast expansion of cocoa production in the Gold Coast, from which the local farmers could profit.

In the last years of the nineteenth century, the first cocoa from the Gold Coast was exported. As early as 1911, the Gold Coast became the leading cocoa producer in the world, with an output of 41,000 tons (Hill 1970: 22). Cocoa plantations were first established in the Eastern Region of modern Ghana (Hill 1963: 15–16) and from there spread out at a fast speed to the west and northwest (Schaaf 1988: 42–45).

Cocoa cash cropping produced two kinds of migrants. On the one hand, farmers who predominantly originated from southern Ghana, migrated in search of new farmland. On the other hand, the clearing of forestland, the weeding of the fields and the cropping of cocoa created a demand for wage labourers. The labour supply for these activities became satisfied by migrant labourers (Hofmann 1994: 5). The migratory system profited from the complementarity of the cocoa cultivation cycle and the farming cycle in the northern savannahs (Rouch 1956: 70). The main workload in the cocoa plantations rose from November to January (Eschenhagen 1990: 35–36). At this time, the harvest in the savannahs was finished and the young men from the north were free to migrate to the south. During the dry season they stayed in the cocoa areas and often returned to their home villages at the beginning of the rainy season in March or April (Fortes 1936: 41). In 1947 it was estimated that about 210,000 workers were employed on the cocoa farms (Colonial Office 1948, cited in Rimmer 1992: 353) and in the 1950s, 20 per cent of the total adult population of the Gold Coast were classified as cocoa farmers (Lewis 1953: 2).

In addition to the cocoa plantations, the centres of industrial gold mining in Ghana—Tarkwa in the Western Region and in Obuasi in the Ashanti

Region—were significant destinations of migration.[2] The number of workers in the mines increased from 2,400 in 1894 to 15,000 in 1914 (Rouch 1956: 25) and to more than 30,000 workers in 1938/39 (Greenstreet 1972: 35–36). In the course of the twentieth century the workers, who were originally dominantly from Liberia, were gradually replaced by workers from the northern parts of the colony, Nigeria and the neighboring French colonies (Thomas 1973: 80). Many of them went home every six or twelve months to assist their families during the planting and the harvest season, which caused a chronic deficiency of workers until the 1930s (Dumett 1998: 224–26), especially during the rainy season.

In the twentieth century, Ghana experienced a rapid urbanisation process. From 1948 to 1960, the urban population grew at an annual rate of over 9 per cent, which was three times the growth rate of the rural population (Caldwell 1969: 13). In 1960, more than 23 per cent of all Ghanaians lived in cities and towns. Over 50 per cent of the increase could be explained by internal rural–urban migration. The capital city of Accra experienced the most significant population growth, which amounted to 12.7 per cent per annum between 1948 and 1960. After its destruction in 1873, the renaissance of Kumasi, was connected to the cocoa boom and the expansion of trade in the first decades of the twentieth century. Situated in the centre of the flourishing cocoa zone, Kumasi took over important functions as a market place for cocoa, Western consumer goods, cattle, sheep, cola and rubber (Korboe and Tipple 1995: 267). Parallel to the development of Accra, the period of the fastest growth was that between 1948 and 1960, when the population grew from 70,000 to 180,000 people at a rate of more than 12 per cent per annum (Hofmann 1994: 19). After independence, the speed of growth decelerated. This was partly a result of the strengthening of Accra as the national capital and the creation of new regional capitals which reduced the importance of Kumasi.

Even to a greater extent than from the Gold Coast itself, the migrants in the Gold Coast came from the neighbouring countries to the cities, mines and cocoa plantations (Arthur 1991: 71). In 1931, 120,000 persons from French West Africa and 57,400 Nigerians lived in the Ashanti Region and the coastal area, according to official statistics (Fortes 1936: 36–37). In 1960, over 12 per cent of the Ghanaian population, which corresponded to over 800,000 persons, was born outside Ghana, mostly in Togo, Upper Volta and Nigeria (Peil 1974: 369). Although other West African countries like the Côte d'Ivoire or Senegal also experienced significant immigration during this period, Ghana was the major destination for labour migration in West Africa up until the 1960s (Zarachariah and Condé 1981: 37).

Within Ghana, the majority of migrants came from the north and the Volta Region in the east of the country, which were economically the most disadvantaged parts of the country.[3] In 1960, 157,000 people from the northern regions and 95,000 people of the Volta Region, corresponding to about 12 per cent of the respective regional populations, lived outside of their region of birth (Census Office Accra 1962: 8). Some parts of Ghana, like the poor and densely populated Upper East Region, experienced an exodus of young men. According to Fortes (1971: 15), up to 50 per cent of young men between the ages of 20 and 45 from Taleland in the upper east migrated to the south in the 1960s.

One important incentive for migration from the rural areas to the cities was differential wage levels. In Accra in the 1960s wages were twice as high as in the Ashanti Region and five times higher than in the northern parts of Ghana (Caldwell 1969: 205).

Until the 1970s, migration was male dominated. Because of the gender selectivity of mobility patterns the number of adult men outranged the number of adult women by 50 per cent in the three largest Ghanaian cities in 1960 (Caldwell 1969: 13). The proportion of women among migrants varied with respect to ethnic group, occupation and the distance of migration. Trading minorities, like the Hausa, were more likely to migrate as families, while seasonal long-distance labour migrants, like Mossi or Zabrama, were normally single young men (Rouch 1956: 122). Women were more often permanent rather than seasonal migrants, and their proportion amongst short-distance migrants was higher than amongst long-distance migrants (Caldwell 1969: 67–68).

Until the 1960s the overall ratio of seasonal to permanent migrants was about two to one (Caldwell 1969: 45). Despite the dominance of circular migration, a significant number of migrants settled more permanently in the cities or as tenants in the rural areas (Eades 1987). In particular, trading minorities like Hausa or Yoruba were among the less mobile migrants. Both more seasonal and more permanent migrants[4] usually maintained intense contacts to their places of origin. They sent money, invested in housing and visited their locality of origin more or less regularly. To return one day permanently to their place or region of origin was intended by the majority of migrants who stayed for longer periods in the receiving areas (Caldwell 1969: 198).

While migrants from the northern savannah were more likely to be seasonal migrants, those from the south tended to stay for longer periods in the towns and cities. This was connected to the differential occupational and educational profile of these groups. Because the average level of formal education was higher among 'southerners' than among 'northerners', more of the former went to the cities to look for more qualified, better paid and more permanent jobs (Caldwell 1969: 84), while the latter were more likely to attain more temporary, low-wage and unqualified jobs.

Generally, the levels of literacy and English language competencies was significantly higher among migrants than among non-migrants (Caldwell 1969: 69). According to Caldwell (1969: 86), the link between rural–urban migration and formal education reinforced social differentiation in the rural areas. Because wealthier families were more likely to send their children to school, more children from wealthy families migrated to the towns and cities; and because they offered better income opportunities, the migrants' remittances increased existing inequalities in the rural sending areas.

The majority of migrants did not turn into permanent migrants (Fortes 1936: 41; Hart 1987: 68). The dominance of circular migration was reinforced by the gender structure of the migrants. Because the families in the villages relied on the labour of the young men during the labour-intensive months of the year, many of them would return. In particular, the low-wage segment of the labour market profited from the link between the subsistence and the wage sectors of the economy. Because part of the means of reproduction of the workers' labour force were provided by the village economies, the workers could accept lower wages as if they were forced to cover the whole expenses for their and their families' subsistence from their monetary income (Gerold-Scheepers and Binsbergen 1978: 25).

The social networks connecting the regions of emigration and immigration provided migrants, or persons who aspired to become migrants, with a social infrastructure enabling them to move back and forth in between them (Fortes 1971: 7). Moreover, relations to the locality of origin and to the extended family provided migrants with a form of risk management. It secured them in cases of sickness or the failure of the migratory project. At the same time, money earned in the cities was important to support families in the villages in times of need, such as drought or sickness of family members. Therefore, the migrants' double inclusion in their places of origin and in the monetary sector of the economy in the receiving areas contributed to their social security and that of their relatives (Gluckman 1961: 77).

In addition to the economic logics of incorporation in the communities of origin, there were also social motivations in the narrower sense to maintain home ties. For instance, Frafra migrants from northeastern Ghana had to maintain good relationships to their locality of origin in order to get the lineage elders' permission to marry (Hart 1971: 34–35). A further reason for the Frafra to maintain home ties was that funerals had to be performed by the lineage elders in their respective home villages. Abandonment of these relationships would have made it impossible for the migrants to attain the full status of an ancestor.

From a societal perspective, mass migration changed the relationship between the cities and the rural parts of the Gold Coast. Before the twentieth century, urban centres had a more island-like character. Often being enclaves of the overseas trade, they remained socially and economically weakly integrated into the rural hinterland (Hopkins 1973: 122). Through circular migration and migrants' simultaneous inclusion, the urban centres became more closely interlinked with the rural periphery.

The movements to the metropolitan areas also affected the 'identity landscape' of the Gold Coast. City dwellers had to make sense out of the situation of meeting new types of persons on an everyday basis. As a result of these encounters, some new identity categories were invented and some older ones were reconfigured. For instance, the category 'Frafra', referring to a cluster of more or less distinct social groups in the Upper East Region, changed from being a colonial label used in the context of recruitment of soldiers and workers to a category of self-identification in the context of rural–urban migration (Hart 1971: 21–22). Another orginary urban migrant identity developed in the *zongo*s, strangers' quarters that were predominantly inhabited by migrants from Burkina Faso, Mali, Niger and the northern regions of Ghana and Nigeria. The predominant role of Islam, the use of Hausa as a lingua franca as well as collectively experienced discrimination created and evidenced a shared *zongo* identity among migrants and their descendants with diverse backgrounds (Schildkrout 1974: 198).

The trend towards an extension of the degree of inclusivity of ethnic identities under the condition of migration was accompanied by a complementary process of the reinforcement of solidarity within smaller social entities, in particular kin groups which, due to their smaller size and stronger moral underpinning, proved more reliable in case of a need for substantive support (Caldwell 1969: 133).

Generally, the changes of the political and economic structures that took place in the course of the first half of the twentieth century had a deep impact on the society of the Gold Coast. They brought many innovations and affected those social entities, which pre-existed these developments like families, villages and local and ethnic groups. Nevertheless it did not destroy or replace them by 'modern' forms, as some academics and policymakers had suspected.

POSTCOLONIAL MIGRATION

To understand the transformation of Ghana from a country of immigration to a country of emigration within a decade, the phenomenon has to be put in its broader political and economic context. In this framework, a connection will be drawn between the economic development of Ghana, the state-propagated imaginary of modernity and migration. It is argued that the migration of Ghanaians to Europe and North America can, to some extent, be interpreted as a reaction to the (temporary) failure of the collective project of modernisation to deliver what it had promised.

In the 1950s, political self-determination was perceived by many people in Ghana as a means of overcoming the colonial predicament of exploitation and subordination. This heavy load of historical significance attributed to independence made the experience of failure and the stigma of poverty even more painful. In the context of Zambia, Ferguson (2001: 141–42) spoke of a state of being disconnected. Due to the general economic deterioration of Zambia that was induced by the decline of the world market prices for copper, the mineworkers amongst whom he had done his field research, had to give up the material and social standards that they had achieved in the past. According to Ferguson experience of 'becoming disconnected' implies a feeling of loss. It refers to the social memory of a period when people felt 'connected' with the larger world. Migration from Ghana can be understood, in reference to Ferguson, as an individualised attempt of connection or reconnection to an imagined global modernity, which is entangled with the disillusion of the hopes directed at the development state. In the following paragraphs I carve out some of the specificities of the Ghanaian 'structures and processes of disconnection' (Ferguson 1999: 238).

Becoming Disconnected

Ghana's independence was accompanied by high expectations. In the 1950s it was one of the most promising colonies in all of Africa, with a comparatively good educational system and a prospering economy. The living standard was increasing and Ghana saw itself as being an avant-garde of African emancipation within the modern world of nation-states. The political vision of the country's first President, Kwame Nkrumah, was that Ghana's example should evidence the ability of Africans to build up an efficient, modern and just nation-state. Thereby, it was supposed to disprove the ideology of racism and colonialism. This historical mission was stressed on the eve of independence:

> Today, from now on, there is a new African in the world and that new African is ready to fight his own battle and show that after all the black man is capable of managing his own affairs. We are going to demonstrate to the world, to the other nations, young as we are, that we are prepared to lay our own foundation ... Here today the work of Rousseau, the work of Marcus Garvey[5] ... the work of Casely Hayford[6], the work of these illustrious men who have gone before us has come to reality at this present moment.
>
> (Nkrumah 1961: 106–7)

The conditions for catching up with the developed world appeared to be good. Ghana's income per capita was about the same as that of Mexico and South Korea and it was three to four times higher than the estimates for Nigeria, Kenya and Uganda (Rimmer 1992: 4). The first postcolonial government took over external bank deposits of more than U.S. $550 million (Siebold 1988: 1). The inflation rate was very low, at 1 per cent, and Ghana was classified as a medium income country (Overseas Development Institute 1996).

Nkrumah's plan was to create a 'socialism adapted to suit the conditions and circumstances in Africa' (Rimmer 1992: 84). Practically, this meant an increase in state investment and activities in the fields of infrastructure, education and social welfare. In accordance with the mainstream thought of Western development economy of those days, the Ghanaian development strategy was based on the idea of a state-induced industrialisation with a preference for capital-intensive technologies (Killick 1978: 52–54). The aspired transition from the colonial economy, relying on cheap unskilled labour and agriculture, to the postcolonial economy, which was expected to be based on skilled labour and industrial production in the future, also entailed high investments in the educational system.

Within the political framework of anti-colonialism, it was impossible to assume that political self-determination could turn out to be less beneficial than colonial rule. Therefore, the new states in general and Ghana in particular faced strong pressure to produce instant proof of economic and social progress (Foster 1965: 184).

Nevertheless, the so-called Big Push that was fuelled by state investment, did not produce a sustainable economic development (Rimmer 1992: 84). Because 'the postcolonial boom in public spending was never justified by domestic economic performance' (Hart 1987: 73), it ended in a severe crisis after a short period of accelerated economic growth induced by increased state expenditures. Instead of being a solution to the structural problems of the Ghanaian economy, the strategy of industrialisation aggravated them. The country had to experience that 'import substitution . . . was itself a fairly import-intensive enterprise' (Tabatabai 1986: 396). Since foreign exchange mainly earned by cocoa sales was used to build up and to maintain the factories and the infrastructure projects, the country became not less but even more dependent on its exports (Killick 1978: 330). As long as the cocoa price was high, this indirect subsidisation was possible. But when the price went down, as was the case in 1958–66, deficits in the balance of payments were unavoidable.

Due to a combination of declining world market prices, the state's high demand for foreign exchange and the increasing inefficiency of the state cocoa marketing board, the producer price for cocoa in Ghana decreased significantly. As a consequence, it became less attractive to plant new cocoa trees and cocoa smuggling to Togo and the Côte d'Ivoire, where the producer prices were higher, became an attractive marketing option. This meant practically that the more the state withdrew profits from the cocoa trade to finance its foreign exchange deficit, the less cocoa was available on the market and, as a result, the higher the budgetary deficit became.

In 1962, the assets that were inherited by the British colonial administration were exhausted and the state started to finance its deficit by incurring debts. Because the Nkrumah administration undertook few attempts to obtain long-term development credits or to mobilise international development aid—which would have meant depending on the goodwill of Western governments—it raised unfavourable medium-term supplier credits (Rimmer 1992: 80). This strategy soon became ruinous and the Ghanaian state was 'over-indebted' by the mid-1960s (Siebold 1988: 44–45).

In 1965, consultations with the World Bank and the International Monetary Fund (IMF) about a restructuring of the debts were abandoned because the Ghanaian government refused to accept the suggested conditions

(Siebold 1988: 38–41). In February 1966, the increasingly authoritarian character of the Nkrumah regime, its loss of legitimacy and its inability to improve the economic situation ended in the first coup in Ghanaian history. There was almost no resistance against the forced change of government led by army and police officers, which was an indicator of the general loss of trust in Nkrumah's capacity to solve the country's pressing problems. The agenda of the coup leaders, the so-called National Liberation Council (NLC), was to restore the economic order of the 1950s and to regain the confidence of the Western world (Rimmer 1992: 106). The NLC government accepted the conditions of the IMF and started subsequent negotiations about debt relief and debt restructuring. Most requirements of the IMF aimed at a reduction of the current account deficit, like the devaluation of the Ghanaian currency and the reduction of the volume of imports. In return for compliance with the structure adjustment programme, Ghana's unfavourable medium-term supplier credits were restructured into long-term development credits with better conditions of repayment.

The military government was backed by a rise in the cocoa price. The world market price for cocoa rose constantly from 1967–1970 (Rimmer 1992: 100). The resulting increase of state revenues combined with a reduction of imports, as an effect of the structure adjustment programme, and the restructuring of the debts led to a relaxation of state finances during this period (Rimmer 1992: 114–17). However, the high dependence on a single export product left Ghana in a very vulnerable position (Siebold 1988: 101–3).

Another structural problem became the increasing numbers of state employees. The cocoa farmers had to pay the bill for inefficient allocation of state resources. Although the producer price for cocoa was raised between 1966 and 1969, the increase was significantly below that of the world market price (Rimmer 1992: 113).

In October 1969, after a transition period of roughly three and a half years the military government handed over power to an elected civilian government led by the Progress Party (PP). Kofi A. Busia, who was one of the prominent political opponents of Nkrumah, became the new president. After almost ten years of stagnation, a major economic goal of the Busia administration was to stimulate economic growth (Killick 1978: 56). The favourable cocoa price and the effects of debt restructuring and development aid led to an increase in private consumption in 1969 and 1970. To satisfy the demands of the population, the new government deviated from the austerity policy of the NLC government and liberalised the import licence regime that was introduced by its predecessor to comply with the requirements of the IMF (Rimmer 1992: 125).

In 1971, the situation again tensed because the cocoa price decreased sharply while the expansive spending policy of the Busia government continued. Moreover, the external debt service grew and international aid was diminishing (Rimmer 1992: 115). The Busia administration reacted very hesitantly. The Minister of Finance, Mensah, insisted on his growth policy (Siebold 1988: 115) and negotiated, unsuccessfully, with the IMF about debt relief and a renewed restructuring of the debts. Because of the imminent inability to pay for necessary imports, Busia pulled the emergency brake in December 1971 and decided to no longer act in accordance with his Minister of Finance who did not want to endanger his growth policy. As a sign of goodwill to the IMF, Busia decided to devalue the Cedi[7] by 44 per cent (Siebold 1988: 122–23). Since devaluation of the currency makes imports more expensive, it was a highly sensitive topic amongst the urban Ghanaian public.

On 13 January 1972, a small group of middle-ranked army officers took advantage of the political tensions and overthrew the civilian government. This forced change of government was the prelude for a period of accelerated political and economic decay of the Ghanaian nation-state, which lasted until the mid-1980s. During these years, only one of five changes of government was due to election. The remaining four were the result of coups or palace revolutions, respectively.

The government, which came to power by the coup of 1972, was the National Redemption Council (NRC) led by Colonel I. K. Acheampong. As a means of legitimation, the NRC took popular measures and underpinned them with an anti-imperialist rhetoric. In accordance with Marxist dependency theory, the NRC government proclaimed a policy of self-reliance (Rimmer 1992: 135). It was argued that the less Ghana depended on the world market and on Western countries the better for the country. This view was supported by larger parts of the Ghanaian intellectual elite of the time. Apart from its ideological relevance, the self-reliance policy of the NRC government reflected the economic necessity to reduce imports because of the insufficient supply with foreign exchange. One reason was that Ghana lost its international creditworthiness because the new government unilaterally intermitted its debts service in the context of medium-term supplier credits for 10 years and rejected some of the debts incurred by the Nkrumah administration. The NRC government nationalised 55 per cent of four large timber enterprises and of the Ashanti Goldfields gold mining company (Siebold 1988: 135). Furthermore, the unpopular devaluation of the Cedi was partially repealed, minimum wages were increased, and the cuts of social benefits for soldiers and civil servants executed by the Busia administration were annuled (Rimmer 1992: 134–35). The overvaluation of the Cedi made it necessary to re-introduce a system of import licences.

Although the huge expenses were not backed by revenues, the government ignored the inflationary risks of deficit spending (Siebold 1988: 132). In 1974/75 the sharp rise of the oil price and a drought increased fiscal pressure on the government. The situation was aggravated by the inefficiency of the import licence system and rising inflation. As a reaction to increasing political tensions, Acheampong became more defensive and the system of power maintenance became more authoritarian. In this framework, the so-called Supreme Military Council (SMC) removed the National Redemption

Council (NRC) from government in October 1976. Practically, this meant a concentration of power in the hands of Acheampong and the exclusion of other members of government whose loyalty appeared questionable (Siebold 1988: 145). Thereby, an enclosed and isolated ruling elite was created (Chazan 1982: 465–66), who exploited the state in their own interests with an increasing unscrupulousness.

The real income per capita declined between 1970 and 1980 on an annual average of 3.1 per cent, industrial and agricultural production decreased significantly and the annual inflation averaged about 35 per cent, with peaks of more than 100 per cent in the late 1970s. In accordance with this general downward trend, the volume of foreign trade also decreased. In the period of 1970 to 1982 exports shrank at an annual rate of 9.2 per cent (Rimmer 1992: 108–10). Parallel to the exports also the volume of imports declined. As a consequence, spare parts became rare and hospitals lacked equipment and medicine to maintain efficient services.

Runaway inflation devalued wages. During the 1970s, the minimum wage fell at an annual average rate of 16 per cent; the real value of the average wage declined between 1974 and 1978 by 69 per cent (Siebold 1988: 163). Cocoa producers in 1983 received one tenth of the real income of what they had in 1970 (Tabatabai 1986: 398). Since it was impossible to live on official wages, it became widely accepted in the public sector that people occupied themselves with other economic activities than the ones for which they were paid for (Goody 2003: 18). Among Ghanaians of all social classes a reorientation towards subsistence agriculture could be observed.

The so-called *kalabule*[8] system, a Ghanaian term for the informal economy of this period, played a decisive role in the dramatic decline of the national economy. It was based on the exploitation of price differences between the formal and the informal sector. Because of the inflation the real value of the Cedi decreased during the 1970s. Since the government did not adjust the official exchange rate of the Ghanaian currency, the difference between the black market exchange rate and the official rate grew larger.[9] This made import licences, allowing their owners to buy imported goods at the official exchange rate of the Cedi, a strategic economic resource. People who had access to them made huge profits by buying imports at official prices based on official exchange rates and reselling them for black market prices, which were based on unofficial exchange rates. This economic rationale gave the members of the political elite who controlled the access to import licences a means of enrichment and power (Siebold 1988: 154).

The kalabule system significantly contributed to the decline of the formal sector of the economy and the tax revenues of the state. The resulting budget deficits increased the inflation rate and the growth of the inflation rate increased the incentives for engaging in the kalabule system. A vicious circle of self-accelerating economic deterioration had been created, half intentionally, half accidentally, in which a small group that ruled the state became rich at the expense of the great majority of the population.

After 1975, opposition to the Acheampong administration grew. The urban middle class, which suffered from relative deprivation, was the social basis for resistance against the regime. In this situation, Acheampong's confrontational stance on the opposition was perceived as risky by other members of the ruling elite. In 1978, he and three other members of the ruling SMC were removed by a palace revolution. The new president, Fred W. K. Akuffo, pursued a cautious reform course, including a devaluation of the official Cedi exchange rate and attempts to reduce the budget deficit (Chazan 1982: 474). The devaluation of the Cedi caused riots and did not turn out to be very effective. The government was unable to initiate a consequent course of reform. It was too deeply involved in the kalabule economy, and it was afraid of the consequences of a deflationary policy that was demanded by the IMF. Facing the ongoing protests of parts of the urban middle class and acknowledging its lack of legitimacy the government decided in 1978 to call for elections in 1979.

The army's reputation had substantially suffered during the Acheampong era, affecting in particular the lower ranks of the armed forces, who did not profit materially from the military rule but faced the disdain of the population, and perceived themselves as victims of their ruling superiors. The executors of the next coup, which took place in May and June of 1979, came from within this group of low-ranking army officers. The leader of the new interim government, which was called Armed Forces Revolutionary Committee (AFRC), became Flight Lieutenant J. J. Rawlings. His declared goal was to stop the excesses of corruption and black market economy, to punish the responsible ruling elite and, after having restored order, to hand over the power to an elected civil government. The violent transitional period of military rule to civil government was euphemistically called a 'house cleaning exercise'. In the course of it, Acheampong and Akuffo were executed and traders who were blamed for the excesses of the black market economy were forced to sell their goods at official prices, which were sometimes below wholesale prices (Robertson 1983).[10] In September 1979, after three months of 'house cleaning', Rawlings, who had become very popular in the course of this process, handed over the power to Hilla Liman, who had won the election in June for the People's National Party (PNP). Liman started negotiations with the IMF but was afraid of the political consequences of a devaluation of the Cedi (Rimmer 1992: 167). To prove his goodwill to an international audience he pursued a stricter budget austerity to slow down inflation and started repaying short-term credits. These efforts at stabilising the economy were undermined by unfavourable terms of trade and declining exports (Siebold 1988: 186–87). The living conditions were still deteriorating and already in June 1980 demonstrations against the government and riots started. The government made a careful attempt to liberalise the import licence system in order to improve the domestic supply and to pacify the angry urban population. But the measures did not yield the expected results (Siebold 1988: 188). The government lost control over fiscal policy. Both the budget deficit and inflation increased considerably. The IMF insisted on a devaluation of the Cedi as a precondition for negotiations on an economic recovery programme, but Liman rejected it because he did not want to risk another coup. In this explosive situation it became public that PNP functionaries were involved in kalabule activities (Siebold 1988: 197–98).

On the 31 December 1981, Rawlings overthrew the third civilian government in Ghanaian history after 28 months in office and stayed in power until 7 January 2001. With an inflation rate of more than 100 per cent, a tremendous budget deficit, diminishing foreign exchange reserves and a demoralised population fleeing the country, he took over the Ghanaian state in an extremely difficult situation.

In the beginning, the governments of Western countries reacted with hostility to Rawlings and the government of the Provisional National Defence Council (PNDC). They immediately cancelled consultations on development aid. This was related to the fact that Rawlings supplemented his populist fight against corruption by propagating a revolutionary ideology inspired by the Libyan model of socialism (Siebold 1988: 201–2). Meanwhile the PNDC persecuted people involved in kalabule practices, enforced the official prices with punishments, confiscated large bank assets and mobilised their supporters.

The question of whether Ghana should cooperate with the IMF and the World Bank to solve its problems became a major point of conflict within the PNDC government. A power struggle arose between the radical left wing, whose members refused any kind of negotiations with Western institutions, and a moderate wing, whose members endorsed them. The fraction supporting consultations prevailed in the end and the more radical wing was excluded from government. The economic situation continued to worsen during this period and the initial support within the population declined. Ghana, at this time, faced one of the most severe droughts in its recent history; large parts of the farming land were destroyed by bush fires and more than 700,000 Ghanaians were expelled from Nigeria. The nadir of economic deterioration was reached in 1982 and 1983. Consultations with the IMF were left as the only alternative to mobilise international support in a situation in which the country itself was no longer able to cope with its problems. In 1983, the PNDC government and the IMF together with the World Bank started an economic recovery programme, which turned out to be successful in breaking with the downwards trend of the economy. During the next decade, a liberalisation policy was applied step by step, which entailed a devaluation of the currency, liberalisation of the markets, budget austerity, dismissal of public employees, an increase of wages in the public sector and a rise of producer prices for cocoa. By 1985, the real gross domestic product per capita grew again (ISSER 2003: 4). Since then, the economic situation has stabilised, and the economy has been growing by 3 to 6 per cent per annum.[11]

In 1992, parliamentary democracy was revived and in 2001, when the leader of the largest opposition party, J. A. Kufuor, won the elections and took over the office as president from J. J. Rawlings, Ghana experienced its first democratic change from one elected government to another.[12] In 2009 the second democratic change of government took place when Kufuor, in accordance with the constitution, had to resign after two presidential terms and J. E. Atta Mill, from Rawling's former ruling party, came to power.

Over the last 20 years Ghana has stabilised in many respects. Nevertheless, economic consolidation started at a very low level. Still, Ghana has by now achieved only the average Gross National Income (GNI) per capita of low-income countries.[13] The economic structure of the economy has not changed significantly since colonial times it still relies on the export of cocoa, timber and gold. Poverty remains one of Ghana's major problems. Decker summarised the situation of Ghana in 2005: 'The considerable degree of democratic consolidation is not matched by economic progress' (Decker 2005: 297).

In the previous paragraphs, I have reconstructed the socio-economic processes of becoming disconnected that initiated mass migration from Ghana. It is argued that feelings of loss and exclusion from an imagined global modernity, which appeared to be within grasp of Ghanaians in 1957, played an important role in stimulating transnational and transcontinental mass migration of Ghanaians.

Reversing Migration

In the 1960s, circular migration, which was typical for the colonial migration system, was gradually replaced by more permanent forms of migration (Hart 1971: 25). As a consequence of falling real wages and fewer available jobs, migrants became more hesitant to give up their jobs and had to work longer periods to achieve their economic goals. At the peak of the crisis in the 1980s, the direction of rural–urban migration even reversed (Twum-Baah, Nabila and Aryee 1995a: 160). More urban dwellers went to the rural areas to do subsistence farming than the other way round.

Shortly after independence, the liberal colonial regime of labour migration became an object of criticism and more restrictive immigration policies were implemented. In 1963, the Nkrumah government passed the so-called Aliens Act, which stipulated that all foreigners living in Ghana were required to have a permit of residence (Peil 1971: 206). The military interim government of the NLC tightened the regimentation of foreigners by additionally requiring all non-citizens to have a working permit. First, these measures were only enforced upon the economically successful Lebanese trading minority that faced the largest resentments, but not on African migrants. In 1968, the situation changed and the newly elected Busia government enacted the so-called Compliance Order, according to which all aliens without a residence permit had to leave the country within two weeks. In fear of sanctions and harassments, between 100,000 and 200,000 persons fled from Ghana (Peil 1971: 206).

Although, up to this time, the expulsion of foreigners from Ghana was the most serious action taken against foreigners in West Africa, anti-foreigner policies were also executed by other countries in West Africa, including Nigeria, the Côte d'Ivoire, Sierra Leone, Guinea, Dahomey and Senegal, in the course of decolonisation (Peil 1971: 205–6; Skinner 1960: 395; Wallerstein 1965: 158). After a period of relatively free mobility during the late phase of colonial rule, the nation-building projects of the decolonising states in West Africa often entailed more restrictive migration policies. Thereby, the emergence of nation-states in Africa led to a general reduction of cross-border migration. This tendency could—with few exceptions—be observed all over Africa in the 1960s and 1970s (Gould 1985: 5–6).

Nationalism is based on a differentiation between nationals, who are citizens, and foreigners, who are not, and excludes the latter from the resources and rights which are granted to the former. Therefore, the possibility of expelling non-citizens, in radical reference to the basic distinction between foreigners and citizens, is inherent to the form of the nation-state itself.

For the Busia government the drastic political measure of expulsion was a way to appease the population for some time and detract attention from the country's structural economic problems. It was primarily meant to oust the Lebanese and Yoruba trading minorities, who became the most significant victims of the policies (Rimmer 1992: 131). Economically, the measure was counterproductive. It created a shortage of workers on the cocoa farms (Adomako-Sarfoh 1974: 148–49) and induced an increase of prices because the expulsion of migrant traders strengthened the market power of local traders (Peil 1971: 227; Brydon 1985: 564).

Up to the 1970s, Ghanaians were not very likely to leave the country (Zarachariah and Condé 1981: 6). In some respects, the subsequent increase in emigration was not only an indicator of the failure of the Ghanaian nation-state but also a result of its successes. During the Nkrumah period, Ghana had developed one of the best educational systems in Africa (Gould 1985: 7). Nevertheless, since the late 1960s, the increasing number of school graduates met decreasing job opportunities and wages. The lack of opportunity left a growing segment of formally educated Ghanaians with feelings of relative deprivation (Rhoda 1980: 69–71). Above all, the lack of prospects in Ghana made migration appear as an attractive exit option. Rado (1986: 563) estimated that from the mid-1970s to the early 1980s between one half and two thirds of Ghana's 'experienced, top-level professional manpower' went abroad. The most noticed loss concerned the emigration of teachers, nurses and medical doctors.

To a great extent the growing migration pressure from Ghana was absorbed by Nigeria, which profited from the oil boom of the mid-1970s and invested extensively in infrastructure, medical care and education (Brydon

1985: 565). For Ghanaians, Nigeria was a good destination for migration. English was the official language in both countries and the administrative and legal structures were similar due to their common colonial past as parts of the British Empire (Swindell 1990: 141). Therefore, it was relatively easy for formally educated Ghanaians to convert their educational degrees and professional experiences on the Nigerian labour market. Many skilled Ghanaians worked as teachers, doctors, lawyers, architects and craftspeople (Peil 1995: 350). In the early 1980s, more than 35,000 Ghanaian teachers were employed in Nigeria (Swindell 1990: 140). Formally less educated Ghanaians worked as labourers on the building sites, in the oil industry or as traders. Altogether, an estimated one million Ghanaians lived in Nigeria in the early 1980s (Brydon 1985: 571).

Apart from Nigeria, Ghanaians also started to migrate in greater numbers to other countries. Within Africa, particularly Gabon, Botswana, South Africa, the Côte d'Ivoire and Libya became popular destinations for migration (Gould 1985: 9–11). Skilled professionals and formally educated migrants preferred English-speaking countries where they could convert their cultural capital more easily on the labour markets, while unskilled migrants also went in greater numbers to non-English speaking countries, like Libya, Gabon and the Côte d'Ivoire.

At the beginning of the 1980s, a slump in the international demand for oil caused an economic crisis in Nigeria. In an explosive political situation, foreigners were accused of being responsible for the increase in general unemployment and in criminality and the intensification of religious conflicts. Finally, the Nigerian president Alhaji Shehu Shagari ordered the expulsion of aliens without valid permits of residence in 1983 (Swindell 1990: 153).[14] Afraid of xenophobic violence, 700,000 Ghanaians fled to Ghana (Adepoju 1986: 21), where at this time the already bad economic situation was aggravated by a severe drought. The inflow of large numbers of returnees from Nigeria under these circumstances was a catastrophe. The situation was difficult in a double sense. On the one hand, the weak administration and the impoverished country had to provide help for the masses of return migrants and, on the other hand, the migrants' remittances from Nigeria, on which many families were dependent, abruptly stopped.

In April 1985, the Nigerian government executed a second wave of expulsion. The Ghanaian embassy in Lagos estimated that again about 300,000 Ghanaians, who had returned after the first expulsions or had not left the country in 1983, were exposed to this second displacement within two years.

The expulsions from Nigeria had catalytic effects on the migration of Ghanaians. A significant number of returnees had been able to save money in Nigeria, which they could use to migrate further to other destinations. Moreover, the experiences of mass migration to Nigeria popularised transnational migration as a way out of feelings of relative deprivation in Ghana (Akyeampong 2000: 206). Because several African countries experienced an economic downward trend during the 1980s, the focus of migration gradually shifted towards Western Europe and North America.

TRANSCONTINENTAL MIGRATION

During the last decades, Ghanaians have spread across many of the high- and medium-income countries of the globe, from Australia to South Africa to the United States and Canada, from Sweden to Israel to South Korea and Japan. It is difficult to determine the quantitative level of transnational migration from Ghana because there is no reliable data on emigration. It is estimated that between 5 and 20 per cent of Ghanaian citizens are living abroad (Peil 1995: 365; IMF 2005: 7), which would correspond to between one to four million people, based on the current size of the Ghanaian population. In Western Europe, Great Britain, Italy, Germany, the Netherlands and Spain are the countries with the largest Ghanaian populations (see Table 2.1).

Because of the relatively high number of naturalised Ghanaians, the actual figures of migrants from Ghana and their descendants in Great Britain may even be much larger than the Eurostat data indicate. In the 2001 census of England and Wales, 55,537 persons were identified as being born in Ghana (cited in Bump 2006). The Netherlands as well as the Scandinavian countries

Table 2.1 Ghanaians in Western Europe (2008)*

Country	Ghanaians
Italy	38,400
Great Britain	38,308[a]
Germany	21,969
Spain	13,129
Netherlands	4,594
Switzerland	1,368
Denmark	992
Norway	698
Sweden	679
Finland	564

Source: Eurostat (2009).
Note a: Persons with Ghanaian citizenship in 2005.
*The data originates from the Eurostat data base and was provided to me by email.

might also have larger populations of Ghanaian origin than is represented in the Eurostat statistics. Estimations on Ghanaians in the Netherlands, which include undocumented and naturalised migrants, go up to as much as 40,000 (cited in Bump 2006).[15] In the course of the last decade, Italy and Spain have become the most important destinations for undocumented migration from Africa. In Italy, Ghanaian migrants profited from legalisation campaigns of the government. The latest took place in 2004 and led to a significant increase of the official numbers of Ghanaians. The same could be observed in Spain, where an immigration amnesty was issued in 2005.

Outside of Europe, Canada and the United States are the most significant destinations for Ghanaian migrants. In the year 2000, more than 30,000 Ghanaians officially resided in Canada, of which more than half were concentrated in Toronto (cited in Owusu 2003: 400). The United States, according to the U.S. Census Bureau, was home to 65,570 Ghanaians (cited in Bump 2006) in 2000, but other estimations go up to 200,000 or even 400,000 (cited in Akyeampong 2000: 211).

Transcontinental migration differs from internal migration in at least one important respect. The sending regions of Ghana from where most transcontinental migrants come from are not the same as those from where the majority of rural–urban migrants used to come. Most transcontinental migrants originate from the southern parts of the country, which were the main receiving areas during colonial times and still attract internal migrants (cf. Twum-Baah, Nabila and Aryee 1995b: 4). The shift from north to south in terms of the emigrants' regional origin supports the hypothesis that transcontinental migration grew as a reaction to the relative deprivation of the more privileged parts of the Ghanaian population during the economic crisis and was neither an expression of absolute poverty nor a simple expansion of the scope of pre-existing patterns of migration.

Socially, the mass migration from Ghana induced a significant transnationalisation. Due to technical innovations, like mobile phones, and a reduction in the costs of travelling and communication, spatial distance became less relevant as an obstacle for social interaction. Furthermore, the liberalisation of the Ghanaian economy simplified the transfer of money and the sending of goods. As a result, many Ghanaians, in Ghana and abroad, participate in transnational relationships, which connect them with relatives and friends in various parts of the world.

CASE-STUDY: MIGRATION FROM THE DORMAA DISTRICT

In the second part of this chapter, I will present a case study on migration from the village of Bonokrom[16] in the Dormaa District. The Dormaa District is one of thirteen administrative subunits of the Brong Ahafo Region and is located in the southwest of the region on the border to the Côte d'Ivoire.

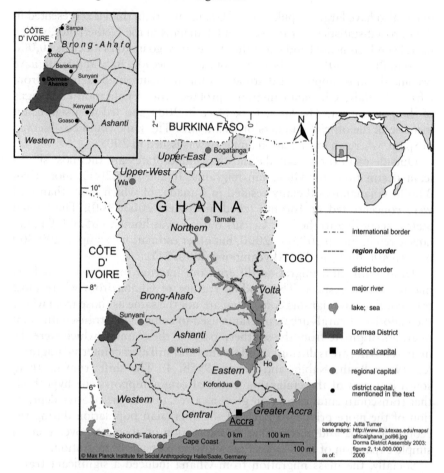

Map 2.1 Research region in Ghana.

The Dormaa District was founded in 1988 within the framework of a national reform of the Ghanaian state administration (Twum-Baah, Nabila and Aryee 1995a: 12). It is situated in the tropical climate zone and was in the past covered by forest. Because of deforestation, which is a result of timber extraction and the expansion of the cacao plantations since the 1930s, only small parts of the district are still densely wooded. Officially, 150,221 people lived in the district in 2003 (Dormaa District Assembly 2003: 2). About 70 per cent of the population is classified as rural, while about 30 per cent live in towns, half of them in the district capital itself. The main income-generating activity is agriculture and the most important cash crops are cocoa and coffee. Additionally, food crops like tomatoes, plantain, maize, cassava, pineapples, citrus, cashews and oil palms are cultivated for marketing purposes. More recently, poultry farming has become a significant economic factor in the region.

Since the early twentieth century, the local economy in Dormaa Ahenkro was strongly dominated by the cultivation of cacao. During the last decades its significance has decreased. Severe bushfires destroyed large parts of the cacao plantations in 1982. After these incidents, many farmers have stopped planting cacao trees. Only in the less densely populated south of the region, cacao farming is still the major economic activity.

At the time of the kalabule economy, the border position of the Dormaa District, providing the Dormaa people with opportunities to exploit differentials in prices and currency exchange rates between the Côte d'Ivoire and Ghana, was a vital resource and alleviated the effects of the crisis. As a result of economic stabilisation, which included the raising of producer prices for cocoa, the incentives for smuggling have decreased. During the recent crisis of the Côte d'Ivoire, the direction of cocoa smuggling even turned around and the farmers from the Ivorian side of the border sold cocoa in the Dormaa District.

Dormaa people perceive themselves as the autochthonous population of the Dormaa District and are part of the larger ethnic group of the Brong or Bono (cf. Arhin 1979). Although the Dormaa people identify themselves as Bono or Brong, identification with the traditional state (*oman*) of which they are part is stronger. The *Dormaahene,* the highest traditional authority of the Dormaa District, and his court in the city of Dormaa Ahenkro symbolises the unity of the Dormaa people.

The Dormaa District was for a long time a receiving area of immigration. The favourable climate for cocoa production, the consequent demand for wage labour and the low population density all supported a substantive inflow of migrants (Caldwell 1969: 2). Between 1960 and 1984 Brong Ahafo, of which the Dormaa District is part, was among the regions with the highest number of immigrants in Ghana together with Greater Accra and the Ashanti Region (Achanfuo-Yeboah 1993: 224). In general, the extent of emigration from Brong Ahafo remained relatively small. This was connected to at least three factors. First, cacao cultivation was still expanding in the south of the Dormaa District when it was already stagnating in other regions of Ghana, and this created economic incentives to stay in the region. Second, the strategic border position and the possibility of smuggling was an economic resource, which made cocoa production more profitable than in parts of the country without direct access to a border. Third, because of the peripheral position of the district the level of formal education was lower than in some other parts of the country and, as it was shown above, the degree of formal education correlates positively with the probability of migration.

The pressure of emigration started to grow in the late 1970s and early 1980s, when many families lost their cacao farms as a result of the bush fires. The most important destinations for migration during this period were the Côte d'Ivoire and Nigeria. More than 75 per cent of migrants from the Brong Ahafo Region covered by the census of 1984 went to the Côte d'Ivoire and about 15 per cent to Nigeria (Twum-Baah, Nabila and Aryee 1995b: 8). Transcontinental migration became increasingly relevant during the 1980s.

My own decision to go to the Dormaa District was influenced by a significant number of migrants from this area whom I met in Berlin. Apart from Berlin, Hamburg, Saarbrücken and Stuttgart are considered to be centres of Dormaa migrants in Germany. A well-connected pioneer migrant from the Dormaa District to Germany estimated that there were about 80 Dormaa migrants in Berlin and a total of about one thousand in Germany.[17] Groups of Dormaa migrants have also emerged in North America and in different Western European countries, in particular in Great Britain and Italy. Over the last decades, the Dormaa District has turned into an emigration area. Most migrants from Dormaa who came to Europe and North America could only find unqualified jobs in the receiving areas and belong to the examined class of transcontinental Ghanaian labour migrants that will be the focus of Chapter 5.

In our case study, we found 728 people living in Bonokrom, who belonged to 60 different kin units.[18] The size of the covered 60 kin units varied from 7 to 80 persons, with an average of 28 persons. Altogether we collected data on 1,410 living persons.

As much as 96 per cent of the 378 villagers about whom we collected occupational data were categorised either as farmers (58 per cent) or as students (38 per cent). The peasants in Bonokrom produced mainly food crops like tomatoes, maize, sugarcane, plantain, cocoyam and cassava (see Table 2.2).[19]

Altogether, 71 per cent of the people in the sample lived in different settlements within the Dormaa District (cf. Table 2.2); 87 per cent out of the 702 persons living in the Dormaa District about whom we acquired data were either farmers or students. The high number of students reflects, on the one hand, the high proportion of children under 15, which is due to the relatively high fertility rate of the population, compared to Western European standards. On the other hand, it indicates that most children have access to school facilities.

Outside the Dormaa District, there were two relevant destinations for rural–rural migration. One of them is the cacao farming zone of the close-by Western Region (Benneh 1988), where 41 persons (3 per cent) of the sample were living. Another destination was the neighbouring rural borderland of the Côte d'Ivoire where 31 persons settled.

The most important destination for rural–urban migration was the district capital of Dormaa Ahenkro (236 persons; 17 per cent). Since many people in the villages of the Dormaa District have friends and relatives in Dormaa Ahenkro, it is easy for them to move to the town. In the district capital educational and administrative functions are concentrated. It is a common pattern in Ghana to send talented children to relatives in town for

Table 2.2 Persons by Place of Residence

Region/Country/Continent of Residence	Selected Areas of Residence	Persons	Percent
	Dormaa District	999	71
	Sunyani District	118	8
Brong Ahafo Region (B/A)		*1,164*	*84*
	Greater Accra	56	4
	Ashanti Region	26	2
	Western Region	47	3
Ghana (except B/A)		*139*	*10*
Ghana (Total)		*1,303*	*92*
	North Africa	9	1
	West Africa	38	3
	Côte d'Ivoire	34	2
	Nigeria	4	0.3
Africa (except Ghana)		*48*	*3.5*
	Europe	55	4
	North America	4	0.3
Europe and North America		*59*	*4.2*
Outside Ghana (Total)		*108*	*8*
Total		**1,410**	

their education, because the schools in the urban areas are better and offer opportunities for secondary education, which do not exist in the villages. This is reflected in the proportion of students in the sample, which made up 47 per cent in Dormaa Ahenkro, as compared to 37 per cent in Bonokrom. Moreover, Dormaa Ahenkro provides job opportunities outside of the agricultural sector. Among the persons covered, only 17 per cent were farmers. Apart from agriculture, the most important income-generating activities in Dormaa Ahenkro were trading (9 per cent), different handicrafts (11 per cent) and personal services, mostly drivers and hairdressers (7 per cent). For the artisans and people employed in the personal service sector formal education might be helpful but is not necessarily required in the context of Dormaa Ahenkro. In this sense, it is remarkable that none of the documented occupations required higher education. Although the sample is not representative for the population of Dormaa Ahenkro, it does indicate a structural problem. There is a considerable proportion of students but relatively few opportunities to convert educational capital on the labour market into status-adequate occupations. This outcome was confirmed by the findings for other urban settlements:

Next to the Dormaa District, the nearby Sunyani District was the area where most people of the sample lived (8 per cent). Out of 118 persons, 86 resided in the regional capital, Sunyani, itself. Students made up more than half of the 55 persons, about whom we collected data. Only three persons in the sample were farmers. The rest were distributed over different sectors: six in personal services, included two drivers and four hairdressers, and two persons performing public and social services, as well as one lawyer.

The most important destinations of migration in Ghana outside the Brong Ahafo Region were the urban centres of the country, in particular Greater Accra, Kumasi and Sekondi-Takoradi; 56 persons migrated to Greater Accra and 20 to Kumasi. A group of six persons, mostly policemen and soldiers, resided in the seaport of Sekondi-Takoradi. Altogether, less than 6 per cent of the sample lived in one of the three mentioned cities. The relatively small number of persons in metropolitan areas reflects, on the one hand, that the Brong Ahafo Region was never a major area of emigration to the cities in Ghana. On the other hand, it shows that the urban labour markets offer little attractive alternatives to persons from the Dormaa District.

More than 50 per cent of the 48 persons living in Kumasi, Greater Accra and Sekondi-Takoradi were students. Among the wage earners, craftsmen and persons performing social and public services, namely policemen and soldiers, made up the largest occupational groups. All in all, the data on the spatial and occupational distribution shows two tendencies: firstly, most of the mobility takes place within the Dormaa District. Secondly, the most important income-generating activity is farming. About two thirds of the adult population (excluding the students) were classified as farmers. The remaining one third was distributed over different occupational fields among which crafts (11 per cent), trade (7 per cent) and personal and social services (12 per cent) were the most relevant. If we consider that most families also engage in some kind of subsistence farming, the economic importance of the agricultural sector is even higher than these figures indicate. Additionally, we can observe that more than 40 per cent of the sample was classified as students, which documents the high relevance of schooling for people in and from the Dormaa District. Because the formal labour market does not provide an adequate number of jobs requiring formal education, the situation is very likely to produce feelings of dissatisfaction and status inconsistency among the educated group of people.

About 18 per cent of the persons covered lived outside the Dormaa District in Ghana. In total, the data shows that the number of internal migrants outside the region of origin is relevant but comparatively modest. This is not the result of a lack of desire to go somewhere else to improve one's life, as I realized by talking to young people, but rather of the fact that the urban labour markets in Ghana do offer this perspective only to a limited extent from the perspective of the Dormaa District.

Forty-eight persons (3.5 per cent) in the sample lived in an African country outside Ghana, out of which 31 resided in the neighbouring border region of the Côte d'Ivoire. Due to the political and economic crisis in the Côte d'Ivoire, only three persons had migrated to Abidjan. Only four persons lived in Nigeria where more significant numbers of persons from the Brong Ahafo Region went in the 1980s.[20]

Ten intra-African migrants were outside West Africa. Eight persons lived in Libya, one in Morocco and one in Gabon. Libya and Morocco are considered as stepping stones on the way to Western Europe. Since the 1990s (Konadu-Agyemang 1999: 28), mostly young men with insufficient financial resources to take an airplane and/or without a chance to get a visa for the European Union have travelled from Ghana through Burkina Faso to Niger in order to clandestinely cross the border to Libya. Because many of them walk off-road through the Sahara to circumvent Libyan border controls, the endeavour is risky and several persons have died on their way through the desert. The migrants' goal is to work in North Africa, in particular in Libya, for some time in order to earn enough money to cross the Mediterranean Sea illegally by boat. People either try to enter southern European countries, especially Italy, directly from Libya, or they go to Morocco in order to enter Spain from there.

Fifty-five persons, or about 4 per cent of the sample, lived in Europe and four people were residents of the United States and Canada. Although the absolute number is not particularly high, it is significant when compared to the 48 migrants who were distributed over the African continent (out of which 31 lived just across the border in the Côte d'Ivoire) and the 76 persons in Greater Accra and Kumasi.

Although internal migration is quantitatively the most significant form of migration in the sample, its relevance is limited. Moreover, it becomes visible that African countries, in particular those in West Africa, have lost relevance as destinations for migration. At the same time, Europe and North America became significant destinations for migrants despite the large distances to be overcome, the legal restrictions and the—in relation to local wages—high travel costs.

The destinations of the 59 transcontinental migrants in the sample display two divergent processes. On the one hand, they have become more diverse over the decades and, on the other hand, personal networks and chain migration lead to a concentration of Dormaa migrants in some places (see Table 2.3).

Table 2.3 Receiving Countries in Europe

Country	Persons	Percent
Germany	17	31
Great Britain	10	18
Italy	5	9
France	4	7
Spain	3	5
Netherlands	2	4
Sweden	2	4
Belgium	1	2
Europe (without specification)	11	20
Total	55	100

About half of all migrants lived either in Germany or in Great Britain. The fact that in the sample the number of persons living in Germany is higher than the number in Great Britain or Italy is probably an outlier effect caused by the extraordinary success of one family's chain migration to Germany and does not reflect a more general regional pattern of migration.[21] Although Great Britain, due to its colonial past and the long history of immigration from Ghana, still plays an important role, the sample shows that the destinations of migration diversified and shifted to continental European countries during the 1980s and 1990s. It exhibits that colonial ties, languages and the recognition of educational qualifications are of decreasing value for a prediction of migration destinations. Indirectly, it reflects that, due to profound global social inequalities (cf. Chapter 4), the dominant goal of this type of migration is the exploitation of the wealth and wage differentials between Western Europe and Ghana, and career or status considerations, such as the convertibility of formal cultural capital, are of secondary relevance (cf. Chapter 5).

It is noteworthy that in 11 cases, it was not differentiated between continental European countries at all. It reflects the exchangeability of these destinations from the local Ghanaian perspective. In terms of the type of migration and the meaning attributed to it, it made no difference to the interviewees whether a relative lives in Belgium, France, Germany, the Netherlands or Italy.

Western European countries were the main destinations of migration in the 1980s and early 1990s. Although these countries still matter, the regional focus of migration has been shifting to Southern Europe since the second half of the 1990s, particularly in Spain and Italy. Measured in five-year intervals the average number of transcontinental migrants in the sample has increased since the mid-1970s. The only exception is the period between 1995 and 1999. This decrease coincides with a period of increasingly restrictive anti-immigration policies being implemented by the governments of northwestern European countries. Between 2000 and 2003, the number of migrants rose again. This is partly a result of the inclusion of Morocco and Libya in the sample.[22] The migration of Ghanaians to North Africa indicates a change of the routes of migration. In the 1980s, many migrants entered Western Europe through Eastern Europe or flew directly by plane to Western Europe. Anti-migration policies and bi-national agreements on the deportation of undocumented migrants with Eastern European countries in the 1990s made these routes increasingly risky for African migrants. As a result, North Africa replaced Eastern Europe as a doorstep to the European Union.

Very obvious is the disproportion between male and female migrants in the sample; 39 out of 47 migrants are men. The assumed risks of the journey match male gender identities better than female ones and it is often easier for men in the Dormaa District to raise funds for migration in their families.[23]

Statistics indicate that in the past Ghanaian transcontinental pioneer migrants were often men and that the increase in the share of women occurred with a temporal delay, because they often depended on male migrants to sponsor or to support their migration in other respects (cf. Chapter 3; Twum-Baah, Nabila and Aryee 1995b: 38). This is also confirmed by the data collected in Bonokrom. Six out of eight women were supported by male transcontinental migrants, while 25 out of 38 men did not receive support from transcontinental migrants.

Transcontinental migration from Bonokrom is not only gender selective but also age selective; 36 out of 39 migrants were between 16 and 35 when they left their country of origin. On the one hand, this pattern reflects the demand structure in the receiving countries, where it is easier for young people to find jobs. On the other hand, migration often takes place in a life stage of economic orientation before a family is founded. In this period, individuals are in a position of relative structural freedom, which makes the imagination and realisation of alternative life sketches more probable than at other points in time. To a certain extent, also the institutional logic of formal education has an impact on the age of migration. For many, the time after finishing school and during the first years of full-time work are a period when they are more likely to migrate than after they have established themselves economically and socially.

The data also shows a relation between education and transcontinental migration. The educational status of the 42 persons, on whom we could collect information, is above the regional average. Only one third of all children in the Dormaa District continued school beyond the level of primary education (Dormaa District Assembly 2003: 8). In contrast to this, 42 out of 43 transcontinental migrants in our sample had an educational degree above primary level. Most of them had medium types of education; 31 out of 43 persons had visited either middle school or junior secondary school, but did not have a secondary school degree or tertiary education. This is noteworthy because persons with medium types of education were particularly affected by the devaluation of educational degrees on the Ghanaian labour market during the economic crisis (Foster 1980: 227; see Table 2.4).

If remittances are taken as an indicator of the economic success of migrants in the receiving areas, the outcomes of the study of the Ghana Statistical Service (Twum-Baah, Nabila and Aryee 1995a: 194–95) support the hypothesis that particularly medium types of education were devalued; 24.2 per cent of the 297 internal migrants with a junior secondary school or middle school degree in the quoted sample sent remittances to their family members in the rural areas. In contrast to this, 52 per cent of the secondary school graduates, 55 per cent of migrants with technical education and 67 per cent of the university graduates remitted money. The share of people with junior secondary or middle school degrees who sent remittances, therefore, was much more comparable with those with elementary school education (17.4 per cent) or without any school education (23.2 per cent) than with migrants with higher education. Although persons with a medium level of education have a degree above the average, it is for many of them not convertible into a corresponding status and income on the Ghanaian labour market and, therefore, creates a situation of status inconsistency.

Table 2.4 Educational Status of Transcontinental Migrants

Type of School	Persons	Percent
Middle School	19	44
Junior Secondary School	12	28
Secondary School	5	12
University	3	7
Vocational School	1	2
Polytechnics	1	2
Teacher Training College	1	2
No formal education	1	2
Total	43	100

This interpretation is also supported by the jobs which the transcontinental migrants in the sample had before they left Ghana; 13 out of 41 were farmers before they migrated; 10 migrants were students or had just finished school shortly before they left. Together these two groups made up more than 55 per cent. Only four migrants had a modern middle class job. 9 persons were involved in petty trade, personal services and crafts, which are highly competitive domains providing only few profit chances.

Since migration within Ghana, as well as alternatives within Africa, only to a limited extent offer opportunities, migration to Europe or North America promises to present a solution to the perceived deprivation, at least in terms of monetary incentives.

Transcontinental migrants were more likely to be urban dwellers before they left Ghana than the rest of the sample; 61 per cent of them had lived in Dormaa Ahenkro, Sunyani, Kumasi or Accra where only 28 per cent of all persons in the sample lived. In contrast, only 9 per cent of the transcontinental migrants had lived in the village of Bonokrom before they migrated as compared to 37 per cent of the total sample. On average, Ghanaians who live in towns have higher incomes than people in rural areas and, consequently, more financial resources to spend on migration. Moreover, the density of transnational networks is higher in the cities. Personal contacts to transnationally connected persons can facilitate migration because they enlarge the subjective scope of individual action and provide access to practical knowledge about the modalities of migration.

Since transcontinental migration is expensive in relation to local incomes, access to funding is an important factor for explaining migratory patterns. According to their relatives in Bonokrom, 28 per cent of the migrants paid all or a significant share of their travelling costs themselves. Eight out of these 15 persons financed their migration without any assistance from anybody else. Three out of these eight accumulated the capital to go to Europe by working in other African countries (Nigeria, Gabon and Libya), one migrant was an executive in the gold industry before he left, one was a pharmacist and one was a teacher.[24] In the seven cases in which migrants did pay a significant share but not all the travelling costs themselves, close relatives contributed the rest.

To finance one's migration by oneself attenuates the moral weight of the relatives' claims to remittances and, in the case of an unsuccessful return, there are fewer reasons for complaint about the failure than in situations in which the migration is seen as a family investment.

Apart from the migrants themselves, their parents—ten fathers and six mothers—were the most important sponsors of migration. Since having a son or a daughter abroad can be an important resource in times of need, some parents considered this assistance to be an active diversification strategy for the family's income. In other cases, the migrants had to convince their parents more actively to support their migration. As many migrants were supported by their mothers as were sponsored by their mothers' brothers. In the framework of the pre-colonial matrilineal Akan kinship system (see Chapter 4), it was the mothers' brothers (*wofa*) who took responsibility for their sisters' children, to whom they also left their estate. Ever since colonial times, attempts have been undertaken to promote the European model of the nuclear family. Although generally in the present-day Dormaa District, men care primarily for their own children, which is also indicated by the higher number of persons being supported by their fathers than by their mothers' brothers, the responsibility for one's sisters' children is still of some relevance, as these figures indicate. Four out of six mothers' brothers who supported their sisters' children lived abroad, while only two out of ten fathers who supported their children were migrants. On the one hand, this is related to the fact that married persons with children are less likely to migrate to Europe. On the other hand, this result indicates that the obligation to support one's matrilineal family becomes particularly relevant in cases in which persons are considered as relatively wealthy and resourceful, as is the case with transcontinental migrants. In this respect the support strategies of the mothers' brothers are qualitatively different from the support of the fathers in the sample, who in most cases supported their children while they were in Ghana, but resemble more the patterns which are typical for support among siblings.

In seven out of eight cases in which persons were supported by a brother or a sister these were migrants themselves. Seven out of eight siblings covered were older than the brothers or sisters they funded. Seniority and responsibility for younger siblings are important values in Akan societies, which consequently also manifests in the context of sponsoring younger siblings' migration. It is noteworthy that the same relevance of seniority also becomes observable in the mothers' brothers' strategy of selecting children for migration. In four of five cases, they chose the children of their older sisters. This means that these migrants picked children of those sisters to whom they had to pay respect as their seniors and, since girls often are from an early age on involved in child-care, they were those who presumably looked after them when they were young. In this sense, the support patterns of matrilineal uncles indirectly reflects the relationship between relatively affluent men and their (mostly) older sisters.

In this chapter, I have presented an historical overview of the more recent migration history to and from Ghana. In this context, the argument was presented that there is a link between the promises of modernity, expansion of mass education and transnational migration. Experiences of status inconsistency and the process of becoming disconnected are considered important in understanding why Ghana became one of the major sub-Saharan sending countries of migrants to Western Europe and North America. In the course of the 1970s, a larger class of people had emerged who, because of their formal qualifications, had status claims but could not satisfy them under the given societal conditions. In particular, after the expulsions from Nigeria, transcontinental mobility appeared to offer one of few ways out of this situation.

This interpretation was confirmed by the case study. It could be shown that in particular young male urban dwellers with a medium level of education were likely to migrate. Furthermore, it was shown that kinship relationships were of great importance in the context of fundraising. As I will argue more extensively in Chapter 4, reciprocity and the redistribution of resources within families are important factors for the understanding and theorising of transnational social relationships.

3 Processes of Localisation

The fast growth of the German post-war economy in the 1950s and 1960s created a huge demand for labour. Until the building of the wall, in 1961, the immigration of East Germans was an important source of supply. Afterwards, the German economy became dependent on the migration of cheap and unskilled workers from Mediterranean countries, which had already started before 1961. The first bilateral contract on the recruitment of labourers was ratified between Germany and Italy in 1955. In 1960 contracts with Spain and Greece followed, in 1961 with Turkey, in 1963 with Morocco, in 1964 with Portugal, in 1965 with Tunisia and in 1968 with Yugoslavia. The official number of foreigners grew from about 500,000 in 1950 to roughly four million in 1973. In November 1973, the government reacted with the declaration of the so-called *Anwerbestopp* (stop of labour recruitment) to an economic downturn and increasing unemployment. Although it changed the legal conditions of immigration, it did not lead to the intended quantitative reduction of the number of immigrants in West Germany. As a reaction to the legal changes, migrants became more hesitant to leave West Germany and tried to bring their families to Germany. Additionally, immigration continued by other legal means (Bade and Oltmer 2004: 72–73). From 1973 to 2008, the total number of non-Germans grew from four million to 6.7 million.[1]

Besides family reunion, political asylum was one of few remaining legal possibilities for non-Germans to migrate to West Germany.[2] The West German asylum law, which was formulated against the historical background of the refugees who fled from Germany during Nazi-fascism, was one of the most liberal ones in the world at that time (Bade and Oltmer 2004: 86). Although the tendency of growth in numbers of asylum seekers was noticeable all over Western Europe, Germany attracted the largest share in the European Union between 1973 and 1993 (Nuscheler 1995: 49).[3] The number of asylum seekers in Germany increased from 5,289 in 1972 to 121,318 in 1989 to more than 322,599 in 1993.[4]

During the 1980s, respective German governments reacted to the growing numbers of asylum seekers by an increasingly restrictive policy, which culminated in the change of the constitution in 1993. In contrast to the 'guest workers', who had come only from a limited number of sending countries with which the German government had agreed on bilateral contracts, the individualised logic of the application for asylum as well as the shifting of the global centres of political crisis and conflict facilitated a diversification of countries of origin. Until the mid-1980s, migrants from non-European countries, like Sri Lanka, Iran or Ghana, made up large groups of asylum applicants. Because of political interventions, which impeded migration by airway to West Germany, their share declined in the second half of the 1980s. At the same time the number of East and Southeast European asylum applicants increased sharply because of the political changes which took place in the Eastern Bloc during this period (Bade 1994: 95–99).

The first step in a series of restrictive measures against migration from the global south was the introduction of visa requirements for citizens of several countries, among them Ghana, during the late 1970s and early 1980s. The visa regime in the following decades turned into a strategic element of the anti-immigration policies of all Western European governments. The embassies gained influence as gatekeepers, whose function in the countries of the global south increasingly became to stop immigration before it could start.

The number of Ghanaians in Germany rose from 1,340 Ghanaians in 1969—with a peak of 25,952 in 1992—to 20,447 in 2008. From 1979, the year of Rawlings' first coup, to 1993, the year when the asylum law was changed, the number of Ghanaians increased sharply, only interrupted by two declines in 1983–84 and 1987–88, respectively. Although

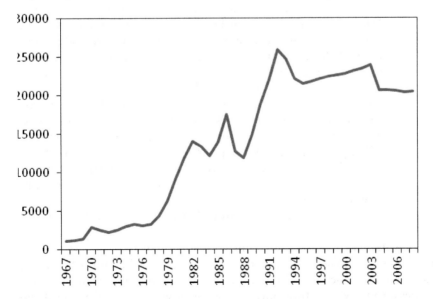

Figure 3.1 Ghanaians in Germany (1967–2008).[5]
Source: Statistisches Bundesamt Deutschland (2008).

the decreases were amplified by periodical corrections of the official foreigner statistics,[6] the number also indicates the temporary effects of anti-immigration policies, such as the introduction of visa requirements for Ghanaians in the early 1980s and a package of measures undertaken in 1986 and 1987 (see below).

Until the mid-1980s, it was still possible for Ghanaians and other migrants to circumvent migration restrictions by travelling to East Germany and then entering West Germany from there. Steve Antwi, a Ghanaian re-migrant whom I met in Accra, gave me a biographical account of his experiences of the transit migration from East Berlin to West Berlin:

S: Suddenly, I was in East Berlin . . . I did not know anything about asylum and how I should apply for it. I mean, I knew that there was East and West Germany but I didn't know that it was really as much separated . . .

B: But you flew from Lagos to East Berlin?

S: Yes, to East Berlin with Aeroflot. This was the end of September—26 September 1984. It was terribly cold . . . At one point, the *Volkspolizei* [police of the GDR; B.N.] told me: "You can go in this direction. The border is there." I was not alone on the plane. There were about 35 people, Ghanaians and Nigerians, who were with me . . . They put us on a train and, then we arrived at this famous checkpoint—Friedrichstraße. We walked from there to West Berlin. I did not know anybody. Most people had an agent. Me and another boy, we did not have anybody. We saw how the agents picked up their people and entered the train. We did just the same. After we had entered West Germany, I think within three minutes or so the police came and wanted to see our passports. Then they took us to a hotel and said, "You can stay here. We will come and pick you up tomorrow" . . . The next day they brought us to the place where you can apply for asylum . . . We, my friend and I, did not know anything at this time . . . Some Ghanaians came to us and said, "Yes, you must fill in a paper and you have to write that you are asylum seekers and refugees and so on. Otherwise they will send you back." Then we wrote something and they gave us tips how we should do it.

(Interview, Steve Antwi, 26 October 2001, Accra)

In 1986, the two German governments agreed that persons intending to travel on to West Germany had to prove they had a valid visa before being allowed to enter the GDR. Moreover, the West German government started to fine airlines which transported passengers without valid travel documents, required transit travellers to produce a transit visa and tightened the asylum procedure law (Bade 1994: 105–8).

Despite some short-term effects of these measures, the Ghanaian population continued to grow until 1993. In the 1980s and the early 1990s between 1,700 and almost 7,000 Ghanaians applied annually for asylum in Germany. Although only few Ghanaians obtained a secure legal status by being accepted as asylum seekers,[7] the application procedure was of strategic importance for the growth of the Ghanaian population in Germany after the mid-1970s. The often several years of asylum decision-making provided migrants with the opportunity to attain a more permanent and secure legal status in Germany by other means. Many Ghanaians married German citizens or foreigners with a secure legal status. After a group of Ghanaians once had established itself in Germany, family reunion became another important way of entering the country.

In 1993, Ghana became one out of eight countries that were classified as safe countries of origin in the annex to § 29 of the German asylum procedure law (*Asylverfahrensgesetz*).[8] Since then, it has become practically impossible for Ghanaians to obtain political asylum in Germany and the decision-making process is substantially accelerated. After 1993, the official numbers of Ghanaians declined sharply and since 1995 they more or less stagnated.[9] Nevertheless, Ghanaians are still the largest group of sub-Saharan Africans in Germany. Apart from legal and policy factors, there were also economic and political developments which made Germany less attractive as a destination for immigrants. A great number of East Germans entered the labour market in the 1990s and aggravated problems of unemployment. Additionally, rationalisation processes and the transfer of industrial production to low-wage and medium-wage countries led to a decrease in the demand for unskilled and semi-skilled jobs in the industrial sector, which often were worked by immigrants. Moreover, Germany stopped being a doorway to Western Europe. As mentioned in the previous chapter, the migration routes of West Africans have shifted from East Europe to South Europe, and the European Union was expanded to the East.

Changes in the gender ratio are the most significant demographical development among Ghanaians in Germany. The share of women increased from 29 per cent in 1985 to 53 per cent in 2008.[10] These numbers indicate that the majority of pioneer migrants from Ghana to Western Europe were young men. After they had established themselves, they frequently assisted Ghanaian women to migrate to Germany. Recently, the number of women even outnumbered the number of men.[11]

Further significant changes concern the migrants' legal and social status. While 30 per cent of the Ghanaian population were students in the late 1960s, their share decreased to 2 per cent in the 1980s and 1990s.[12] In recent years, a modest increase in the numbers of students is noticeable[13], which is connected to the expansion of university programmes in English. Nevertheless, the share of students still does not count for more than 4 per cent of the total Ghanaian population in Germany.[14]

As an outcome of being exposed to the asylum procedure the lives of many Ghanaians in Germany were shaped by instabilities and insecurities between the mid-1970s and the early 1990s. After 1993, a legal consolidation of the Ghanaian population became noticeable. The share of asylum seekers decreased from 30 per cent in 1980 to 1 per cent in 2000. Although a relevant number of Ghanaians lives as undocumented migrants in Germany, the majority has attained a secure legal position by now. On an average, the legal status of Ghanaians is more secure than that of comparable African migrant groups, like Togolese or Ethiopians, who came to Germany more recently.[15]

Ghanaians in Germany concentrate in comparatively large cities in the north and west of Germany. The most important centre of Ghanaian migration to Germany is Hamburg with more than 4,900 legal Ghanaians, making up 24 per cent of the Ghanaian population in Germany. Large groups also live in Berlin (9 per cent), Düsseldorf and Bremen (see Table 3.1).

Hamburg's exceptional role is related to its importance as a centre of European sea trade. Trade relations between Hamburg and the former Gold Coast have existed for more than 100 years (Hopkins 1973: 130). In the late 1970s and 1980s, Hamburg became famous among Ghanaians for providing job opportunities and relatively favourable conditions of stay (Ter Haar 1998b: 135). Berlin was, as already mentioned, of special significance as the gate to Western Europe for migrants who came through Eastern Europe in the 1980s and early 1990s.

Table 3.1 Cities with Large Ghanaian Populations in Germany (2008)[16]

City	Ghanaians
Hamburg	4,949[a]
Berlin	1,788[a]
Düsseldorf	1,021[b]
Bremen	975[a]
Frankfurt	662
Stuttgart	612
Hanover	525[c]
Cologne	457[d]
Dortmund	401
Munich	392
Total	12,041

Note a: Statistisches Bundesamt (2008).
Note b: Einwohnermelderegister, Stadt Düsseldorf (2008).
Note c: Ausländerzentralregister, Stadt Hannover (2008).
Note d: Amt für Stadtentwicklung und Statistik, Stadt Köln (2008).

Processes of Localisation 73

The larger Rhine-Ruhr area in the West of Germany, where Düsseldorf, Dortmund and Cologne are located, is a densely populated traditional immigration area where heavy industry and coal mining provided job opportunities for migrants in the past. Moreover, Ghana Airways flew directly from Düsseldorf to Accra until 2004.

However, although economic and social factors influence migration decisions, the differentiation of centres of immigration is partly a self-reinforcing process: to some extent migrants migrate to places where other migrants of the same type have already migrated to.

GHANAIANS IN EAST GERMANY

Shortly after independence, the Nkrumah government signed a bilateral agreement with the government of the GDR on the admission of Ghanaian students at East German universities.

The first students matriculated in 1959. The majority of the more than 100 Ghanaians who lived in East Germany at the peak of Ghanaian educational migration in 1966[17] arrived between 1963 and 1965. In 1966, when the Nkrumah government was overthrown, the cooperation between Ghana and the GDR stopped. The new Ghanaian government changed its political alliances and abandoned its diplomatic relations to East Germany. In April 1966, they ordered all Ghanaian students in the GDR to leave the country and cut financial support. Although some students the GDR permanently, the majority remained in the country or returned after a short period; 25 out of 37 Ghanaian students who matriculated at the University of Leipzig in 1966 continued their studies.[18]

In 2002, at least eight out of 79 former GDR students who I could identify, all of them medical doctors, lived in West Germany. Some of the other students returned to Ghana and others migrated to the United States and Canada. Not until the late 1970s did the GDR gain, again, some relevance as a destination for Ghanaian students. In the 1980s, a so-called Committee for Peace and Solidarity offered a small number of scholarships for the GDR to Ghanaian students. About 40 Ghanaian students lived in the GDR in 1988.[19] Although the GDR was an important transit country from 1980 to 1986, it did not become a destination for labour migration of Ghanaians.

Different from West Germany, African students were a privileged group in relation to the local population in the GDR. In the 1960s, they received a monthly grant both from the GDR and from Ghana. The Ghanaian administration paid the stipend in foreign exchange, with which the students could buy items at special foreign currency shops.[20] Moreover, they were allowed to travel to West Germany and West Berlin. After the building of the wall, the restricted mobility of GDR citizens and the limited access to Western consumer goods created an opportunity structure for those persons who could freely cross the border between East and West Germany from which also Ghanaian students profited.

74 Theorising Transnational Migration

After the reunification of Germany in 1990, mostly asylum seekers and students from Ghana came to East Germany. Asylum seekers in Germany do not have free choice of residence but are distributed by the *Bundesamt für Migration und Flüchtlinge* (Federal Office for Migration and Refugees) according to quotas all over the country. Because of a lack of economic opportunity structure, high unemployment and racism, only very few Ghanaians voluntarily settled in the east of the country. Altogether, only about 2 per cent of the Ghanaian population in Germany lived in one of the five eastern federal states (excluding Berlin) in 2008.[21]

GHANAIANS IN BERLIN

According to official statistics about 1,800 out of 15,000 Africans in Berlin have a Ghanaian passport.[22] This means that Ghanaians constitute the largest group of Africans in Berlin. Additionally, 563 Ghanaians—which corresponds to more than one fourth of the total population—were naturalised as German citizens between 1991 and 2005. In 2002, 91 per cent of all Ghanaians lived in districts that had been part of West Berlin before 1990.[23] They concentrated in areas with a high proportion of residents with a migration background. The growth of the Ghanaian population in Berlin since 1973 has followed similar patterns as the trend for Germany as a whole:

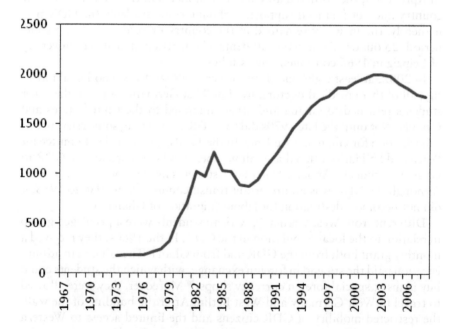

Figure 3.2 Ghanaians in Berlin (1973–2008).[76]
Source: Landesamt für Statistik Berlin

However, unlike the general trend there is no sharp decline after 1993 but the population in Berlin increased until the late 1990s. This indicates that compared to the average, disproportionately many Ghanaians with a secure legal status had already settled in Berlin at that time. Therefore, the decrease in the number of asylum seekers had a less significant effect on the total Ghanaian population in Berlin than it had on the total Ghanaian population in Germany. Since the early 2000s a slight decrease is noticeable that is related to naturalisation, the decrease of new immigration and onward migration of Ghanaians to other places.[25]

In Berlin, as in the rest of Germany, the first group of Ghanaians after World War II were students. After the mid-1970s, asylum seekers became the dominant group among Ghanaians. After 1993 the population consolidated and many of the former migrants and their families achieved a more secure legal status. At the same time, undocumented migration presumably increased due to the lack of legal alternatives.

A significant change within the composition of the Ghanaian population in Berlin, which was already described for Germany as a whole, is the sharp increase in the number of women and children. In 1982, 791 Ghanaian men and 239 women including 40 boys and girls under 15 were documented in Berlin. In 2008, 978 men and 810 women were living in Berlin. The proportion of Ghanaian women rose from 23 per cent in 1982 to 45 per cent in 2008. Although marriage migration surely played a significant role in the increase in the number of Ghanaian women, it cannot exclusively be attributed to it. Some women, as will be exemplified in Chapter 4, migrated on their own or were assisted by female relatives. Moreover, the trafficking of women in the context of prostitution also played a minor role in the migration of Ghanaian women to Berlin.

Parallel to the increase in the number of women the number of children under 15 grew from 57 in 1982 to 180 in 2008. The statistical data confirms what became obvious to me during fieldwork: Many of the migrants have founded families in Berlin. Because of the attainment of a more secure legal status and the successive delay of their return to Ghana, a significant part of Ghanaians settled in Berlin more permanently and started to raise their children in the city.

Ralph Boakye who came to Germany in the 1980s described another change:

> At the parties at the beginning [the late 1980s, B.N.] we were sometimes fifty-fifty; Germans fifty and Ghanaians fifty. Then we became about seventy per cent Ghanaians and thirty per cent Germans. When you go now to a Ghanaian party, it is one hundred and five per cent Ghanaians because the intermarriage with Germans has stopped. Before, we were forced to marry here in order to get papers. Now, they pick their wife from home and, I mean, there is the difference.
> (Interview, Ralph Boakye, 2 May 2002, Berlin)

Although Ralph Boakye's account might be a bit loosely formulated, as a tendency it appears to be correct. Although there are some locations, like some churches or bars, which are spaces of personal encounters between Ghanaians and Germans or other non-African migrants, among the migrants I could observe a tendency toward a 'Ghanaisation' of the private sphere. This is, as Ralph describes it, related to a decrease and failure of marriages between ethnically defined Germans and ethnically defined Ghanaians. This seems to be related to the fact that the incentives for interethnic marriages have declined after many migrants had achieved a secure legal status in Germany.

A frequent pattern, which is also known from internal migration within Ghana, was that migrants left their children and/or their spouses in Ghana and brought them to Germany only after they had established themselves there. A Ghanaian woman, born in 1976, who came to Berlin with her mother in 1982, where her father had migrated some years before, described the situation like this:

> There are quite a number of Ghanaians of my age in Berlin now. Nevertheless, I remember the time when I first arrived, or at least when my memory starts: There were only Gifti and me. We were the only ones here. So, for me it is a luxury that so many others are here now and that we are not alone any longer ... Most of them came later than I. Many of them were already teenagers, or even older.
> (Interview, Belinda Oppong, 18 April 2002, Berlin)

In the last two decades, the age structure of the Ghanaian population in Berlin became more heterogeneous. Most obvious is the ageing process. The share of persons between 45 and 65 years has significantly increased from 2 per cent in 1982 to 35 per cent in 2008.

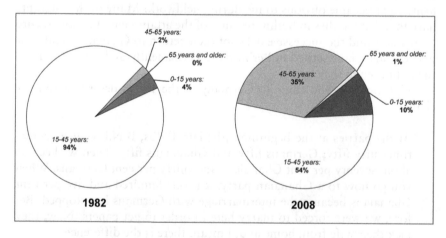

Figure 3.3 Ghanaians in Berlin by age group, 1982 and 2008.
Source: Landesamt für Statistik Berlin

This development indicates that the inflow of new migrants, who normally are between 20 and 35, has become less relevant in relation to the total population.

An effect of the localisation and consolidation of the Ghanaian population in Berlin is the emergence and proliferation of Ghanaian-initiated institutions, which supply the demands of the migrants in Berlin. In this respect, so-called afro shops and churches are of special importance. Both types of institutions first appeared in Berlin in the late 1980s and are related to an increase in the numbers of Ghanaian families.

The growing number of women created a larger demand for Afro-American and African cosmetic products as well as West African foodstuff. In the late 1980s, retail shops began to be founded to satisfy the needs of the West African population. These 'ethnic enterprises' (Portes, Guarnizo and Haller 2002: 279) are typical economic niches for immigrant entrepreneurship. Afro shops sell American and African beauty products, like skin creams or cocoa butter, Rasta attachments for hair, and African foodstuff like yam, plantain, deep frozen fish or bouillon cubes adapted to West African tastes. Some are more specialised in beauty products, others in foodstuff, but often both types of products are sold. Other goods that are frequently offered include telephone cards for long-distance calls, clothes with West African patterns, shoes, Afro-American sportswear, religious music and Nigerian or Ghanaian video films. Often hairdressers are attached to afro shops who do Rasta attachments for women and come once or twice a week to shave the hair of their male customers. Some shops have back rooms where they offer drinks and sometimes food, mostly to African men. Although there is also some demand from 'European' women for Rasta attachments and some Europeans with experience of Africa or interest in exotic cooking buy food products, the majority of the customers are Africans to whose specific needs these shops are adapted. Since the late 1990s, more and more telecommunication shops were founded by Africans, in which telephone cards for long-distance calls are sold and where there are telephones and internet facilities. Some Ghanaians have opened African art shops in which they sell woodworks, drums, 'ethnic' clothes and jewelleries and the like to mostly non-African customers.

During the late 1980s and early 1990s, Ghanaians, as the largest African group, became forerunners in the ethnic niche of afro shops in Berlin.[26] Since the mid-1990s, retail enterprises are being increasingly founded also by other Africans. This was, on the one hand, a result of the growing market for Africa-specific products and, on the other hand, it was related to the problem of unemployment, which increased significantly in Berlin after reunification and by which Africans were affected to a higher degree than Germans. To found a shop or other small-scale enterprise often was a way out of unemployment. Since the market became saturated and some shopkeepers lack capital or skills to efficiently run a shop in a bureaucratic society like Germany, however, several shops went bankrupt.

Altogether, a dynamic scene of opening and closing shops has emerged. The shops are social meeting points for Africans in Berlin. The shopkeepers' ethnic, national or religious background contributes to the differentiation of public spheres around different shops. Nevertheless, I found that none of the shops was visited exclusively by customers from one region or one ethnic group. In the end, it appears that other factors, like management, accountancy, the variety and quality of the offered products, the location and the prices, were more crucial to the economic sustainability of an afro shop than the shopkeepers' ethnic background. Although women dominate the retail trade in Ghana and there were also some female shopkeepers in Berlin, the majority of afro shops were owned by men.

Another type of social institution which has a strong impact on the Ghanaian public sphere in Berlin are churches. In 1982, when already about 1,000 Ghanaians lived in the city, no Ghanaian-initiated church existed. At that time, some migrants attended an Afro-American church, which was frequented by black U.S. soldiers in Berlin, other migrants visited German-dominated churches with different denominational backgrounds and many young men did not go to church at all.[27] In 2002, I identified twelve Ghanaian-initiated and/or Ghanaian-dominated churches in Berlin. The foundation and expansion of these churches is connected to four developments: First, it was the result of the growth of the Ghanaian population in Berlin since 1988. The churches profited in particular from the immigration of women since the second half of the 1980s. Although the majority of church functionaries are men, the majority of church attendants in Ghanaian-founded churches in Berlin are women. Second, the number of Ghanaian families has increased since the late 1980s. Because churches are meeting points for young Ghanaian families with children, an increase of families indirectly fostered the growth of Ghanaian-initiated churches in Berlin. Third, a group of legally secured and relatively established migrants had developed before the late-1980s who could act as functionaries and pastors of these churches. And lastly, the neo-Pentecostal revival, which Ghana has been experiencing since the late 1970s (Gifford 2004), was brought to Germany by migrants with a delay and led to an intensified interest in Christian religion among Ghanaian migrants from the late 1980s to today.

In total, approximately 550–800 persons attended the Sunday services of the 12 churches in summer 2002. The investigated migrant churches had different organisational forms. Five congregations were Berlin-founded and did not belong to any other church. Four congregations were branches of Ghana-founded or Nigeria-founded, respectively, mother churches and the Ghanaian congregations of Roman Catholics and Adventists were organisationally considered to be part of the German branches of the respective churches.

While Pentecostal and neo-Pentecostal churches are dominant among Ghanaian-initiated churches in Berlin, the mainline churches, which in Ghana form the largest cluster in terms of church members (Omenyo 2002), are the smallest cluster in Berlin. Ghanaian Presbyterians and Catholics founded their parishes only in 2001 and in 2000, respectively. Methodists and Anglicans, who are popular in Ghana, were not represented at all.

Because most of the neo-Pentecostal churches in Berlin did not exist in Ghana, the members have changed their church affiliation in the context of migration. In contrast, churches that exist in Ghana, like Adventists, Church of Pentecost, Presbyterians, Deeper Life Ministries and Roman Catholics, recruited their members largely among people who had already been members of these churches in Ghana. The dominance of (neo-)Pentecostal churches also reflects the fact that the foundation of a mainline congregation is institutionally more demanding than that of independent Pentecostal congregations. (Neo-)Pentecostalism provides religiously ambitious migrants with the opportunity to found churches, to become pastors or act as functionaries without authorisation by a mother church and formal theological education.

SOCIO-SPATIAL CONFIGURATIONS OF IDENTITY

Migration affects the social identities of mobile populations. This means that migrants' knowledge about who they are in relation to others and who the relevant others are from whom they distinguish themselves has to be reconfigured with regard to a different political context, other identity discourses and differently composed populations (Schlee 2001a). It entails the learning of new identity categories that are relevant in the receiving context as well as the reproduction and adaptation of pre-existing ones under different social conditions.

Boundary making and re-configuring identities (Wimmer 2008) will be picked out as examples of cultural processes of localisation. It is highlighted that cultural localisation is not only done by local means but makes use of interpretive schemes that relate to and originate from different socio-spatial contexts.

The case of transnational migrants, who frequently maintain relationships to different geographical entities, highlights that social identities do not only refer to collectivities but also have spatial dimensions. The socio-spatial referentiality of identity discourses provides a good case to study the dynamic of localisation and transnationalisation of migrants' life worlds. It manifests in two interconnected but distinct ways: On the one hand, socio-spatial entities like nation-states, regions or cities are often objects of identification. On the other hand, identification practices and discourses are affected by the local context in which they are situated and enacted. For example, in a social environment in which the majority are Ghanaians, the identity category means something different than in a context in which they present a marginalised and racialised migrant minority although in both cases they refer to the same nation-state. The following identity discourses were selected because they were considered interesting in respect to their socio-spatial referentiality. They are not meant to be exhaustive.[28]

Students and Asylum Seekers

A relevant identity discourse found among Ghanaian migrants, which refers to Germany and the legal-political conditions of migration, was the differentiation between 'students' and 'asylum seekers'. Peggy, a medical doctor who came as a student to East Berlin in 1989, related the subsequent incident to exemplify the difference between these two groups:

> I sat in the first compartment of the underground train . . . You are not allowed to take bikes to this part of the train. Two Africans entered the compartment with their bikes and because they spoke Twi I recognised they were Ghanaians. I wanted to say something but a man was faster and told them, "Excuse me, but it is not allowed to take your bikes to this part of the train" . . . The two Ghanaians started to talk in Twi, "What does this guy want?" They had not understood the man and one of them said to his friend: "He must be a racist" . . . After some time, the driver of the underground train opened his door and said the two guys must leave the compartment with their bikes. They answered something in German but [it was so bad that; B.N.] I could only understand single words like "foreigner", "shit" and "racist" . . . Then I stood up and said to them in Twi, "This is how you create troubles for us Ghanaians here. Nobody insulted you. The only ones who are really impolite are you."
> (Interview, Peggy Antwi, 2 November 2002, Berlin)

In Peggy's narrative the men were characterised by a lack of German language skills, by a general ignorance in respect to the wider societal environment, by vulgarity and by the instrumentalisation of racism accusations. Peggy herself is the protagonist of her story who embodies all the positive attributes, which were negated by the two men. She speaks German and Twi, knows the rules of the society, is polite and acts socially responsible.

Peggy stressed that the misbehaviour of the two Ghanaians in public is not just an individual incident but of broader social relevance ('This is how you create troubles for us Ghanaians here'). It seems that the possibility of being identified with them together as Ghanaians implied for Peggy an element of collective devaluation. In her narrative she restored a positive Ghanaian identity by distinguishing herself and passing criticism on them.

Peggy's concern about the public image of Ghanaians in Germany has to be seen in the political context of the 1980s and 1990s. Related to an intensified competition on the labour market and a nationalist revival after reunification, xenophobic tendencies increased among the German population in the early 1990s. In this context, the asylum law became a central issue in the debate on migration. Expressions like 'asylum fraud' (*Asylbetrug*) and 'flood of asylum seekers' (*Asylantenflut*) were used in the public debate to evoke the impression that asylum migration threatens the persistence of societal order. Although the majority of the asylum seekers in Germany came from Europe and the Middle East at this period, sub-Saharan Africans became, presumably because of their social visibility, symbols of this type of unwelcome migrants. Peggy's concerns about being affected by the negative public image of asylum seekers and her wish to distinguish herself from the two Ghanaian men implicitly refer to this broader political situation.

The story functions in the interview as what can be called *everyday myth* or a *mythicising narrative*. The notion of everyday myth was developed by Roland Barthes (1964 [1957]). For him an everyday myth is a semiotic form which is based on a constitutive ambiguity (ibid: 105): On the one hand, it delivers a more or less realistic account of persons, objects or incidents and, on the other hand, it implies an ideological discourse about their generalised and 'true' being. Based on its characteristic fusion of the concrete with the general, the everyday myth becomes a semiotic device for the simplification and reification of the social world. Its ideological superstructure transfers a particular, complex and often ambiguous reality into a more coherent and generalised representation, which Barthes (1964 [1957]: 130) called a world of 'purified essences'. At the same time, the concrete and often experiential content of the everyday myth functions as an illustration and supposed evidence for the reality of the ideological superstructure.

However, since the term 'everyday myth' implies a notion of collectivity, which is inappropriate in the case of Peggy's story, I prefer the term *mythicising narrative* (Nieswand and Vogel 2000). In Peggy's case it combines the narration of a personal encounter with two Ghanaians in an underground train with a general identity statement about the difference between asylum seekers and persons, like Peggy, with higher education.

The differentiation between asylum seekers and persons with higher education could also be identified among other Ghanaians. Henry, a Ghanaian-trained insurance salesperson, who at the time of the interview did a vocational retraining in the IT sector, attributed the conflicts between students and asylum seekers to the confined worldview and the lack of German language skills of the latter.

> I think the members of the Ghana Union[29] did not want to have anything to do with the intellectuals. They didn't want that. They wanted to stay in their small groups speaking their local languages. The students also speak English and German and they had their difficulties with that.[30]
>
> (Interview, Henry Oppong, 3 May 2002, Berlin)

Nancy, an unemployed engineer, underlined the fundamentality of the difference between students and asylum seekers, which was already stressed by Peggy and Henry:

> When I came to Germany in 1982 I did not want any contact to Ghanaians. Most of them were asylum seekers and simply had a different attitude towards life. I mean, everybody chooses their own friends. I don't mean to sound arrogant, but this was not my world.
> (Interview, Nancy Behrend, 6 March 2002, Berlin)

One aspect which affected the relationship between students and asylum seekers was that the former were suspecting the latter to have spoiled the social conditions of a return to Ghana. The economic success of some labour migrants in Ghana has created, in the view of several university graduates, exaggerated expectations about the potential material benefits of migration. Sebastian Appiah, a former student in East Germany who had returned to Ghana in the 1970s, described the situation like this:

> In the 1970s, it was different. You came home and just said: I studied, but did not work there. People did not expect much. When the *Gastarbeiter* [guest workers; B.N.] came back; they had worked hard and brought a lot of money. If now somebody comes back from Germany without money he is insulted as a ne'er-do-well.
> (Interview, Sebastian Appiah, 1 December 2001, Kumasi)

Yao Dotse, an engineer who had returned to Ghana in the 1990s, gives a similar account:

> Many asylum seekers came with buses and trucks. And the people asked: What is this? He is only one, two, three years there and he comes back with cars, buses and trucks? People think when you go to Germany you will get it automatically. I mean the asylum politics was different in Germany before. You could earn good money as an asylum seeker . . . With this money you could do a lot. This is why the opinion developed: In Germany, only one or two days and you make it.
> (Interview, Yao Dotse, 13 December 2001, Accra)

It is remarkable that a significant proportion of the asylum seekers as well as the members of the Ghana Union to whom Henry referred, were not as 'uneducated' as they were depicted by the university graduates. Several of them had secondary school degrees or some university education. Nevertheless, the stereotypical perception of asylum seekers as 'uneducated' and 'rude' remained dominant. As the result of the local identity politics between the two groups, students in particular merged legal categories with a discourse on class differences between migrants in order to distinguish themselves from larger segments of the Ghanaian population in Germany and from the racialised stereotypes with which asylum seekers were confronted.

The strongest reservations against asylum seekers I found were among female Ghanaians who came as students to Germany. The rejection of the milieu of asylum seekers as an 'entirely different world' from which they were eager to keep their distance is linked to a Ghanaian discourse on class and gender. In particular, middle-class women in Ghana have to take care not to be associated with places such as bars, dance halls or so-called drinking spots, and practices such as smoking, drinking alcohol or sexualised behaviour, that are perceived as morally contaminated. The 'world of the asylum seekers' was conceptualised by the interviewed female students as morally too ambiguous. Therefore, it was rejected to reinforce the gendered self-image of middle-class decency.

On an institutional level, the distinction between students and asylum seekers found an expression in Berlin by the organisational differentiation between the Ghana Union in which asylum seekers played an important role (Nieswand 2008a) and the Ghana Students Union. A frequently returning point of conflict between the two groups was the question of which of the two associations represented Ghanaians in Berlin more adequately. While the Ghana Union could claim to represent a larger segment of the Ghanaian population, the Ghana Student Union emphasised the seniority of their organisation and their educational resources. One of the last conflicts between the two organisations arose in 2002, when the Ghanaian President came to Berlin on an official visit. During the preparation some members of the Ghana Student Union did not feel adequately recognised by the Ghanaian embassy. They wrote a letter of protest and, thereby, created a public commotion. At this point in time, only a small minority of the members of the Ghana Student Union were in fact students. Most of them were university graduates who had stayed in Berlin. Moreover, none of the members of the Ghana Community[31] was factually an asylum seeker. Obviously, the social distinction between the two groups turned out to be more persistent than the administrative classification to which it had once referred.

Interestingly, those who were classified as asylum seekers were much less concerned about the students than it was the other way round. Nevertheless, some narratives could be found. Students were sometimes perceived as arrogant and elitist persons who 'do not want to mix with normal people'.[32] Other people emphasised that students were over-adapted to German cultural standards and, by this, were alienated from their Ghanaian cultural background.[33] One former asylum seeker used a macho narrative to highlight the superiority of the asylum seekers. In his view, students were 'bookworms', who were too soft and not smart enough to cope with the tough social realities outside the protected space of university.[34]

The examples demonstrate that legal categories of the receiving country can be transformed into social identities. In this respect it is important to note that they did not remain at the level of formal regulations but entailed different experiences of migration and a discrepancy in migration goals. To a significant extent, the asylum procedure flattened pre-existing social differences among those Ghanaians who were subjected to it. Everybody, independently of their class background or education, had to go through the same investigative procedure, face the same suspicions, encounter the same resentments and live with the same feeling of insecurity. In contrast, students' encounters with the German state were very different. They did not, as long as they had matriculated at a German university, suffer from legal insecurity and did not face the same levelling down of their social status. Therefore, the distinction between asylum seekers and students entailed different modes of inclusion in the receiving country and varying experiences of migration. Nevertheless, it seems that it only achieved broader attention especially among female Ghanaians with higher education because it also resonated with pre-existing discourses on and experiences of class, education and gender in Ghana.

Pentecostalists and Traditionalists

More recently, religion has gained in importance as a distinctive criterion among Ghanaians in Berlin. In particular, the dominance of (neo-)Pentecostal forms of Christianity in Berlin has polarised the migrants. Religious neutrality became more difficult to maintain and even those for whom before religion had not played an important role had to position themselves either in favour or in opposition to (neo)-Pentecostalism. One reaction was that some so-called mainline Christians felt dominated by (neo-)Pentecostal Christianity and started to react to its hegemony by founding their own congregations.

> Let us say for the Ghanaian community 50 per cent are Catholic, but you see them today at the charismatic[35] and the Pentecostal churches. It was my . . . idea that we have to sit down and to bring back our Catholic people who are going out of the Catholic community.
> (Interview, John Asiedu, 20 May 2002, Berlin)

(Neo-)Pentecostal Christianity seeks to have a strong impact on personal identities. It is highlighted that believers have to 'be born again in the Holy Spirit' in order to receive personal salvation. This process is considered a far-reaching transformation of the self. As a consequence, conversion to Pentecostal forms of Christianity is modelled as a fundamental break with the past (Meyer 1998). In the Ghanaian context, this also includes a break with certain cultural and religious traditions. This becomes controversial at points at which Pentecostalists condemn practices as idol worshipping which other persons perceive as legitimate expressions of their culture. It concerns in particular those rituals, like libation, funerals or female nubility rites (*bragoro*), that involve a religious reference to the ancestors. Occasions at which the differential evaluation of cultural practices became relevant were the visit of President Kufuor in Berlin in 2002 and in the framework of the Ghana@50 celebrations in Berlin 2007 (Nieswand 2010b). In these contexts the respective organisation committees decided to perform libations as symbolic markers of Ghanaian culture. Some influential neo-Pentecostal Christians expressed their opposition to these practices. Since the relationship between cultural traditions and Christianity is a matter of common concern, the Ghana Community organised a panel discussion on the issue in 2005. The question of whether the pouring of libation and the performance of Akan *bragoro* rites are in accordance with Christian beliefs were the main points of debate. As it was expected, Pastor Henry, the invited neo-Pentecostal pastor, and his supporters rejected these customs, while their opponents depicted them as traditions which are of special importance for the maintenance of a Ghanaian cultural identity under the conditions of migration.[36]

In 2002, Pastor Henry explained his views to me in an interview:

> My father was a Chief in the Eastern Region and he was an Elder in the Methodist Church. He went to pour libation to his idols and on Sundays he sat in the church. So, where does he belong to? Does he belong to God? Or does he belong to the idols? When the Pentecostal Movement came in, they said: No, you cannot serve idols and serve God at the same time . . . Either you are standing for God or you are standing for the idols. There is no middle way.
> (Interview, Pastor Henry, 4 April 2002, Berlin)

This devaluation of traditional practices is very critically received by migrants who feel more strongly connected to them. As a reaction, some of them referred to the neo-Pentecostalism churches as sects and openly accused them of dividing the Ghanaian community. Although there are some specificities of the case of Berlin, like the comparatively weak institutional role of mainline Christianity among the Ghanaians, the main reference of this identity discourse—the conflict between (neo-)Pentecostalists and traditionalists—is Ghana where it can be observed in greater intensity (Darkwa and Kwabena 2009). In this sense, it is an example for the localisation and adaptation of a Ghanaian identity discourse in the context of Berlin. At the same time, the transnational character of the (neo-)Pentecostalist discourse of breaking with the past adds a global element to it that cross-cuts the simplistic analytical distinction between 'here' and 'there'.

Ethnicity

Apart from legal categories and religious distinctions, ethnic and regional identities were significant for Ghanaians in Berlin as well. Ethnic identities in general are normally organised in taxonomies comprising identities with different degrees of inclusivity (Schlee and Werner 1996; Schlee 2004b: 136). For Ghanaians in Berlin this meant in practice that they could switch from an identification with a very inclusive identity, like 'human being' or 'African', to an identification with a national identity ('Ghanaian') or 'transethnic' identity (e.g. 'Akan', 'northerner') to a more exclusive ethnic identity (e.g. Asante, Ewe, Brong) or hometown identity (e.g. Dormaa Ahenkro, Kumasi).

In the case of southern Ghanaians, the 'traditional states' with their royal heads were of special importance as units of identification. The more narrow ethnic or local identifications normally corresponded to some shared cultural features, such as a particular dialect, participation in specific festivals, food habits, myths of common origin and the identification with certain historical events. Although also being a Ghanaian was of particular relevance, several of my informants emotionally privileged more exclusive ethnic and hometown identities. However, the situation of migration induced a paradoxical dynamic: The identities that people perceived as closer to themselves than others were devalued in the broader social context of the receiving society. In the public space in Germany and at their working places Ghanaians were mostly identified as 'blacks' or 'Africans' because the majority of the non-African population was not able or willing enough to distinguish Africans along national or ethnic lines. At the same time, the diaspora situation also re-evaluated the significance of national categories in relation to African migrants of different national origin as well as ethnic or local identifications within the group of Ghanaian migrants. Because the number of migrants from a particular ethnic group or home district tends to be relatively small, these features become more distinctive and, therefore, more valuable as a social resource. This was particularly relevant for newly arrived migrants who were in need of practical help.

Factually, in the context of Berlin, ethnicity did not refer to fixed groups with a clearly defined membership. Instead of being a permanent feature of persons or groups it functioned as a knowledge resource that could be mobilised situationally (cf. Gluckman 1961). One incident, which helped me to understand the situational character of ethnic identification in Berlin, occurred when I met Kojo Yeboah, who was recommended to me as an elder of the 'Dormaa community' in Berlin, at his wife's afro shop. Although some of the customers and friends who regularly visited this shop were from the Dormaa District, most of them were not. I would meet people from different regions of Ghana, people from Nigeria, Sierra Leone, Jamaica, Sudan and Poland. The afro shop provided a semi-public sphere of exchange and sociality that was used by different persons, often African migrants, but was not defined in ethnic terms. Without having this context information about the shop, at my first meeting I approached Kojo as an elder of the Dormaa community.

> I explained my research project to Kojo and asked him for help. At the beginning, he tried to get rid of me politely by stating that there was nothing special about the Dormaa people in Berlin. The situation changed when I produced a bottle of gin, which I had brought as a gift.

In southern Ghana gin or schnapps are gifts traditionally presented to a traditional authority by visitors. I used this symbolic language playfully during my research in Berlin to indicate some knowledge of the cultural background and to communicate a certain degree of recognition to some of the authorities among Ghanaian migrants. Normally, the persons reacted with mild irony to my gesture. This time it was different. I did not know when I handed over the bottle that people from Dormaa and the *Dormaahene* himself regarded Kojo, in fact, a legitimate representative of the Dormaa community in Germany comparable to a traditional authority. Because of this, the bottle induced a switch in the code of communication. Kojo reacted to my gesture in the cultural language of Dormaa chieftaincy and welcomed me officially as a guest. Practically, he poured a libation on the floor, which included a short prayer to the ancestors, and welcomed me in the name of the Dormaa community in the shop. I had to repeat my request, which was then formally accepted by him. Afterwards, Kojo gave me a short introduction to the history of the Dormaa people and handed me a brochure about the 'Dormaa traditional state' as well as a video tape documenting the *Dormaahene*'s visit to Berlin in 2000. I encountered this welcoming ritual in a similar way when I introduced myself and my project to traditional authorities in Ghana.
(Field Protocol, 27 June 2002, Berlin)

This case description captures a situational evocation of ethnically framed behaviour. My gesture of handing over the bottle of gin induced a switch from an informal everyday code of communication to a formal ethnic code of communication. Of course, this change in the repertoire and framing of behaviour could not only be stimulated by me but was also induced by migrants from the Dormaa District themselves who appealed to Kojo's moral obligation of ethnic solidarity in a foreign country.[37]

In general, some public spaces of Ghanaians in Berlin function as institutionalisations of the situational relevance of ethnicity. National or ethnic associations, occasional social events and some meeting places provided migrants with social contexts in which the identity categories that they considered important aspects of their selves could regain meaning in a social environment which was normally not able to decode them. Nevertheless, these social spaces remained niches in a broader context in which the power relations between minority and majority led to a general devaluation of more narrow ethnic categories of identification.

Among Ghanaians, shared ethnic origin created some moral expectations to show solidarity in the context of migration. For this particular reason, the discourses and practices of ethnic solidarity turned out to be very ambivalent. Beside the discourse that stresses the value of helping somebody of common origin, also other, often less public, discourses can be identified, which highlight exactly the opposite, namely, the threats of maintaining close contact to co-ethnics. A Ghanaian migrant who worked as a carer in an old people's home explained the mutual suspicions and forms of distancing among Ghanaians, which I could observe during my participant observation, like this:

> People are afraid of others—that others will go and report them or ... do something about them to spoil their lives. People are careful to come close to their people ... When they know your background ... sometimes, they like to pull you down. This has happened to some people ... People were deported because of friends and some people told me that their friends are not good to them, because they are jealous of what they do ... So, everybody likes to be distant from others.
> (Interview, Daniel Adamu, 23 September 2001, Berlin)

Thomas Annan, a Berlin-trained engineer who had returned to Ghana, gave me a comparable description for the case of petty crimes:

> An asylum seeker, if he knew your identity he can go and steal it and when he was asked his name he will mention your name ... So, you will be home and then the police will come to you, "You have been caught at Aldi [a German supermarket chain; B.N.]". "Oh, I don't know anything about this. How did you get me?" Those things happened ... Among the students nobody had any problem with the police. But, you had to be careful that nobody used your identity in case of crime. This was happening a lot.
> (Interview, Thomas Annan, 30 November 2001, Kumasi)

These narratives on co-ethnics who 'pull others down', 'spoil their lives' for envy or commit crimes by using innocent persons' identities resonate with Ghanaian imaginaries of witchcraft, according to which social closeness can be used to spiritually harm others. It appears that in the context of migration and asylum seeking, information about persons becomes a functional equivalent to what hairs or fingernails are in the context of traditional witchcraft practices: essences of personhood that, if they are controlled by an evil-minded person, can ruin one's life. On a more general level, the discourse on the dangers of closeness reflects the ambiguity of moral obligations. On the one hand, stressing ethnic solidarity allowed migrants to get closer to and claim support from persons who would otherwise be more socially distant. On the other hand, emphasising the dangers of closeness enabled migrants to distance themselves from people whom they considered structurally close to them. The combination of the two discourses provided migrants with a repertoire for manoeuvring within the field of personal relationships and negotiating the extent and limits of ethnic solidarity.

Besides their role in the context of managing social closeness and distance, ethnic ascriptions were also a means for classifying other Ghanaians. This opened up a field of half playful, half serious stereotyping of persons. These clichés which people used to label and tease each other are well-known and wide-spread in Ghana. For instance, Asante were considered as entrepreneurial and proud of their culture, but at the same time as arrogant, not highly educated and materialistic. Brong or Bono people were described affirmatively as hospitable and honest, and derogatively as 'backward' and unsophisticated; Ewe as ambitious with regard to education, but as bad businesspeople and dangerous because of their spiritual powers. Hausa were considered straightforward but aggressive.

It can be summarized that most of the employed categories of ethnic identification and ethnic stereotypes originated from Ghana, but were adapted to the migration setting and enacted under the specific local conditions of being a minority among minorities. Obviously, processes of racialisation in German reinforced the relevance of the category of being 'African' in many spheres of social life. This led to the paradoxical effect that more narrow ethnic identities, depending on the context, became simultaneously devalued and revalued.

Turks and Ghanaians

One important group of relevant others for Ghanaians in Berlin is Turkish migrants and their descendants who are Berlin's largest ethnic minority group. In the immigrant neighbourhoods of the city, Ghanaians compete with Turks for similar resources, such as jobs, flats and social recognition. Sometimes the resulting tensions between Turks and Africans are openly addressed:

> During the football World Cup in South Korea and Japan in 2002, Turkey won against Senegal in the quarter finals. Celebrating the victory, Turks drove in convoys through Berlin horning and displaying Turkish national emblems. I sat in an afro shop in Neukölln and watched the scene together with Gifty, the shopkeeper originating from the coastal region of Ghana. After a while, she commented on the behaviour of the Turkish football fans on the streets: "Look, how these people behave. They act as if they were at home in this country. This is not civilised. They are bush people. I am happy they won because otherwise they would have killed an African."
> (Field Protocol, 22 June 2002, Berlin)

Noteworthy in this passage is the emotionality of the shopkeeper's reaction and the reference to a discourse of civilisation ('bush people') she used to deprecate Turkish migrants. Although the affects were augmented by the football match, in which a 'black' West African team that was supported by

Gifty lost against a 'white' Turkish team, the reaction also expressed more general feelings of resentment against Turks. The term 'bush people', which Gifty used, refers to an evaluative colonial distinction between the 'civilised' urban space with its modern institutions and the 'uncivilised' countryside. In a sense, the superiority claims that are implied in the equation of Turkish migrants with bush people inverts the power relation between the two immigrant groups in Berlin. To understand the emotionality of the reaction it is of special importance to take into consideration that many Ghanaians suspect Turks of having racist attitudes.[38] Yaa Serwah, a young Ghanaian woman, who grew up in Berlin described it like this:

> Racism ... was always present in the public ... In most cases, it was foreigners who insulted me; other foreigners, mostly *türkisch-arabische Mitbürger* [Turkic-Arabic fellow citizens].
> (Interview, Yaa Serwaa, 18 April 2002, Berlin)

Yaw Agyeman, worked temporarily as a sub-contractor in the building sector. In order to exemplify the problematic relationship between Turks and Africans - he told me that he found out that one of his Turkish employees in front of other Turkish workers pretended that Yaw was his business partner and not his boss because he perceived it as a particular discredit to work for an African. Esther, a friend of Yaw Agyeman, summarised his narration with the words: 'These Turkish people, they don't respect us.'[39] In this sense, Gifty's reproach of Turks as being uncivilised implicitly relates to the fact that she as an African can become an object of racist disrespect.

Obviously the depicted tensions between Turks and Ghanaians refer to experiences in the migrant neighbourhoods of Berlin in which Turks play a significant role. Nevertheless, Gifty's representation links up to a southern Ghanaian discourse on civilisation and Islam. Within the colonial labour migration system, the migrants from rural areas in the north to the urban centres in the south of the Gold Coast became the prototypes of 'bushmen' (Little 1973: 411), and the *zongo,* as the area of the city where they lived, was depicted as an underdeveloped and dirty part of the city. Since Hausa-speaking Muslims dominated the *zongo,* the socio-economic position of its inhabitants became an attribute of their northern origin and their religion. The socio-economic marginalisation of the *zongo* population and the everyday experiences of otherness solidified in stereotypes about the Muslims being less civilised that can easily be applied to Turks in Berlin. Although this connection normally remains an implicit background assumption, in an informal talk John Appiah, a Southern Ghanaian who was working as a cleaner in Berlin, explicitly drew a parallel between Neukölln, relatively poor migrant neighbourhood in Berlin where he lived and in which Turks are the most important minority group, and the *zongo*:

The *zongo* is the part of the city where the Muslim people live. You can find many run-down houses and it is dirty. The people in the *zongo* are not like us Christians. They are different. They speak Hausa among themselves and do not want to mix with others. Muslims love themselves very much. They are very proud and aggressive. Even the small kids in the *zongo*—they will insult you. It is like Neukölln. Here, you can see the same.

(Field Protocol, 8 May 2002, Berlin)

In this sense, the representations of Turks as being uncivilised and disrespectful which I encountered among Ghanaians picked up elements of imaginaries, which were produced at different localities and modulated to make sense of local encounters in the neighbourhoods of Berlin. An important function of the discourse on 'civilisation', which is implied in the notion of being 'bush people', is to counter experiences of racialisation. It reflects a competitive element not to be at the bottom of the ethnic hierarchy in Germany between two groups of which a significant proportion experiences devaluation and marginalisation in the broader German societal context.

East Germans and Ghanaians

The discourse on 'bush people' was also relevant in the relation of Ghanaians to East Germans. The distinction between West Germans and East Germans became of particular importance in Berlin in the course of the reunification of Germany. In Berlin, where the wall had divided the city into East and West, the effects were felt much more directly than in most other parts of Germany.

After the fall of the Wall, East Germans in Berlin—whose professional qualifications were often devalued in West Germany—competed with non-German migrants for some segments of the labour market. Moreover, in the industrial sector many jobs were lost because state subventions, which had been paid during the Cold War to maintain jobs in the city, were cancelled after reunification and the industrial production in East Berlin collapsed after 1989 (Häußermann 2001: 72). New jobs were especially created in the high-wage service sector (e.g. finance, producer services) and the low-wage service sector (e.g. commercial cleaning, health and care services, catering, trade, tourism).[40] Generally, the total number of employed persons in Berlin decreased by 6 per cent between 1992 and 2005.[41] In particular migrants were affected by these developments and lost their jobs. The official quota of unemployment among foreigners in Berlin at 35 per cent was almost twice as high as the quota of the total population, which amounted to 18 per cent.[42]

In addition to intensified competition on the labour market, racist violence increased in Germany in the early 1990s and was perceived by many

Ghanaians and western Germans to be a particular problem of former East Germany.[43] Many Ghanaian migrants in Berlin attributed the aggravation of their economic and social situation after 1990 to the reunification. Yaa, who experienced the reunification in Berlin as a teenager, described her impressions like this: 'In particular since the reunification, I do not feel accepted anymore, not wanted anymore (Interview, Yaa Serwaa, 18 April 2002, Berlin).'

Thomas Annan described his anxieties of falling victim to racist violence after the fall of the wall:

> And then after this [the fall of the Berlin wall; B.N.], I don't know what happened, but this hatred against blacks started. Because when the 'easterners' came to the West, they saw how bad their situation was in terms of their standard of living. I don't think that they were very happy to see foreigners living in Germany doing well ... There were stories of attacks on blacks here and there. The attacks were not only coming from East Germans but also from westerners. They were also doing that kind of things. So, you became very cautious ... if you went out in the evening ... you were looking around to see whether someone is going to attack you.
> (Interview, Thomas Annan, 30 November 2001, Kumasi)

For most Ghanaians, the east of Germany, including the eastern part of Berlin, became an area which was believed to be potentially dangerous for Africans. This manifests in particular in the housing patterns. Only a small minority of Ghanaians live in parts of the city which belonged to East Berlin before 1990. The expectation that East Germans are more racist than West Germans was so strong that sometimes people, when facing disrespect from a German, concluded the person had to be an East German. Lydia Abrefa, a nurse in her early 40s, experienced a conflict with a taxi driver:

> Because Lydia was delayed when she brought her daughter to school, she had to take a taxi to come to work in time. In the taxi an argument arose between Lydia and the driver about the best route. It escalated and Lydia asked the driver to stop and declared that she was not going to pay him for his services. First, the driver did not want to let her go but, finally, they agreed that Lydia would go to work without paying the taxi fare but leaving the address of her work place and that he would call the police. Some hours later two police officers visited Lydia in the hospital. While one police officer informed her neutrally and politely that she was legally obliged to pay the taxi driver even if she was not satisfied with his services, Lydia perceived the second police officer as hostile. She described her as "inhuman", "bureaucratic" and without empathy for her point of view. Lydia concluded that she must be an *Ossi*[44] while her colleague had to be a *Wessi*.
> (Field Protocol, 20 October 2002, Berlin)

Ghanaians in Berlin have developed interpretative schemes to explain the supposed difference in the behaviour of East and West Germans. Several emphasised, like Thomas Annan, the economic problems of East Germany as the reason for hostility. Some Christians attributed it to the comparatively high number of atheists. Others argued that xenophobic tendencies were a result of the wall. Because East Germans were not allowed to travel and, therefore, did also not learn to speak foreign languages, in particular English, they were less prepared for encounters with persons from other parts of the world.

Altogether, there were striking parallels between the interpretative schemes for explaining differences between West and East Germany and those which Ghanaians usually apply on the north–south divide in Ghana. Eastern Germany and northern Ghana both present the economically weak parts of their respective countries, have a lower proportion of Christians (as defined through church membership), English is less widely spoken[45] and the inhabitants are said to be less experienced in travelling outside their own country. These characteristics accumulate, according to the dominant Ghanaian discourse on the north, in a 'confined worldview', which makes the population think dominantly in ethnic categories and, finally, leads to ethnic motivated violence. The notion of being 'bushy' which is constituted by these factors can easily be applied to East Germans:

C: It is because the East Germans did not travel that they are bushy.
B: What does 'bushy' mean?
C: It means 'from the bush'. They are like people who come from the bush.
(Interview, Comfort Busia, 28 June 2001, Leipzig)

This parallelisation of the discourses on East Germans and northern Ghanaians results in a new, non-ethnic space of identification. Cosmopolitan migrants from southern Ghana, who are mostly English-speaking Christians with travelling experience and come from the more prosperous part of their home country, identify with cosmopolitan West Germans, who are supposed to possess similar features. East Germans and northern Ghanaians in this discourse turn into 'uncivilised' and 'violent' others, from whom one's own identity is distinguished. By applying this discourse, Ghanaian migrants can imagine themselves as cosmopolitans and can counter the humiliating experience of being a potential or factual victim of racist violence. This described identification with an urban cosmopolitanism also works the other way around:

At my working place, they do not care so much for the colour of your skin ... They see me more as somebody from West Germany. They say, "we Wessis" and this includes me. I am also a Wessi.
(Interview, Ralph Boakye, 2 May 2002, Berlin)

Multicultural cosmopolitanism also provides west Germans with the chance to distinguish themselves positively from the bad reputation of their allegedly racist and 'uncivilised' compatriots from the east and represent themselves as the better Germans and the better Berliners. Racialised minorities like Ghanaians can assume a special importance in ratifying this aspirational self-image. Nevertheless, for both sides, the discourse of being cosmopolitan opens up a field of non-ethnic identification that temporarily transcends racial stereotypes and social inequalities between West Africa and Western Europe.

Processes of Localisation

In this chapter, I have focused on the processes of localisation of Ghanaian migrants in Germany. I distinguished roughly three periods of migration from Ghana to Germany. In the first phase, which lasted from the mid-1950s to the mid-1970s, students were dominant among Ghanaian migrants. The period between 1975 and 1993 was shaped by asylum migration. After 1993, the number of new Ghanaian immigrants decreased and the existing population consolidated.

For the case of Berlin, I showed that the localisation process was largely connected to the achievement of a safe legal status, family establishment and the consequent increase in Ghanaian women and children. Since the inflow of young immigrants dropped off, the age structure of the Ghanaian population has become more diverse. Moreover, since the late 1980s an increasing number of institutions, particularly churches and afro shops, satisfying the demands of the Ghanaian population in Berlin, were founded.

For the example of identity discourses and practices, I showed the complexity of localisation processes. It was emphasised that cultural and cognitive localisation is not achieved entirely by local means. On the one hand, I presented identity discourses—'Turks' and 'Ghanaians', 'asylum seekers' and 'students', 'southern Ghanaians' and 'East Germans'—which only became relevant at the locality of immigration, but were supplemented by and contextualised in Ghanaian discourses on regional divisions, religion, class and civilisation. On the other hand, I showed how ethnic and religious identities referring to Ghana were applied to the local situation in Berlin. Moreover, the cases of Islam and charismatic Christianity exemplify that some local discourses, both in Germany and in Ghana, resonate at the same time with global discourses.

Nevertheless, localisation is only one part of a more complex process of social inclusion of Ghanaian migrants. The next chapter will examine the complementary dynamic of transnationalisation.

4 Processes of Transnationalisation

The assumption of the existence of transnational social fields requires further explanation. Nation-states have borders, laws, passports, police forces, parliaments, and a migration balance; and they are identifiable as coloured shapes on a world map. In contrast to this, transnational social fields are a mere abstraction, which refers to the structural dimension of social relationships, communication and the circulation of money, persons and goods across borders. Lacking geographical materiality and the means of power to enforce their persistence, transnational social fields appear theoretically to be more transient, occasional and temporary than states. Against this background, the question emerges how and why transnational social fields are reproduced if their continuity is not secured by force. It is argued that it is above all an interplay of incentives and obligations that motivates many migrants to maintain cross-border relationships in their daily practices. Through the migrants' and their relevant others' agency, transnational social fields become a relatively persistent and reliable social structure.

Relative stability means that the social practices, which constitute a transnational social field, imply relatively predictable, reproducible and persistent patterns in the selection of means, partners and contents of communication which connect migrants with persons and institutions in Ghana. The term 'social field' refers, thereby, to both the structural effects of these social practices as well as the formal and informal rules and institutions that regulate and shape individuals' actions.

Statistically, the structural importance of transnational activities of Ghanaian migrants became noticeable due to the significant increase in the volume of remittances and the economic relevance of migrants' 'home visits' over the last decades that were mentioned above. According to the IMF (2005: 7), private remittances to Ghana increased from U.S. $500 million in 2000 to U.S. $1.3 billion in 2004. They amounted to 15 per cent of the Ghanaian GNP (Gross National Product) and were in 2004, for the first time, the largest single source of foreign exchange, followed by cocoa and gold. Moreover, the tourism sector profited substantially from the so-called 'visiting friends and relatives tourism' (Asiedu

2005). The income generated by the tourism sector in Ghana quadrupled between 1991 and 2002, amounting to U.S. $520 million in 2002 (ISSER 2003: 146–48). Ghanaian migrants were, with 27 per cent, the largest group of visitors, and many of the tourists who were classified as Europeans and North Americans were de facto former Ghanaians who had been naturalised in their receiving countries. As a reaction to the migrants' increasing economic significance, the Ghanaian government started political attempts to maintain and increase their commitment to their home country. 'Ghanaian diaspora' became a key term, employed by Ghanaian state officials as well as migrants, to negotiate transnational political inclusion.

During large parts of the Rawlings period the relationship between the Ghanaian state and the transcontinental migrants in Western Europe was tense. Many Ghanaians claimed political asylum in the receiving countries, which made them suspicious to the Ghanaian government. It suspected them of being supporters of the opposition and accused them of deserting the country in difficult times. In the late Rawlings' period the general assessment of migration changed. Although 'brain drain' was and still is raised as an issue in the context of the emigration of physicians and nurses, it was increasingly highlighted that migrants' remittances and their loyalty to the Ghanaian nation-state are a resource for the development of the country. This tendency became more dominant and explicit during the NPP government led by President J.A. Kufuor between 2001 and 2009 (Owusu 2003: 406). It introduced double citizenship in order to give Ghanaians the possibility of acquiring the citizenship in the receiving country without losing their Ghanaian one. In 2001 a *Homecoming Summit* was organised in which the President and several ministers of state participated. In this context it was discussed how the Ghanaian diaspora could contribute to the development of the country. As a result, in 2003 the Non-Resident Ghanaian Secretariat was established to co-ordinate diaspora activities. Another step aiming at the promotion of migrants' inclusion was the so-called Representation of the People Amendment Act passed by the Ghanaian parliament in February 2006. It grants Ghanaian citizens living outside the country the right to vote. In the same year Obetsebi-Lamptey became the first Ghanaian Minister of Tourism and Diasporian Relations.[1] By employing the concept of diaspora and creating state institutions for migrant inclusion, Ghana has adapted its discourse of national belonging to the conditions of mass migration. This process included an adjustment of the political definitions of citizenship. The state's interest in migrants is directly related to the depicted increase in remittances. This paradigm shift in the assessment of migrants and their transnational relationships not only affects institutions in Ghana but those also in the receiving countries. Generally, 'new diaspora policies' create opportunities for Ghanaians abroad to become involved in transnational activities (Nieswand 2008b).

THE ECONOMICS OF TRANSNATIONALISATION

Transnational social fields emerge within an ambivalent relationship between migrants and nation-states. On the one hand, the existence of transnational fields factually often relies on nation-states and their infrastructures. On the other hand, they transcend national social orders and open up an alternative social space of interaction. In order to understand the economic rationality of migrants' transnational activities and its relationship to the involved nation-states, it is important to take historical developments of global social inequalities into consideration.

In particular, the core countries of industrialisation in Western Europe, North America and, with a temporal delay, some Asian countries, benefited from profound economic and political changes in the nineteenth and twentieth centuries. Contrary to what revolutionary thinkers, especially Marx, predicted, the economic development of the industrial core countries did not lead to increasing tensions and inequalities within the industrialised countries. Instead, political struggles between national labour movements, governments and the economic elites led to a partial redistribution of wealth. Welfare institutions and tax systems became central means for the reallocation of resources.

The hegemony of the nation-state as a form of political organisation deeply affected both the structures and the perceptions of social inequality (Kreckel 2008). Still the inequality between citizens of the same nation-state is considered the most highly politicised form of social inequality. Although questions of global inequalities periodically receive some attention, nation-states are considered by most of their citizens as the political units in which equality has the highest significance. Moreover, the nation-state of residence is also statistically the strongest single predictor of a person's average income (Bronschier 2002: 107). It indicates that despite undeniable globalisation processes nation-states still have an important impact on the allocation and distribution of resources within a global economy.

The nationalisation of social inequality has had profound consequences for its global structures. Since the nineteenth century, a process of increasing economic inequality between countries has been observable (Bata and Bergesen 2002). Because the unequal distribution of resources is mainly treated as an internal problem of particular nation-states, the inequalities between different states became 'imaginable and factually stable in unlimitedly crass forms' (Stichweh 2000: 69). They only matter in a political sense, if they are perceived within the same public 'horizon of perception', which was and still is above all the nation-state (Beck 2008: 24).

The different degrees of freedom of the mobility of goods and capital, on the one hand, and of persons, on the other hand, which in comparison to the former is much more constrained by border regimes and immigration laws, stabilises these global differences in wealth and buying power. The fact that the mobility of labour is more constrained by border regimes than the mobility of goods and capital has effects on global social inequalities. Those nation-states that profit from the relatively free circulation of goods and capital restrict the resulting migration in order to protect their welfare institutions and their national populations.

Particularly during the second half of the twentieth century, a sharp increase in economic inequalities was statistically observable. While in 1960 the per capita GDPs (gross domestic products) of the 20 wealthiest countries were 18 times higher than those of the 20 poorest countries, the disparity had more than doubled by 1995.[2] In the cases of Ghana and Germany, the ratio of the national GDPs per capita changed from 1 to 48 in 1973 to 1 to 81 in 2004.[3] In the same period, the ratio of the GNI (gross national income) per capita, which is a more significant measure for the economic situation of the inhabitants of a country than the GDP, almost quintupled. It increased from 1 to 17 to 1 to 81.

The simultaneous development of the increase in economic inequalities between different nation-states, on the one hand, and their decrease within the core countries of industrialisation, on the other, can be identified as a dominant trend until the 1970s (Bronschier 2002). Since then, the tendency towards national equality was partially reversed while global inequalities still increased. From World War II until the late 1960s, industrial mass production, mass consumption and the expansion of welfare institutions led to a broadening of the middle classes in the countries of the global north. During the last quarter of the twentieth century, the increased speed of globalisation and the deregulation of national markets reversed this trend and led to an increase in social inequalities in most OECD countries (Alderson and Nielsen 2002; Bronschier 2002: 102–3).

One reason for these developments is the transformation of the global economy. During the last decades a knowledge- and electronic-based 'new economy' gained importance at the cost of the industrial sector. Moreover, the reorganisation of production and the liberalisation of global capital markets affected the distribution of income. The changes in the bargaining positions of managers and experts in relation to the rest of the staff were reflected in a significant increase in the salaries of the class of top managers and experts, while workers and minor office workers often lost real income (Sennett 2002: 218–25). On top of that, the core countries of industrialisation experienced a partial deindustrialisation that went along with a growth in the service sector. As Sassen (1994) and others (Basch, Glick Schiller and Szanton Blanc 1994: 25–27; Portes, Fernández-Kelly and Haller 2005: 1007) have argued, the growth of the service sector was matched by a polarisation of incomes. On the one hand, jobs for qualified professionals within a high-wage sector were available, often created in the knowledge and consultancy industry; on the other, new income opportunities developed in a low-wage service sector, which partly supplies the demands of the former. Although in the high-wage segment the transnational migration of highly skilled professionals plays a role, in particular within the low-wage segment of the labour market disproportionally many migrants are employed.

The tendency towards a bifurcation of the employment structure at the expense of the middle-income segment was described as a 'new hourglass labour market' (Portes and Zhou 1993; Portes, Fernández-Kelly and Haller 2005: 1007). When Ghanaian migrants first came to Western Europe, unemployment was growing and the number of migrant jobs in the industrial sector was slowly decreasing in favour of jobs in the low-wage segment of the service sector. On average, these latter jobs were paid less and were less secure than the former.

This combination of an increase in income inequalities between states and world regions, on the one hand, and the economic polarisation within the industrialised countries, on the other, provides an economic opportunity structure for the participation of migrants in transnational social fields. It creates incentives for the transfer of resources from high-wage countries, like Germany, to low-wage countries, like Ghana. Due to the devaluation of educational degrees and professional skills, many Ghanaians have no or only very limited chances to achieve upward mobility in the receiving countries. At the same time, global inequalities provide Ghanaians and other migrants from the global south with the opportunity to achieve a significant increase in buying power and socio-economic status in their countries of origin by spending money earned in the low-wage segments of high-wage countries. In this respect, disparities between currencies also matter. Migrants from weak currency countries can gain purchasing power in their countries of origin by converting strong Euros or Dollars into the weak currencies of their home countries (Hankel 2001). Moreover, the transnationalisation of migrants' life-worlds has profited substantially from a reduction in the transaction costs of long-distance relationships in the course of the last wave of globalisation. In particular, the costs of transport, telecommunication and money transfers have significantly decreased (Vertovec 2009: 54–60).

Generally, many transnational migrants employ the inversed strategy of transnational business corporations. The latter often produce goods in countries with a lower wage level and weaker currencies, and sell them, preferably, in high-wage and strong-currency countries. In contrast, transcontinental migrants from the global south preferably work in countries with relatively high wages and strong currencies and transfer some parts of their profits to low-wage and weak-currency countries. In the global south these transfers often manifest as a significant increase in social status, which is based on the described economic inequalities. This effect is amplified by the generally lower level of wealth. Because the material standard of living is generally much lower in Ghana than in Germany, fewer resources are necessary to build up the symbolic representations of a middle-class lifestyle.

The statistical data and empirical studies on money transfers to Ghana indicate that a large number of migrant transfer more or less regularly resources to Ghana (Mazzucato, Boom and Nsowah-Nuamah 2008). Simultaneous economic inclusion in two countries rely on a careful management of the limited resources the migrants have at their disposal (Salih 2003: 158). The economic rationality of simultaneous inclusion of migrants in two nation-states becomes obvious when we consider concrete examples. A secondary school teacher at a government school in Ghana, who is perceived as a member of the modern middle class, earned, the Cedi equivalent of €82 in 2004. A school director received about €116. A policeman earned, after finishing the police academy, about €40 and a chief police inspector about €100. A full-time worker on a cacao farm earned about €20 per month (Mazzucato, Kabki and Smith 2006: 1057).

In contrast to this, a cleaner in west Germany earned, according to the generally agreed wage, between seven and eight Euros per hour in 2004. This means it takes between two and four days of work in Germany as a cleaner to earn the monthly wage of a secondary school teacher in Ghana. In the 1980s and early 1990s, when many Ghanaian migrants came to Germany, the average wages in Ghana were even lower than they are today.

In this respect, the differentials between wages and buying power make it theoretically possible to save the Euro equivalent of a middle-class salary in Ghana every month by doing one or more working-class jobs in Germany if the migrants manage to keep their living costs in Germany low. Since the economic capital accumulated in low-wage jobs in Germany is often not sufficient to secure a permanent middle-class status in Ghana, many migrants, in particular those with medium-types of education subjectively feel locked in a situation of double inclusion. They do not have the economic and educational resources to achieve a middle-class status in the receiving countries and, at the same time, by a permanent return they would risk losing or, at least, failing to consolidate their material and social achievements of migration.

Another factor that leads to the stabilisation of transnational social fields is the precarious economic and legal position that many migrants face, at least during certain phases of their migratory trajectory. As former asylum seekers and members of the working class, many Ghanaian migrants face higher risks and insecurities than the non-migrant population which makes them socially and economically vulnerable (cf. Beck 1986: 143). The chance of a return with dignity, which has to be prepared by investments in Ghana, in this context, offers an outlook of social security. Additionally, as I have argued in the last chapter, for several Ghanaians in Berlin it was a way out of unemployment to work in the informal sector or to start a small-scale business. In contrast to formal wage labour, these forms of income generation often do not include unemployment or pension insurance. In particular the outlook to receive only a small pension, which is not sufficient to secure a dignified old age in Germany, affects the strategies of working class migrants' transnational inclusion:

The ... advantage is that because of the economic differences between the countries, it is better to settle back in Ghana than to be here. Let's say I get 500 Euros pension. Here, 500 Euros is not much. But when I live in Ghana, I can live like a king ... I can buy a land there, a big land. Here, you have to pay your rent. In Ghana, I can build my own house ... And it's possible. What do I need to build a house? Not a tenth or so of what I need to build a house in Germany.

(Interview, Ralph Boakye, 2 May 2002, Berlin)

In this sense, inclusion in Ghana provides migrants with a system of social security separately from state institutions in Germany. In case of failure of the migration project, desperation or retirement, the maintenance of cross-border relationships and the investment in houses and people in Ghana makes a life in another place possible. Consequently, transnational kinship relationships play an important role in creating and keeping up the option of a 'respectable return' during the process of migration.

TRANSNATIONALISATION OF KINSHIP RELATIONSHIPS

As has been argued, cross-border kinship relationships contribute significantly to the stabilisation of transnational social fields. Reciprocity and solidarity within families connect migrants and non-migrants residing in different nation-states. In order to understand the logic of the transnationalisation of kinship relation in the case of Ghanaian migrants it is important to make some remarks on their specificity.

Most pre-colonial Akan societies privileged matrilineal in relation to patrilineal descent. This means that children belonged—and still belong—to the extended matrilineal family (*abusua*) of their mothers and not to that of their fathers. Despite the dominance of matrilineal decent, tensions between the principles of patrilineal and matrilineal kinship relations in determining obligations were already documented in pre-colonial Asante society (Fortes 1950: 261). However, colonial rule and the increasing influence of Christianity led to a strengthening of the role of patrilineal descent. In particular the relationship of men with their children gained significance at the expense of the relationship of men and their sisters' children, for whom they were traditionally obliged to care (Okwuasa 1975). Nevertheless, in many regions of southern Ghana, matrilineal descent is still of relevance and particularly men have to manage to some extent two competing sets of obligations.

Reciprocity and the redistribution of resources within families represent the most important institutions of social security in Ghana. In this respect, chiefly the relationship between parents and children is of significance. Because divorces are frequent in Ghana and children normally remain with their mother's family, the relationships between fathers and children are more fragile than the relationships between mothers and their children. This is also reflected in the context of kinship reciprocity. The degree to which children practically and financially support their fathers depends, more than in the case of mothers, on how much the former assisted their children while they were young. Van der Geest (1997; 1998: 337) showed in his case study about ageing in Ghana's Eastern Region, that, above all, two variables determine the material and social well-being of old men. This is, on the one hand, building a house and, on the other hand, having supported one's children sufficiently in young age, which concerns in particular the payment of school fees. Because houses often have rooms in which other family members can stay, and they are bequeathed by the owners to their relatives, both activities, building houses and paying school fees serve to create reciprocity claims among those who profited or will profit from it.

Obligations arising from kinship relationships necessitate that transnational migrants engage in cross-border activities. Particularly in cases in which significant inequalities exist between different members of the extended family, the transfer of resources is often a condition for the maintenance of contact with the family.

Generally, the system of delayed intergenerational reciprocity, on which the social security of old people in Ghana relies, is based on the distinction between persons belonging to the generation of one's parents and those belonging to the generation of one's children. While in the first case the support is understood as a reciprocal act for support which one received in the past, in the latter case new claims of reciprocity are created on which one in turn hopes to be able to rely on in old age. The support of younger persons abstractly can be interpreted as a form of accumulation of social capital from which support claims can be deduced at a later point in time. In cases in which one's own children live in Western Europe and will, therefore, not be able to provide their parents with practical assistance, other relatives in Ghana, like nephews or younger siblings, can also be supported to generate reciprocity claims.

A typical problem connected to reciprocity and redistribution is the average size of Ghanaian families. Kin groups in Ghana usually have more potential receivers of support than the migrants have resources they can or want to spend in this field. Consequently transnational forms of reciprocity and redistribution normally imply strategies of limiting the scope of reciprocity and redistribution.

Obligations play an important role in the selection of persons who are to receive remittances and those who are not. Kofi Boadum described the hierarchy of obligation as follows:

> I have two children at home, a boy and a girl, and my mother is still alive. And there is, of course, the extended family, brothers and sisters[4], who I support from time to time. Two years ago, when I went to Ghana the last time, a daughter of my uncle came to me because she had no

money to continue her education as a teacher. I told her that if she wanted to become a teacher, I would support her ... Most importantly, I have to support my own children and my mother. This is our responsibility in Ghana that we care for our parents ... Beyond this, you support other people from time to time. Some time ago, even a friend of my son called me and said that he needed support. He has no flat anymore and to rent one is expensive. He has only half of the money to rent a flat.[5] He asked me to support him. You listen to the story and then you think, "How much does he need?" If I send him, let's say, 300 Euros he has a home for two or three years. What would you do?
(Interview, Kofi Boadum, 26 June 2002, Berlin)

In this passage, Kofi explicated the link between closeness in terms of kinship relationships, moral obligations and remittances. He distinguished the support of his mother and his children from all other relationships. Siblings are of secondary importance, followed by more distant relatives. In relation to them, he highlights the lower degree of obligation and the lower frequency of support.

As a third category Kofi mentioned persons he is not or not very strongly obliged to support, like his uncle's daughter or his son's friend, but whom he helps because he is a charitable and generous person. The less Kofi depicts a relationship as defined by obligations, the more he emphasises the explicit moral considerations that are involved in the decision-making process.

It is noteworthy that probably the least substantial support, the case of his son's friend, evoked the most extensive reasoning. It is the voluntary aspect of the action which requires, on the one hand, more efforts of legitimation than the other cases and, on the other hand, distinguish it as a particularity of Kofi's personality.

Apart from moral obligations, as I will show below in the case studies, strategic consideration can also play a role in the selection of relatives to be supported. Nevertheless, kinship obligations are embedded in a moral discourse to which migrants and their relatives in Ghana refer in their ongoing negotiations on the degree of support and reciprocity.

In one of the most exceptional cases in my data with regard to the family situation, the relationship between morals and material interests within kinship relationship was made an explicit point of discussion. Peggy, who grew up in Ghana as the daughter of a Ghanaian father and a Polish mother, addressed the issue of moral obligations to support one's family in a relatively radical way:

My family does not expect anything from me. My father has lived in Europe himself ... He knows how we are living here and how difficult it is sometimes ... The rest of the family puts up with the situation that I come empty-handed [laughs artificially; B.N.]. At the beginning, they always said that I did not want to share and that I was selfish [laughs, again, artificially; B.N.]. You see, in Ghana people label you very quickly. They always said, "You don't care for us because your mother is white and she taught you to behave like this." I was always labelled that way. I have lived with that for a long time and now I don't care anymore.

(Interview, Peggy Antwi, 2 November 2002, Berlin)

Peggy claimed to have broken with the expectations of her extended family and dismisses the moral contempt of her father's family she received for not supporting them. Nevertheless, bitterness shone through her description about the rejection and the lack of understanding by her relatives. The form of the narrative, in particular the sarcasm in her expressions and in the tone of her laughter, indicated that the issue was more emotionally disturbing for Peggy than the content of the narrative suggested.

At a later point of the interview, she changed from the initial sarcastic tone to a tone of complaint about what she perceived as the materialistic expectations of her relatives. By blaming them for not backing their demands by what she considered sufficient intimacy, she turned around the accusation of being selfish:

> I have problems with the ones I have no contact with; I don't even know how they are related to me. And, then, I get a ten page letter, "I want, I want, I want, I want, I want, I want." Not even asking, "How are you", but always telling you, "I want".
>
> (Interview, Peggy Antwi, 2 November 2002, Berlin)

At this point, her husband Peter, a Nigeria-born social worker in Berlin, intervened in the interview in order to relativise his wife's representations in front of the German interviewer:

> You see, one time when I was in Nigeria my brother came from America ... I went to this man and I said, "Give me one of your shoes, because we were wearing the same size." Then he said. "No, no, no!" ... You cannot imagine how badly I felt ... I never forgot that ... It is not that I was really in need of shoes. It is just like that, "Okay, my brother has come from America and [I wanted; B.N.] to show [his shoes to; B.N.] my friends ... and [wanted; B.N.] to get some satisfaction from wearing his shoes".
>
> (Interview, Peggy Antwi, 2 November 2002, Berlin)

Peter emphasised in his narrative that the materiality of the gift for which he asked his brother was secondary to its symbolic value. According to his representation, the aspired gift primarily was to express social proximity and recognition. Since this narrative was meant as comment on Peggy's representation of her relatives, he indirectly indicated that they were not primarily materialistic but were interested in attracting Peggy's recognition as an admired migrant. Although the issue of who acted selfish and materialistic remained contested in the relationship between Peggy and her relatives, on the one hand, and Peggy and Peter, on the other hand, there is a close linkage between the moral and the material aspects of kinship relationships. Despite Peggy claiming not to care about the moral evaluation of her relatives, her bitterness indicated that she could not, as she pretended to, simply ignore the moral dimension of transnational kinship relationships. At the same time, Peter's defence did not deny the relevance of material redistribution within kinship relationships. Instead, he argued that Peggy over-emphasised the material interests of her relatives and undercommunicated the symbolic and emotional aspects of gifting.

Generally, the deep cultural anchoring of family obligations makes it rare that migrants do not assist anybody in Ghana. Even Peggy, as became clear in the course of the interview, sends money to a cousin of hers from time to time.

In order to examine in a more detailed way how strategies of transnational kinship reciprocity and redistribution work out, I will present three case studies. The selection of cases is not representative in a statistical sense. It was made to demonstrate a wider range of transcontinental migrants' strategies of manoeuvring in the field of transnational kinship relationships and of dealing with the entanglements of the logics of moral obligation and material exchange.

Family 1 *Kojo Yeboah*

Kojo was born in the late 1940s as the third child of Yaw Kumi and Abenaa Kyeremaa. His parents were cacao farmers who came from villages in the area around Dormaa Ahenkro. Kojo turned out to be a good student and his parents supported him in achieving secondary education. Afterwards, he attended a teacher training college. In the early 1970s, he started to work as a secondary school teacher in the Brong Ahafo Region. After having worked for some time, he invested his savings in a piece of land in the south of the Dormaa District to start a cacao plantation.

During the 1970s the incentives to smuggle cocoa to Côte d'Ivoire increased decidedly. In the border region of the Dormaa District, much of the locally produced cacao was marketed on the other side of the border and Kojo intensively engaged in smuggling. The diversification of sources of income—teacher, cacao farmer and smuggler—turned out to be at least for some time a relatively successful economic strategy in a general societal climate of economic decline. In 1975, Kojo realised that the economic situation was still worsening and decided to leave the country. Because he had saved money, he did not rely on the money of other family members to cover his travel expenses.

Kojo left for London and stayed there for two years. In London, he met a German woman in a discotheque who invited him to come to Berlin. Since

Kojo had heard from other migrants that the labour market situation was better in Germany than in Great Britain at the time, he decided to follow the woman to Berlin. In 1979, Kojo married her and this way managed to secure his legal position in Germany.

In Berlin, he found work as an unskilled labourer in the building sector. The marriage with the German woman was dissolved in the mid-1980s. Before, Kojo already had been married twice in Ghana and had four children by three women, all of them living in Ghana at this time.

In the late 1980s, Kojo married Comfort, a woman from Dormaa Ahenkro whom he had met on the occasion of a home visit. Comfort was the daughter of a wealthy cacao farmer and *odikro* (village chief) who altogether had 32 children by four women, who all achieved secondary education. The majority of Comfort's siblings and half-siblings live in Germany, Great Britain, Switzerland and the United States. Kojo and Comfort have three children.

In the early 1990s, Kojo started to work as a self-employed sub-contractor in the building industry. His small enterprise, which employed four to five workers in 2002, specialised in clearing out old buildings before they were renovated. After working as a cleaning woman for some years, Comfort opened an afro shop in the mid-1990s.

Since the demand for clearing out old buildings had been shrinking over the years, Kojo's company faced financial problems in the early 2000s. In 2004, he had to shut down both his company and Comfort's afro shop. After a period of commuting between different European cities, the family settled in London in 2008 where some of Comfort's relatives live.

Despite these more recent difficulties Kojo was one of the more successful labour migrants in Berlin. He owned three houses in Ghana and was building a fourth one in 2003. Moreover, five persons came to Europe through his support, and he paid the travel costs for two further persons whose attempts at migration failed.

Among his relatives, Kojo gave top priority to the support of his own children. He left his cocoa farm to his first-born son Kwasi. In the late 1980s and early 1990s, he funded the migration of his first-born daughter, Akosua, and her brother, Kwame, to Germany. His fourth son, Kojo, to whose mother Kojo had not been married, lived in Ghana in 2003 and attended secondary school. Kojo Yeboah paid for his school fees at a boarding school, occasionally sent him smaller amounts of money and allowed him to stay in his house in Dormaa Ahenkro during school holidays. Kojo's three last-born children, Kwame, Kwasi and Kwaku, were born in Berlin and have moved with him and their mother to London.

Apart from his children, Kojo also funded the migration of his brother Kwabena Yeboah to Germany in the early 1990s.

By bringing his children and his younger brother to Europe, Kojo fulfilled his moral obligations as a father and as an older brother. By assisting younger relatives in migrating, Kojo transformed potential dependants into

Processes of Transnationalisation 107

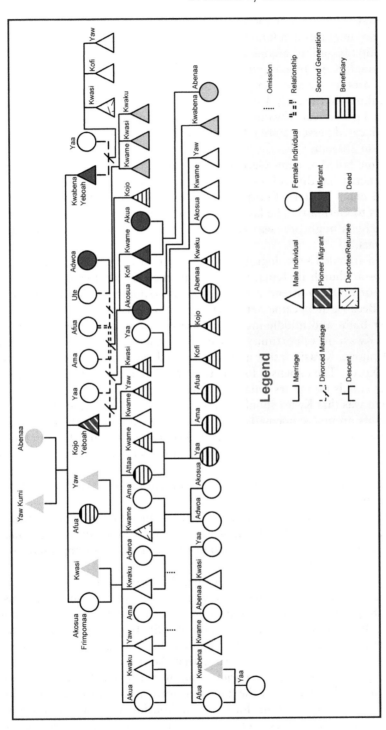

Figure 4.1 Kinship diagram Family 1 *Kojo Yeboah*.

additional supporters of the extended family in Ghana. To increase the number of migrants in a family is a means of distributing the potential load of kinship obligations among a larger number of people.

Although Kojo Yeboah put his main efforts of support on his children and his brother, he also sponsored the migration attempt of one of his sisters' children in the early 1990s. He chose Kwame, a son of his older sister Akosua Frimpomaa. Kwame had finished secondary school and was the most educated person among Kojo's matrilineal nephews at the time of his migration attempt.

Kwame failed to enter Germany and had to return to Ghana. Because of the increasing difficulties that migrants from Africa faced when they tried to enter Western Europe, Kojo stopped funding the migration of relatives to Germany. The last attempt to finance the migration of a family member's migration was the case of Kojo Yeboah's brother's oldest son Kwasi.[6]

Kwasi attended a theological training program at the branch of a Korean Pentecostal church in Tema. Once a year, the church offered its students the opportunity to attend a theological workshop at its headquarters in Seoul. Because it became very difficult for Ghanaians to obtain a visa to enter high- and middle-income countries, an invitation by the church offered Kwasi the opportunity to leave the country. After consultations on the telephone, Kwasi's father and Kojo Yeboah agreed to support the journey to Korea. The expenses for the trip amounted to about €2,500 which roughly equals two-years' salary of a secondary school teacher in Ghana. The plan was that Kwasi should escape from the seminary and try to make a living as an undocumented migrant in Seoul. Kojo Yeboah contacted a Ghanaian friend in Seoul who agreed to help Kwasi. Finally, the plan failed because, as Kwasi told his relatives, one year earlier a substantive portion of the Ghanaian participants of the seminary had already gone underground. Therefore, the church took tight security measures to restrain people from leaving the church campus.

When the message arrived that Kwasi had failed to stay in South Korea and had to come back to Ghana, it was a shock for the family in Dormaa Ahenkro. Kwasi, anticipating the trouble he would face, disappeared from the scene for a while.

Some members of the family in Dormaa Ahenkro blamed the misfortune on super-natural forces which were working against the family and suspected Kojo's wife as the potential source. In the following weeks, money matters that came up in the family's everyday life frequently became linked up to the incident and it was highlighted that the family had to suffer because of Kwasi's failure. It appeared that the strong reaction was a dramatic expression of the general grief about the waste of collective resources which the incident meant for the family in Dormaa Ahenkro. Factually, due to my financial contributions for food and housing, the household income at this point of time was even higher than a couple of months before.

Interestingly, in Kwasi's case the head of the household and the young men living in the house most openly expressed reproach at the abuse of collective resources. While the former controlled the incoming remittances and was afraid of receiving less money after this incident, some of the latter, who would have liked to get the same chance of leaving Ghana, had felt disadvantaged by the support of Kwasi. In a sense, the idiom of collectivity gave the discontented individuals the chance to express personal feelings and interests. Generally, the relation between collective responsibility and individual autonomy was a frequent point of conflict between transcontinental migrants and their families in Ghana. While migrants tended to attribute the agency of migration and the achievements to themselves and complained about the expectations of the family, the relatives in Ghana stressed the role of the collective in making migration possible and criticised what they considered the irresponsible and egotistic behaviour of the migrants. However, it is important to see the relation between both of these positions. Both are complementary in a process of negotiation in which the extent and limits of transnational forms of kinship reciprocity and redistribution are determined.

Sponsoring the migration of relatives is one expression of transnational forms of kinship reciprocity, house building in Ghana is another form. As mentioned earlier, Kojo built four houses in Ghana. The first, relatively small, house Kojo constructed for his mother in her home village in the Dormaa District. Later, he built a more prestigious house in the close-by district capital of Dormaa Ahenkro. The representative part of the house, which was used only on Kojo's occasional home visits, was meant to be occupied by him and his wife after their return to Ghana. The rest of the building was inhabited mostly by Kojo's relatives. In 2003, 25 persons lived in the house. Kojo's sister, Afua Firi, was the head of the household. By asking her to run the household, he supported economically the weakest of his siblings.

Additionally, Attaa—Kojo's sister's daughter—her husband, Kwame, and their seven children lived in the house. Because Afua Firi had no children of her own, Attaa and her children fulfilled important functions for the maintenance of the household, especially cooking, cleaning, subsistence farming and marketing of plantain and cassava. With Afua and Attaa, two particularly needy persons profited from resources which Kojo made available to the family. In return, they maintained the infrastructure in Dormaa Ahenkro.

Kojo's third house was a building in a suburb of Accra, in which two families and Yaw, his youngest sister's son (*wofaase*), who took care of the house, lived. In 2003 Yaw was a student of political sciences at Legon University and Kojo paid for his university fees. By taking care of the education of one of his sisters' children, he fulfilled his traditional obligations as a mother's brother (*wofa*). As an act of reciprocity, Yaw carried out activities in Accra on behalf of Kojo. In 2003, he supervised and organised the construction of a two-storey house in Accra, which was Kojo's latest building project. Moreover, Kojo Yeboah commissioned Yaw to operate as his representative in business affairs in Accra. As a university student, Yaw was dexterous in dealing with Ghanaian bureaucrats and business partners. Occasionally, Yaw received shipments from Germany or sent goods to Germany, which were sold in Comfort's shop. Both Yaw and Kojo profited from their relationship. Yaw was offered the opportunity to study, and Kojo had an agent in the transnational gateway city of Accra who could act on his behalf.

In his support strategies, Kojo had to find a balance between different criteria, in particular the closeness of kinship relationships, the individual neediness of the beneficiary and his strategic interests in a person. Kojo could not choose freely to whom he sent money or granted privileges, but was restricted by the moral order of kinship obligations and the priorities of support which were defined by it. The case of Kojo's relationship to his matrilineal nephew, Yaw, demonstrated that the morals of kinship obligations and individual strategies of profit maximising do not necessarily contradict each other, but can even reinforce one another.

Because Kojo Yeboah engaged in morally sanctioned kinship relationships, he was also able to utilise the supported dependants for his own purposes. If he had not selected Yaw according to the logic of the Akan system of kinship obligations, he would not have developed an instrumental interest in him. Long-distance kinship relationships provided Kojo with a social infrastructure for his transnational activities. They enabled him to build houses, to prepare the ground for a return in old age and to initiate business projects in Ghana.

Family 2 *Yaw Asare*

Yaw Asare, who was in his mid-40s at the time of the research, was the pioneer migrant of Family 2. Yaw had graduated from middle school in the early 1970s. His father owned a cacao farm in the south of the Dormaa District and supported him to buy a piece of land in order to start a maize farm. In the late 1970s, Yaw's dissatisfaction with the economic conditions in Ghana grew and he decided to go to Abidjan in Côte d'Ivoire, where he worked for five years. From other Ghanaian migrants in Abidjan, Yaw heard about the possibility to go to Sweden and got interested in it. In order to cover the travelling expenses, he sold his maize farm in the Dormaa District, invested what he had saved in Côte d'Ivoire and was supported by his father. In 1985, Yaw Asare left for Sweden.

After some time in Sweden, Yaw married a Swedish woman. In 1989, they visited Ghana. At this time, he had secured his legal position and had accumulated enough money to present himself as a successful transcontinental migrant to his family. His Swedish wife died in the early 1990s. In the mid-1990s, Yaw married a Ghanaian woman from Sunyani whom he had met during a home visit and took her to Sweden.

Processes of Transnationalisation 111

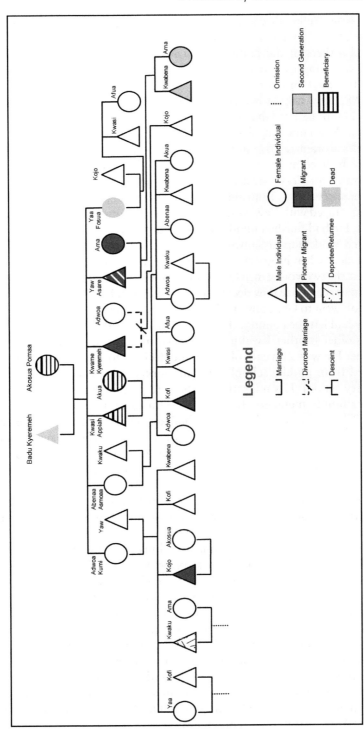

Figure 4.2 Kinship diagram Family 2 *Yaw Asare*.

As in Kojo Yeboah's case, an important form of Yaw Asare's support for his relatives in Ghana was the sponsoring of migration. The oldest of the four brothers of the family, Kwasi Appiah, a teacher in the Dormaa District, was supposed to stay in Ghana. After the death of his father, he looked after the family's property.

In 1989, Yaw helped his second oldest brother, Kwame Kyeremeh, to migrate. Before he left Ghana, Kwame had been a self-employed carpenter in Sunyani. Yaw contributed a part of the travelling expenses and the family contacted a distant relative in Germany who was able to help Kwame. For some time he lived in Hamburg and later moved to another German city. In 1992, Kwame and Yaw decided together to support the migration of two of their older sisters' sons, Kojo and Kofi. The two young men came to Sweden, where they stayed with Yaw Asare. At the time of migration, Kojo was twenty years old. He had finished middle school and had done an apprenticeship as a fitter in a workshop in Sunyani. Kofi was seventeen and was a secondary school student when he got the chance to migrate to Europe.

Because the two young men felt uncomfortable in a situation of dependency on their maternal uncle they decided to leave Sweden. Following personal networks, Kofi went to Germany and Kojo to the Netherlands. In 2002, ten years after they had left the country, they visited Ghana for the first time.

Kojo's older brother Kwaku was the last member of Family 2 to come to Europe. He was 28 years old when he decided to migrate. Kwaku had graduated from middle school and had worked as a teacher in a private elementary school. His migration costs were paid by himself, Yaw Asare and other family members. In 1995, he went to Berlin where he claimed asylum. When it became clear that he had no chance to obtain refugee status, he went underground. In 1997, he was caught by the German police, sent to jail and, finally, deported to Ghana. According to his representation, the German police confiscated his money and he arrived in Ghana without any financial resources or assets.[7] In 2002, he lived as a farmer in his hometown and occasionally received remittances from his younger brother. In his family, he had the stigma of being the only person who had not been successful abroad.

As mentioned above, the fulfilment of kinship obligations in relation to one's own parents has the highest priority. All of the four successful migrants of *Family 2* have built houses for their parents or, in Kofi's case, for his mother, respectively. Additionally, two of the four migrants provided relatives in Ghana with investment capital or producer goods they could use for income generation. Yaw Asare sent his older brother a minibus, which he rented to a driver. Kofi provided his mother with money to open a kiosk in her hometown. Moreover, Yaw Asare bought a red German second-hand compact executive car for his father in Ghana. With this gift, he expressed, on the one hand, his gratefulness to his father, who had, as mentioned above, supported his migration. On the other hand, it served as an icon of Yaw Asare's own economic success.

In 2002, shortly after having completed the house for his mother, Kojo visited Ghana himself. It was the background for a triumphant home visit and expressed his commitment to the moral discourse of kinship reciprocity. During his visit, Kojo became acquainted with a teacher from Sunyani whom he married in 2003. The conspicuously celebrated marriage and the house documented his newly acquired social status as an affluent migrant to his relevant others in Ghana.

Yaw Asare and Kwame Kyeremeh actively fulfilled their family obligations by building houses, supporting the migration of and providing business capital for relatives. In the absence of children in Ghana, they supported their parents, their siblings and two matrilineal nephews. Additionally, Yaw and Kwame built a big house for themselves in Sunyani and started to set up a two-storey building to rent out opposite to the other house.

Their matrilineal nephews, Kojo and Kofi had started to fulfil their family obligations. At the time of research, it was not clear how far they would proceed with it. Kojo's marriage with a woman from Sunyani and the building of a house in his hometown indicated that he intended to carry on his transnational engagement.

Family 3 *Afua Konadu*

Afua Konadu, the pioneer migrant in the third case study, is a woman from the Ashanti Region. She was born in Kumasi in 1961. Her matrilineal family originates from one of the villages in the vicinity of Kumasi. She is the first-born child of a fitter from Bekwai in the Ashanti Region and a trader who traded in sweets. Afua completed middle school in Kumasi and was afterwards trained as a hairdresser. She married and delivered her first daughter in 1978 and her son in 1981. In the early 1980s, when her marriage broke up, Afua looked for economic alternatives that would enable her to care for her children. Because she did not want to enter her mother's business, she made efforts to leave the country. Afua's mother provided her with money to travel to Europe. In 1984, Afua left her children with her mother in Kumasi and went to London. Similar to Kojo of Family 1 a couple of years before, Afua was dissatisfied with the labour market situation in Great Britain in the 1980s and heard from other migrants that it was easier to find work in Germany. Afua contacted the husband of a former schoolmate who lived in Berlin and he helped to accommodate her in the city. In Berlin, she attained secure legal status by marrying a German man. The marriage broke up after some years and she remarried an Asante migrant from Berlin with whom she got two children. After some years, this marriage also broke up. In 2005, she lived alone with her two last-born children in Berlin.

Afua worked as a cleaner for different companies and households in Berlin. Commercial cleaning is probably the most widespread type of work for Ghanaian women in Berlin. Informal and illicit work plays a significant

114 *Theorising Transnational Migration*

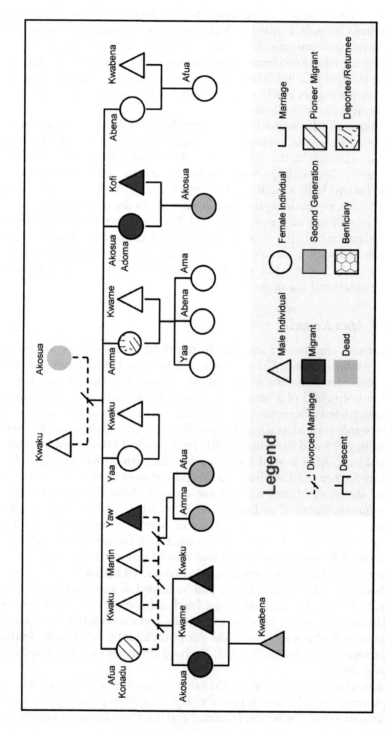

Figure 4.3 Kinship diagram Family 3 *Afua Konadu*.

role in this sector. Without social security and pension insurance these women often are in a precarious situation, particularly when they lose their work or retire.

In 1990, Afua's mother died and Afua, in addition to her own children in Ghana, had to take on responsibility for her younger sisters.

> So, I had to take the responsibilities at the house . . . I had to take care of these [she points at the respective symbols in the kinship diagram that I sketched during the interview; B.N.] three sisters of mine . . . There were no boys and I was the elder . . . My father and my mother were no more together, so, I had to support.
> (Interview, Afua Konadu, 11 June 2005, Berlin)

In this passage, Afua explicated the criteria of assigning responsibility for her dependent sisters. Because the father had left his family long ago, her mother was, as long as she was alive, the main person responsible for her children. After her death, age and gender categories were relevant in determining who had to care for them. In the absence of a son, it was structurally pre-determined that Afua, as the oldest daughter, had to take over the main load of responsibility. In the following years, she sent a significant share of her monthly savings to Ghana. She particularly stressed her role in funding her younger sisters' education. This included coverage of the expenses of one sister's education at a midwifery school in London. In addition, Afua also supported the education of her own two children in Kumasi up to secondary school level.

Another major form of support was the funding of migration. Together with her younger sister she sponsored the migration of her fourth-born sister, Akosua Adoma, to Canada. Additionally, she paid for the travel costs of her younger daughter to Great Britain in 2000. In 2001, she and her daughter financed the migration of Afua's son, Kwame, to Great Britain. After having taken care of the education of her three younger sisters, her two children and the migration expenses of one sister and two children, Afua had fulfilled her obligations, except for the two last-born children in Berlin.

At the time of the interview, her former dependants had become economically independent and did not any longer claim support from Afua.

> They are all grown up now. They are all married. That is why I do not have that responsibility anymore.
> (Interview, Afua Konadu, 11 June 2005, Berlin)

Because of the substantial remittances Afua sent to Ghana for the maintenance of the livelihood of her family, she was not able to buy assets in Ghana herself. When she is in Ghana, Afua stays in her late mother's house, where she also intends to move after her withdrawal from working life in Germany.

Occasionally Afua also supported her father financially although she was not particularly obliged to do this because he had not cared for her when she was a child:

> Sometimes, I give him something . . . Yes, especially because my father did not take care of me, I do not have to support him. You know, because in Ghana the fathers divorce the mothers and leave the children for the women. So, in a case like that, I don't have much interest in my father's side.
> (Interview, Afua Konadu, 11 June 2005, Berlin)

As mentioned before, the support of fathers depends particularly on the assistance they provided for their children. As her comment demonstrates, Afua was, like most Ghanaians, aware of the rules of delayed reciprocity within kinship relations. It includes a constant tension between the moral logic of obligation and the more rational exchange logic of delayed reciprocity. Afua addressed this ambivalence in the interview:

> When I was young and didn't have anything, somebody had to support me . . . My mother takes care of bringing me up and I have to take care of her . . . I have to take care of my other sisters who don't have [money; B.N.] . . . I do not think it is proper for you to see your sister suffering. If my sister has something, I do not need to worry about. But, you know, sickness can come at any time to a person to make him suffer, death can come . . . So if my sister . . . didn't care about me, when we were all in Ghana, and . . . she never helped me . . . I shouldn't force me to help her. Because it is like this: *nsa ko nsa ba*.'[8]
> (Interview, Afua Konadu, 11 June 2005, Berlin)

Afua's statements remain ambiguous. On the one hand, she emphasised the significance of delayed reciprocity in the context of kinship relationships which is, according to Afua's representation, rooted in the condition of human existence ('When I was young and didn't have anything, somebody had to support me.'). On the other hand, she employed a moral discourse on kinship solidarity. She argued that it is 'improper', according to moral standards, to let close relatives suffer despite one having the means to support them.

At the end of the passage, Afua synthesised the different logics of morals and reciprocity within one argument. She highlighted that the strength and resourcefulness which distinguishes the giver from the taker is transitory. Even if somebody might be strong and independent today, he or she can be weak and dependent tomorrow ('sickness can come at any time'). Even if their suffering will never be ours, the fact that it could be ours should change our attitude towards them. The common nature as human beings and the unpredictability of the future should, according to Afua, guide our behaviour in relation to our relatives.

Nevertheless, Afua also made clear that the obligation of solidarity deriving from her argument has its limits. Support of and reciprocity among close kin rely on acknowledgement of the general validity of the rules of kinship solidarity by both sides ('if my sister ... never helped me ... I shouldn't force me to help her'). Those who violate the rules of reciprocity too fundamentally are threatened with exclusion from the potential benefits.

The support of Afua was concentrated, unilaterally, on her sisters and her children. It aimed at securing the family's livelihood in Ghana, providing education and sponsoring migration. Although Afua aims at being independent of financial support in her old age, she has created a social security net by her transnational activities apart from the welfare institutions of the receiving country on which she can rely in cases of need:

> *B:* Are you planning to go back to Ghana?
> *A:* Oh yeah, in my old age.
> *B:* Will your junior sisters and your children support you then?
> *A:* When I am there, yes. If I am in need, they have to support me.
> (Interview, Afua Konadu, 11 June 2005, Berlin)

Kinship Relationships and the Stabilisation of Transnational Social Fields

The three case studies showed that remittances, the sponsoring of chain migration and migrants' home visits play an important role in the production and reproduction of transnational social fields, connecting Ghanaian migrants with their relatives in Ghana.

If migrants have to care for dependants like children or parents, money is sent regularly. Otherwise, remittances are often project- or problem-oriented. Migrants negotiate with their relatives from case to case whether they support somebody in a certain respect or not.

Typologically, six main types of kinship support can be identified:

1. Regular remittances to households in which close relatives live (in particular children and parents)
2. Funding of migration costs (chain migration)
3. Provision of housing or farmland
4. Contribution of investment capital for business activities or provision of producer goods, like second-hand vans, minibuses, computers or photocopiers to be used for income generation
5. Gifts (e.g. televisions, hi-fi systems, clothes, money and shoes) distributed on the occasion of home visits

6. Assistance in case of extraordinary expenses or at times of need (e.g. hospital bills, family rituals)

Because the first four forms of support were already exemplified in the case studies, I will just add some comments on the fifth and sixth type of support. Gifting on the occasion of home visits is an important redistributive practice of migrants, from which often a larger number of recipients profit. Persons who are omitted from the gifting practice frequently feel disregarded. Therefore, most migrants who travel to Ghana bring gifts and money with them, which they distribute among relatives and friends in order to avoid dissatisfaction, envy and conflict.

As already mentioned, family rituals, in general, and funerals, in particular, are of great importance in the Ghanaian context. Because of their publicity and their social relevance, they are stages for the display of family status at the local level (van der Geest 2000; de Witte 2003: 555; Mazzucato, Kabki and Smith 2006: 1064–65). The way funerals are celebrated creates instances of honour and shame for the extended family and its representatives. As a matter of fact, these family rituals lead to a temporary intensification of transnational activities among families whose members reside in different countries and on different continents (Mazzucato, Kabki and Smith 2006). The members of these families have to interact with each other in the course of the preparation of an event. The coordination of holidays and travelling schedules often makes funerals a logistically demanding and time-consuming project.

It was shown that intergenerational forms of reciprocity and redistribution provide social security in cases of old age, sickness or failure of the migratory project. Van der Geest's study of old people in the Kwahu Region (1998; 2000) indicated that there is an interrelation between the support of relatives and the social and economic wellbeing in particular of old men. Although most migrants try to save money to be independent in old age, sponsoring the migration of children, younger siblings or nephews and nieces is a way of generating reciprocity claims a migrant can rely on in cases of need.

The economic importance of migration for a family is felt very strongly in Ghana. An adolescent boy in Dormaa Ahenkro explained to me: 'If you do not have anybody abroad you have to suffer in Ghana.'[9] Therefore, chain migration was, in the cases of the examined families, considered an attractive form of patronage that was normally preferred to the provision of capital to start a business in Ghana. In all cases presented, the sponsoring of the migration of dependants, in particular one's own children and younger siblings, had priority. Chain migration often leads to a dispersal of family members over different countries. Although some families were concentrated in certain places in Europe, even close relatives often migrated to different countries following opportunities. In this sense, Ghanaians distinguish themselves from groups of migrants which tend to build local clusters in the receiving countries along kinship criteria or region of origin. It seems to be related to the deeply ambiguous relation towards social closeness that can be found among Ghanaian migrants and was discussed in the last chapter.

In the cases of Kojo Yeboah and Yaw Asare matrilineal kinship obligations were of some relevance. Moreover, the two cases from the Dormaa District documented, apart from marriage migration, a preference for the selection of male relatives in sponsoring mobility. In contrast to this, in Afua's case, women got supported by their family to migrate independently from men. Beside differences in the gender ratio within the selected families, this difference presumably also refers to regional differences between Greater Kumasi and the Dormaa District.

For pioneer migrants the sponsoring of the migration of close relatives is a way of reducing the burden of responsibility in the present. Because siblings have the same relatives, their migration improves the ratio between potential receivers of remittances and potential givers within a family.

Since the three cases were selected because of their significant share of migrants, they are not representative of Ghanaian migrant families. In this context, the Bonokrom data helps to contextualise the case studies. While all three described families included more than five migrants, only 25 per cent out of the 46 families covered from Bonokrom comprised more than three transnational migrants, and 31 per cent included only one (see Chapter 2, p. 55ff). In the case of transcontinental migration, the share of kinship units with only one migrant was 63 per cent, while only 20 per cent of the families incorporated more than three. These results indicate that although chain migration is a noticeable pattern, not all migrants support their families in this way. One important factor that explains these differences is that only migrants who have established themselves economically and legally in the receiving areas can support others effectively. In five out of ten kinship units with only one transcontinental migrant, he or she had been abroad five years or less. In six out of seven families with three or more transcontinental migrants, the pioneer migrant had been abroad for more than ten years.

Moreover, the data of the Bonokrom sample shows a co-variation between the maintenance of transnational relationships and migrants' transfers of resources; 17 out of 21 transcontinental migrants who had visited 'home', which is a strong indicator of the maintenance of home ties, had built one or more houses in Ghana and had supported their families in one or more respects. Three out of the four remaining persons were students who were not expected at their stage of life to have achieved substantive wealth.

Collecting data on the use of remittances raised methodical problems that provided some insights into the social logic of negotiation between migrant and non-migrant relatives: Shortly before I left Dormaa Ahenkro, two relatives of migrants in Berlin independently of each other approached me and held short speeches in which they emphasised their neediness and their suffering in Ghana. They asked me to deliver this message to their respective relatives in Germany. The degree of neediness that was claimed in these cases, in which I knew the families, was exaggerated. The families were definitely not poor by local standards. In this sense, people who represented themselves as resourceful at other occasions, emphasised their poverty and suffering in relation to me and asked me to convey this message to their relatives in Germany.

It appears that the language of neediness was aimed not so much at giving a realistic representation of their life situation but was a communicative code to express claims for redistribution between more wealthy and less wealthy members of the same kin group.

Besides general declarations of poverty, concrete needs, like school fees or hospital bills, were also common reasons for asking migrants for support. Although there is no doubt that migrant remittances factually play a very important role for assisting family members in Ghana in times of need and distress, the communicative logic of the negotiations for redistribution, generally, creates incentives to over-emphasise one's neediness. I observed, for instance, a case in which a person exaggerated the amount he had to pay for his wife's hospital treatment in relation to his maternal uncle who lived in Germany. In another case, the amount paid for school fees was overstated by a migrant's son. Nevertheless, both parties, migrants and relatives in Ghana, normally regarded these exaggerations not as 'cheating', rather because they were aware of the functionality of the communicative code. It could even easily be perceived as impolite and disrespectful in relation to a potential patron to stress other reasons for support than urgent and important ones.

Another incidence, in which the sometimes difficult relationship between relatives and migrants became obvious, was a transnational building project in which I played a marginal role. A Ghanaian migrant in Berlin asked me to visit his relative in Accra and to take pictures of the progress of the building for which he had sent money. When I wanted to take pictures his relative asked me to come back a few days later. Within these days, the building project made significant progress. Obviously, the migrant in Berlin was aware of the potential risk that his money could be spent on other purposes than the intended ones and imposed social control as a precautionary measure. Both sides are often aware of the conditions and typical pitfalls of the interaction between migrants and relatives in Ghana and adapt their practices and representations to this knowledge.

Within the negotiations between families and migrants, the respective groups control different resources. Moral sanctions are, as I have shown, the major resource of the extended family. In case of conflict and disappointment of expectations, pressure can be put on a migrant. In the context of a conversation about Kwabena Yeboah (cf. Family 1), who has lived in Germany for more than ten years without having made a significant contribution to the well-being of the family, one of his great nephews announced that his maternal grand-uncle 'has to die abroad.'[10] Thereby, he referred to a central sanction of the matrilineal family. The *abusua* fulfils important functions for the organisation of the funeral of a person. Theoretically, the elders of the family have the power to reject the burial of a person. Since 'the ultimate proof of respect and the decisive act of reciprocity is to organise a worthy funeral for someone upon his/her death' (van der Geest 1997: 552) the refusal of burying somebody is the ultimate punishment for those persons who violate the rules of reciprocity too profoundly. Although Kwasi was not in a position to decide whether his maternal granduncle will receive a worthy burial, his remarks reflect that the members of kin groups in Ghana interpreted themselves not as mere dependants, but that the moral discourse of individual indebtedness to one's *abusua* empowers family members to claim their share in a relationship that is considered to be based on the principle of reciprocity. Both parties know that even if migrants do not depend on their matrilineal family as long as they live abroad, they will depend on them at the time of their death.

Ghanaians are often very explicit on the functionality of kinship relationships. Ironically, for instance, Ralph described his simultaneous inclusion into two different systems of social security as being charged twice for the same service:

> I support other people's grandparents by paying my social insurance, which they take from my wage. But, I have to pay for my own grandparents in Ghana as well ... That's why you always become poor, when you are in a foreign country.
> (Interview, Ralph Boakye, 2 May 2002, Berlin)

However, as I argued before, the functionality of kinship relationships is only one aspect. Moral considerations are the other side. As both aspects are entangled with each other, it is in most of the unproblematic cases impossible from an observer's point of view to judge whether the support of relatives is motivated more by the former or the latter. Only in problematic cases actors have to differentiate the motivations in order to evaluate and weigh them. One decision, for instance, in which emphasis was placed on the side of moral considerations, was in the cited case of Kofi Boadum, who sponsored the education of his uncle's daughter as a teacher. A case in which the strategic dimension became dominant in the course of the interaction was the case of Kojo Yeboah's relationship to his maternal nephew Yaw. At the beginning, Kojo's support of Yaw's education had stronger moral connotations. The more important Yaw became as Kojo's agent and caretaker of his house in Accra the more important the strategic interest of both actors in each other became.

PROCESSES OF TRANSNATIONALISATION

While Chapter 3 focussed on processes of localisation, this chapter dealt with processes of transnationalisation of the life-worlds of Ghanaian migrants.

As several students of transnationalism have argued, multiple and simultaneous forms of inclusion in different nation-states and the transnational fields which connect them are often complementary rather than contradictory (Levitt 2001; Levitt and Glick Schiller 2004; Smith 2006; Grillo and Mazzucato 2008). This chapter has examined how and why transnational social fields connecting Ghanaians in Germany with Ghanaians in Ghana and elsewhere stabilise in practice. Beside the more recent developments towards a Ghanaian politics of transnational migrant incorporation, economic incentives and kinship relationships were identified as basic motivations for transnational engagement.

On a macro level, I described the economic opportunity structure for simultaneous incorporation. Economic disparities between different countries and world regions have significantly increased in the last hundred years. At the same time, social inequalities within the industrialised countries also started to grow since the 1970s. This process of double polarisation of incomes together with the decrease in the costs of telecommunication, money transfers and transport has created an opportunity structure for migrants to maintain transnational relationships. Because the cultural capital of Ghanaian migrants is often devalued in the Western European receiving countries and many of them are incorporated in the low-wage service segment of the labour market, their incomes and chances of social mobility are rather low compared to the average of the non-migrant population. At the same time, there are significant economic incentives to transfer profits from labour in Germany to Ghana.

Particular emphasis was placed on the obligations of migrants to support their relatives. Kinship obligations were identified as a major reason why migrants maintain transnational relationships.[11] Although the economic incentive structure for transnational incorporation and the social logic of transnational kinship relationships are practically interlinked, they have to be distinguished analytically. This becomes particularly clear for the relation between transnational forms of inclusion and socio-economic integration of migrants in the receiving countries. While according to a socio-economic logic of assimilation, we could expect that those migrants most marginalised in the receiving country have the strongest interest in the maintenance of transnational relationships, it is the other way around according to the logic of kinship relationships. The more resources migrants control, the more they can intensify and extend their transnational kinship networks. For instance, four out of five medical doctors whom I interviewed travelled to Ghana annually or biannually to visit friends and relatives. The majority of non-academic migrants with a lower income often could only afford to go to Ghana every three to ten years. Migrants with very low incomes and/or no secure legal status could not visit Ghana at all. Often these migrants were only able to maintain sporadic contacts with their relatives in Ghana or had to stop the contact for some time. The cultural logic of shame and honour, which underlies the practices of reciprocity and redistribution in kinship relationships, normally urges transcontinental migrants, who do not want to lose face, either to transfer resources to Ghana or to limit communication.

It was shown that chain migration leads to the dispersal and transnationalisation of families and in this way contributes to the stabilisation and expansion of those transnational fields into which the families are incorporated. Another issue discussed was the relationship of strategic (e.g. securing one's living standard in old age) and moral aspects (e.g. solidarity among relatives) of kinships reciprocity and wealth redistribution. It was argued that it is inappropriate to perceive strategic interests and moral obligations as in fundamental opposition. They manifest themselves practically in different constellations in the framework of transnational kinship relationships. Depending on the situation, they can reinforce, contradict or simply coexist with each other.

5 The Status Paradox of Migration

The notion of status provides a good entry point for an anthropology of social inequality and transnational migration. It offers a framework to explore and theorise the links between unequal distribution of resources, representations of social identity, imaginaries of society and, last but not least, an affective side of personhood that reacts to social misrecognition and is sensitive to feelings of loss and insecurity. An important aspect of the concept of status, which suits very well the purposes of this chapter, is that it implies a theoretical accent on the context-dependency of the value of resources and the relativity of social positions. In this respect the concept of status is more useful to theorise the switches between different status identities relating to different national contexts than other concepts, in particular the notion of class. The latter puts a stronger emphasis on the objectivity and unambiguity of social positions and patterns of stratification (Beck 1986: 121–60). The relativity of social positions and personal resources as well as the affective sides of social status are vital to understand why the status paradox comes into being. At the same time, the idea of status is not ideologically neutral. It transports particular ideas about the character of modern society and the mechanisms for ascribing and attaining social status. What makes it nevertheless of analytical value is that these theoretical presumptions resonate with the discourses on stratification and social mobility that I encountered in the course of my field research. In this sense, the concept of status is not used as an analytical concept that can be simply applied to the examined case but represents an articulation between the analytical interests and the social discourses and practices that are the objects of study. Therefore, it is neither aimed at a mere reconstruction of discourses on social status nor at a explanatory social theory; rather, the concept of status marks a space of intersection in between the observer's and the participants' points of view from which analysis and theorisation starts.

As indicated before, the status paradox found among Ghanaian migrants emerges in interaction with the opportunity structures for transnational transfers of resources on the one hand and the specific problems that occur by converting the material and symbolic resources earned in one socio-spatial context into social status in another. Global inequalities in wealth and the buying power of currencies make it possible for migrants from the global south to build up symbolic representations of middle-class status in their countries of origin by doing working-class jobs in the countries of immigration. This situation has a profound impact on the status identities of the affected persons as well as on the status systems of the sending countries. Since these effects are underrepresented and undertheorised in the migration studies literature this chapter hopes to contribute to a better understanding of these unintended consequences of the transnationalisation of modes of status production. In this context I will explore a modern social imaginary of social status and, in relation to it, the status paradox of migration from three interconnected perspectives:

First, I explain the structural-functionalist theory behind classical ideas of social status. Second, I elaborate on the historical changes in the social imaginaries of social status in Ghana. Third, I describe the empirical case of the *Burger* as an ideal type of a labour migrant to whom the status paradox applies. This triple step from theory to history to ethnography is necessary to bring some of the self-evident background knowledge to the foreground which helps to explain why the status paradox of migration emerges, how it operates and what impact it has on society.

SOCIAL STATUS IN THE SOCIAL SCIENCES

Social status will be understood in the following sections as a specific form of social identity, which reflects the socio-economic positioning of an individual in a social field. Although status identities rely on resources—in contemporary societies particularly on wealth, educational degrees and office—they are not entirely determined by them. As status has to be claimed, acknowledged, performed and negotiated, it is an originary social and relational ascription.

The resources that legitimate individual status claims often cannot be directly observed in everyday interactions. Therefore the participants in a context have to decode the signs by which it is communicated, like dress codes, business cards, habitus, language codes or the size and position of offices. Since social status itself in everyday life is often a contextual and diffuse phenomenon its representation and performance leave sufficient space for 'impression management' (Goffman 1990 [1959]). Persons might over- or understate social status in relation to others in unclear situations, compete with others for status superiority or subordinate to their status claims, deceive others or just try to convey an 'appropriate' impression of what they perceive to be their status in a given context. Both aspects, the resources that legitimate the representations and the practices of representation themselves, are relevant in the context of the status paradox of migration. It is argued that it is above all the transcontinental migrants' status inconsistency between their occupational status in the receiving country and their displayed wealth (measured by the standards of the country of origin) that contests normative assumptions about social status. This concerns a tight coupling of status preformances and key status variables (i.e. wealth, education, office), on the one hand, and of status performances and underlying resources, on the other hand. Since a normative expectation of status consistency is inscribed in *modern imaginaries of social status*, the described type of transnational migrant challenges ideas of legitimate status attainment.

The term 'social imaginary' was introduced by Charles Taylor to theorise the connection between philosophical ideas about society and self-evident forms of everyday knowledge that are shared by members of a society at a given point of time and that are objectified within its institutions.

> What I'm trying to get at with this term is something much broader and deeper than the intellectual schemes people may entertain when they think about social reality in a disengaged mode ... I speak of imaginary because I'm talking about the way ordinary people "imagine" their social surroundings, and this is often not expressed in theoretical terms; it is carried in images, stories, and legends.
>
> (Taylor 2002: 106)

In a certain sense, Taylor's concept of social imaginary is complementary to Weber's concept of ideal type (Weber 1985 [1904]: 190–214). While Taylor looks at the relationship between social imaginaries and academic concepts from the perspective of the former, Weber observed the same link from the side of the latter. Both authors highlighted the fact that the boundary between academic concepts and theories about the social world and social imaginaries prevalent in a given society are porous in both directions: social imaginaries shape theoretical concepts *and* theoretical concepts influence social imaginaries. Social science knowledge not only passively reflects dominant ideas about the character of a society, but also influences them and, at the same time, gets influenced by them.

In the following paragraphs, the relationship between the theoretical model of social status and social imaginaries of social status in Ghana will be explored. It will be argued that classical sociological theory of social status explicates a set of otherwise mostly implicit normative assumptions inherent in social imaginaries of social status. In this sense, it is not the adequacy of the theory as a representation of patterns of social stratification in Ghana, which I am interested in, but its significance for social imaginaries.

The concept of status was predominantly employed to theorise the connection between functional differentiation and the stratification of societies, which is based on the unequal distribution of central resources, like wealth, power and prestige. In distinction to Marxist views of society as a struggle between classes, functionalism advocated a more consensual model of society. Prominently, Durkheim (2002 [1897]: 210) interpreted differences in wealth and prestige as an outcome of the societal consciousness of the structural importance of different functions for the society as a whole. He assumed that those who fulfil the most important functions in a society, according to an underlying societal consensus, earn the highest material and symbolic rewards. The tight coupling between the importance of a function for a society and its gratification was seen by functionalist authors as an 'unconsciously evolved device' (Davis and Moore 1945: 243) to assign the best personnel to the most vital positions.

In this context, structural functionalists differentiated between modern and traditional societies and their respective modes of status ascription. While traditional societies were expected to assign status on the basis of ascribed features (i.e. age, gender, ethnicity and kinship), modern societies were supposed to employ achievement and performance as the central mechanism for the attainment of social status. Because of the higher efficiency of performance in relation to ascription as a device to assign persons to positions, modern societies were said to use their human resources more effectively than traditional ones. Above all, it was assumed that formal education attained a key role for the allocation of status positions in 'modern societies'. The tight coupling between the three status variables of education, office and income was considered the normal case. Kreckel (1992: 94–106) called it the *meritocratic triad*.

Since the 1940s, multi-dimensional models of social status were developed by American sociologists (Warner, Meeker and Eells 1949: 266; Parsons 1954 [1940]: 75–76; Wiley 1967: 157), which highlighted the importance of the combination of so-called objective factors (in particular education, occupation and income) and so-called subjective factors (like prestige and lifestyle; Kreckel 1982: 632) for the determination of personal social status. In this context, it was stressed that the 'process of differentiation' led to an 'increasing looseness in the connections among the components of total social status' (Parsons 1966: 715). These centrifugal forces of functional differentiation are counteracted by a system of shared values and norms by which the status components become, again, integrated. Nevertheless, there is a normal amount of vagueness and inconsistency in the determination of status positions. For instance, a renowned scientist might earn less than a less esteemed lawyer (Parsons 1954 [1940]: 86–88). However, since the differential incomes are partly compensated by social recognition and status positions generally imply an element of under-determination by objective resources, according to Parsons, the system as a whole remains in force.

The total status of a person is usually described as membership in a social segment or class within a strata model of society. Authors normally distinguish three main classes, upper class, middle class and lower class, which are frequently further differentiated by subdivisions, such as upper middle class or lower upper class (Warner, Meeker and Eells 1949).

Because the relative consistency or 'crystallization' (Lenski 1954) of status variables was considered to be normal within the model, status inconsistency became the focus of empirical research (Lenski 1954; Jackson 1962; Geschwender 1967; Stehr 1971; House 1975; Hornung 1977; Zimmerman 1980; Kreckel 1985; Meulemann 1985). Persons were considered to be status inconsistent if the components of their total social status diverged too significantly; for instance in the case of a person with a high income and a low degree of formal education (e.g. a drug dealer) or a person of high formal education and low income (e.g. a university graduate working as a cleaner). In these cases, it is not possible to assign a homogenous total social status to a person. Status inconsistency was expected to be experienced by the affected individuals as a stressful deviance from a normative standard (Kreckel 1982: 643).[1]

The structural functionalist concept of social status has been criticised many times. Some scholars argued that the approach neglected societal conflict and disguised power relations, which were, in their interpretations, central to the explanation of social inequality in capitalist societies (Parkin 1971: 83; Kreckel 1982: 632). Another important point of criticism was formulated by individualisation theoreticians during the 1980s and 1990s. Beck, for instance, (1986: 121–60) argued that the individualisation of life trajectories and the increasing relevance of so-called horizontal forms of inequality, like gender, age, generation and lifestyle, made status inconsistency a normal experience of individuals in Western societies. Therefore, a theory that presumes status consistency as the standard and inconsistency as deviation seemed outdated.

In the recently revived discussion on social inequality, the methodological nationalism of existing research paradigms became a central point of critique. In this context several authors advocated a change in the methodological framework and argued for European (Heidenreich 2003; Verwiebe 2006), transnational (Weiß 2002; Beck 2008) and global perspectives (Bornschier and Trezzini 1997; Theborn 2001; Kreckel 2008) on social inequality.

Independently of the critique, status consistency empirically remains important as a normative model against which empirical deviance is evaluated. In this context, in particular the central role of education for status attainment is emphasised. Within modern imaginaries of social status this is reasoned by the functionalist argument that if the most well-trained and talented persons fulfil the most important functions in a society, all members will profit from it. The sociologist John Meyer (1992: 24) in this context highlighted that all controversies on school knowledge and school curricula 'build around a strikingly shared vision: . . . the . . . society could arrange rational instruction that would prepare children to be better and more effective adults who would both have better lives and contribute more to social development'.

The discourse on modern education implies the double promise of societal development and individual prosperity. Meyer and Kamens (1992) argued that the functionalist consensus in regard to education should be viewed critically. If education was functional for the development of a concrete society, it would imply a high degree of diversity in terms of school curricula. An oil-producing country in the Middle East has different functional needs in regard to the education of its population than a post-industrial country in Western Europe or a cash crop-exporting country in West Africa. However, instead of identifying a high diversity of school curricula, Meyer and his colleagues (Meyer, Kamens and Benavot 1992) in their comparative study found striking global similarities. The functionality of modern education in several cases appeared to be rather a legitimation that accompanied the expansion of standard models of mass education than something to be proved by empirical evidence.

In this sense, social discourses on the individual and collective functionality of education are, as Meyer and his colleagues argued, sometimes only loosely linked to their factual importance. This is particularly correct in the case of the Ghanaian nation-state, which extensively propagated the modernistic promises of collective and individual progress by education but was, particularly during 1970s and 1980s, not able to provide the economic structures to keep them. Nevertheless, the idea that education must contribute to personal wellbeing and societal progress was maintained against empirical counterevidence. In the following paragraphs, I will show how the importance of education and a belief in the efficiency of the meritocratic triad historically became a powerful social imaginary in the territory of present-day Ghana.

EDUCATION AND CLASS FORMATION IN GHANA

The south of Ghana experienced far-reaching social and economic changes during the nineteenth century. In this context, modern imaginaries of social status gained in significance. Nevertheless, in particular the Ashanti Region maintained a relatively high degree of autonomy until the late nineteenth century. The Asante political system, its economy and its system of status ascription were relatively successfully defended against growing capitalist influences (Wilks 1979; 1993; Arhin 1983; McCaskie 1983).

Most important for the unity of the Asante society was the central position of the *Asantehene* as the head of state. He held two insignia which symbolised his sovereign power over the economic and the political sphere. The Golden Stool[2] (*sika dwa*) was the symbol of his ultimate political power and the golden elephant tail (*sika mena*) stood for his control of the modes of capital accumulation (McCaskie 1983: 30–32). These two items corresponded to two different status hierarchies.

Formally, the political rank of a person was determined by office in the Asante state. The functionally most important ranks within the state hierarchies were those of 'village chief' (*odikro*), the head of a state's division (*ohene*), the head of a state (*omanhene*) and that of the *Asantehene* at the top of this hierarchy (Arhin 1983: 5). Ideally, office holders were recruited from 'royal' matrilineages, which legitimised their power through descent from a real or imaginary first settler or founder of a state or one of its subdivisions, respectively.

Until the late eighteenth century, slaves were the most important economic resource in the Asante state. By controlling the military forces, which executed slave raids, the state also controlled the central means of economic accumulation. After the formal abolition of the transatlantic slave trade by the British in 1807, which caused a severe economic crisis in the Asante state, slaves were gradually replaced by agricultural products as a major economic resource (Hopkins 1973: 144). The economic restructuring and the loss of the state's power over economic accumulation facilitated social differentiation. This process was reinforced by a global trading boom in the 1830s. As a result, a class of affluent merchants gradually emerged in the Ashanti Region that threatened the unity of the established status system (Wilks 1993: 156).

The tensions between the old state elite and the new trading elite were counteracted by the provision of possibilities to convert wealth into legitimate status. In Asante Twi the word for wealthy people is *asikafo*. *Asikafo* could attain formal recognition of their status by displaying a certain amount of gold dust—the currency of the time in the Ashanti Region—in a public ritual to the *Asantehene*. Thereby, they acquired the privilege of wearing a cloth with a special design, which was called *nyawoho* ('you have become rich'; Wilks 1979: 12). Another way to convert money into status and power was to create networks of dependants. If somebody controlled a significant number of subjects, he could acquire the title of *asafohene,* an honorary title, which originally meant 'war captain'. An *asafohene* with more than a thousand subjects was entitled to a horsetail switch which he carried at official occasions (Wilks 1979: 13). The most powerful representatives out of this group of rich men could be granted the title of an *obirempon*. Connected to the title of *obirempon* was the privilege of carrying an elephant tail switch (*mena*). The *Asantehene*, at the top of the hierarchy, held the golden elephant switch (*sika mena*).

The purchase of political offices was another way of converting economic capital into public recognition and political power. In order to solve a conflict about the succession of a 'traditional office' in Kumasi in the early twentieth century the colonial administration made investigations (Wilks 1979: 9). It was found that matrilineal descent 'was practically ignored' (ibid.) in the history of this office. The British interpreted the influence of money and bribery in the context of so-called stool disputes as an indicator of a recent decay of the pre-colonial moral order. In contrast to this, Wilks (1979: 10–11) argued that buying offices was rather a means to stabilise the political system than an expression of its deterioration. The potentially destabilising effects for the state by the new merchant class' economic power could be reduced by accepting informal ways of converting economic capital into political power.

An important state device for controlling the 'self-acquired movable property of a deceased citizen' (Wilks 1979: 19) was the so-called *awunnyade* (death duty), which was introduced between 1720 and 1750. The system distinguished between collective family properties, in particular land which was not subjected to the *awunnyade*, and private property, to which it was applied (Wilks 1993: 148). All private property in the Ashanti Region was legally inherited by the *Asantehene* and was redistributed by his representatives among the relatives of the deceased after deducting a substantive death duty (Wilks 1979: 19-20). This system expressed the political ideal that all individual wealth ultimately belonged to the nation and its highest representative. Although people found means to circumvent *awunnyade*, it remained in force until the late nineteenth century. By limiting the extent of cross-generational capital accumulation, the *awunnyade* system slowed down the formation of a capitalist class, which constituted a possible threat to the existing political order.

In the last decades of the nineteenth century, opposition against the *awunnyade* system grew. Before the *Asantehene* Agyeman Prempreh was enstooled in 1888, he was forced to take an oath to abandon the system of death duties (Wilks 1979: 30-31). This ended the *Asantehene's* formal monopoly of the control over economic accumulation and the acription of legitimate status and led to the consolidation of the new economic classes.

In the coastal Fante towns, the differentiation in the system of social stratification took place earlier than in the Ashanti Region (Arhin 1983: 13-14). This was due to a higher degree of economic inequality in the coastal region and due to the greater influence of European powers. The Fante states were dependent on protection by British military forces against the Asante army. Being politically less powerful than the *Asantehene*, the pre-colonial authorities were also less able to control the accumulation of wealth. Additionally, the European lifestyle provided an alternative frame of reference in the urban spaces, which relativised the power of the 'traditional' states to control the means of status ascription (ibid.). By the second half of the nineteenth century, a group of so-called Fante 'merchant princes' (Arhin 1983: 17) had developed, whose families had benefited substantially from the palm oil boom of the 1830s (Hopkins 1973: 132). An important role in the process of formation and consolidation of an affluent trading class was played by the accessibility of formal Western education.

Schools for the local population spread in the Fante territory from the beginning of the nineteenth century onwards (Foster 1965: 48-51).[3] At first, schools founded by the British administration offered some basic education in reading, writing, English, Christian religion and arithmetic to the urban African population. In subsequent decades, the missions became the main providers of education. From the 1830s onwards, the Wesleyan Mission built up schools in the Fante Region. The Basel Mission started its first schools in Christiansborg, which today is part of Accra, in 1843 and in Akropong in today's Eastern Region in 1848. Due to the higher degree of political autonomy, resistance against European influences, such as Western forms of education, was much stronger in the Ashanti Region. Only in 1874 was the first school founded in the region and a significant expansion of educational institutions did not take place until the first decades of the twentieth century (Foster 1965: 52).

During the nineteenth century, most students on the coast came from a relatively small urban segment of the population which was involved in trade or other forms of intense interaction with Europeans (Foster 1965: 62). Although the British administration encouraged the Fante chiefs to send their children to school, only few of them attained formal education. In contrast to this, the emerging merchant class perceived formal education as a means for the consolidation of their class position and started to send some of their children to England for education (Jenkins 1985). The differences in the educational strategies widened the gap between the old political and the new trading elite.

Gradually, the number of formally educated persons from less privileged families, who occupied mostly clerical positions in government, church institutions or commercial enterprises, grew in the coastal towns during the second half of the nineteenth century. Compared to farming activities in the rural hinterland, the small white-collar segment of the Gold Coast's labour market offered significantly higher wages and more convenient working conditions. Consequently, formal Western education and the jobs attainable by it implied a material and symbolical distinction from the majority of the population. Altogether it can be concluded that formal education and individually accumulated wealth had become relatively independent variables of social status ascription in the coastal area by the second half of the nineteenth century.

In the following decades educational institutions spread parallel to the influence of the colonial state from the south to the north, and formal education became particularly important as a condition for the achievement of medium and higher ranks in the expanding colonial administration. The developments of the twentieth century entailed fast processes of social differentiation along multiple lines, including inequalities between the urban and rural sector, between the north and the south, between workers and clerks, between subsistence farmers and cash crop framers, between petty traders and merchants, between formally educated and non-educated persons and between new and old elites. On the level of representation of these inequalities, the symbolic divide between the 'modern' and the 'traditional' became one of the master narratives for interpreting and reducing the empirical complexities of these stratification patterns. To become educated normally meant to learn English, to adopt elements of the European lifestyle and to become Christianised (Arhin 1983: 18).

Although formal education was an 'admission ticket' to another realm of symbols, the empirical situation was much more blurry. Often kinship ties crosscut this divide. Moreover, also formally non-educated parts of the population, such as cacao farmers or traders, profited from the economic growth. Nevertheless, the state expansion and the growth of the public sector led to an increase in the significance of formal education for status attainment and entailed a sharp rise in the demand for formal education. In the 1960s Phillip Foster pointed out that in Ghana 'education' and, I might add, the modernist imaginaries gravitating around it, played, in fact, 'a more crucial role in relation to status and social mobility than it did at comparable stages in Western development' (Foster 1965: 300). Nevertheless, as I showed in Chapter 2, these expectations with regard to formal education and its material rewards, which were particulalry raised by Ghana's independence, were disappointed by the post-independence developments. Due to inflation and unemployment many Ghanaians could not convert their educational degrees into occupational prestige and/or a sufficient income to finance a modern middle-class lifestyle. The educated middle classes' trust in the functioning of the meritocratic triad of education, occupation and income was shaken. Reflecting on these developments, Foster (1980: 228) concluded fifteen years after his first remark: 'Education is no longer the golden key that it once was to occupational social mobility'. In this societal context, many formally educated persons felt deprived of the rewards which had been promised by the state and its educational institutions. Nevertheless, the feelings of exclusion from an imagined global modernity did not invalidate the modernistic promises of education but made them appear even more desirable. James Ferguson (1999) described comparable emotions of disappointment of the 'expectations of modernity' for the case of Zambian Copperbelt mineworkers:

> When the Copperbelt mineworkers expressed their sense of abjection from an imagined modern world "out there", they were not simply lamenting a lack of connection but articulating a specific experience of disconnection, just as they inevitably described their material poverty not simply as a lack but as a loss.
> (Ferguson 1999: 238)

It appears that partaking in the school system itself generates expectations of status attainment, which are only loosely related to the question of how realistic they are. The extent to which many young Ghanaians refer to the meritocratic triad in order to raise the status claims became evident to me in numerous discussions with students and school graduates in Ghana. Amma, for instance, a fifteen-year old schoolgirl in Dormaa Ahenkro, answered when asked about her plans for the future that she wanted to be a pilot. In this situation, I was surprised that a girl from the Ghanaian periphery could self-confidently claim to acquire what I considered a male profession. In the course of the conversation, I came to understand that, in contrast to me, for Amma the gender issue did not play a role. In fact, she knew very little about the educational requirements and career possibilities of pilots. Her point was a different one. Pilot in her view, was a prestigious modern-sector job by which she could achieve a high income. In a sense, she did not explicate a concrete plan for her future, which she was making an effort to realise; rather, she spelled out the modernistic imaginary that those who perform well at school can obtain good jobs in the modern sector and achieve a sufficient income. Daniel, a student at a polytechnic school in Sunyani in his early 20s, wrote in a classroom essay style the following text on my laptop:

> WHAT I WANT TO DO IN FUTURE
> If God permits, I would like to be a BUILDING ENGINEER in the future. The first reason why I like to do this work is that I will gain a lot of money from it. Secondly, technicians are those people who can give more skills to people or give more jobs for people to earn their daily bread. Before every country can develop, it practically depends upon the technicians in the country. That is why I want to be a TECHNICIAN in my future. Finally, it will help me a lot to care for my family and to help those who do not have, especially infants in my society and the country. This is why I want to be a BUILDING ENGINEER in the future, may God help me come out with this dream.
> By Daniel Kwame Boateng[4]

Different from Amma's more implicit reference to the modern imaginary of social status, 'Daniel's Dream' is a precise explication. He combines the idea of individual achievement ('I will gain a lot of money from it') with a notion of the individual's functionality for the collective ('to care for my family', 'give more jobs for people') and a vision of national progress ('Before every country can develop, it practically depends upon the technicians in the country'). However, Daniel's reality turned out to deviate from 'his dream'. After having finished his polytechnic education in the building sector, Daniel could neither find an appropriate job nor continue his education. In 2006 he hoped for somebody in his family to provide him with the necessary capital to sell jeans in Sunyani.

This might be only a snap-shot and Daniel might find a way to improve his socio-economic conditions. Nevertheless, the misfit between his hopes and aspirations of social mobility through education and the difficulties of realising them explains why for many who are in Daniel's or Amma's position migration appears an attractive alternative. Kofi, a 17 year-old junior secondary school student in Dormaa Ahenkro, wrote on my laptop an ironic comment on Daniel's dream. Instead of an essay about his future plans, he only wrote three words: 'Kofi goes abroad'.

However, as I will show in the next paragraphs, Kofi's alternative to Daniel's and Amma's dream is not a solution for the described experiences of status inconsistency and disconnection from an imagined global modernity, but it moves the problems into a larger transnational social space.

THE BURGER'S PARADOX

The term *Burger* (cf. Jach 2005: 206–10; Martin 2005: 9–15;) is a colloquial expression in Ghanaian English, which refers to a transcontinental labour migrant who has achieved wealth abroad but lacks the formal cultural capital to legitimise it according to modern imaginaries of social status.[5] There are several versions of the etymology of the term *Burger* (Martin 2005: 11). The most widespread is that it refers to the city name of Hamburg. As mentioned above (cf. Chapter 3), in the 1980s Hamburg was a major destination for Ghanaian labour migrants of a new type. At a time when the differentials in wages and buying power were even larger than today, *Burgers* impressed people in Ghana with the money they often earned in low-wage jobs abroad. Reflecting the irritation of modern imaginaries of social status, a new term was introduced to give the social phenomenon a name.

In Western Europe in general, and in Germany in particular, the migrants met with relatively unfavourable conditions when mass labour migration started. For those Ghanaians who went through the asylum process, the adaptation to the procedure and the legal insecurity caused by the uncertainty of its outcome left an impact on their experience of migration (cf. Chapter 3). The levelling down of status, which was connected to asylum seeking, was particularly painful for those who felt that their cultural and social capital, which they had achieved in Ghana, was devalued.

Being an asylum seeker was one of the lowest possible status positions in the receiving countries. In addition to the precarious legal and economic conditions, asylum seekers often were portrayed either as poor victims or as swindlers who have no legitimate reason to claim asylum. In both respects, their status equality was denied. The situation became even worse for those who went underground in order to escape the threat of deportation or overstayed a tourist visa.

I encountered the bitterness caused by these experiences of degradation during the course of the migration process on several occasions during my research:

> I sat together with Kojo Yeboah and his friend, Kwabena. After some beers, Kojo started to tell me about his early time in Germany. He talked about the hard work on the building sites in winter and the

disrespect of his non-African colleagues. The longer he talked, the more of the bitterness and humiliation he connected with those experiences became apparent and was turned against me. In the course of the situation my role gradually changed from being the audience for the narrative to being a representative of the ethnic majority in Germany that was made responsible for these experiences of loss. In this tense atmosphere, to which the alcohol had contributed its part, Kojo and Kwabena started speculating that I was a policeman whose only goal was to spy them out. After trying to defend myself against the accusation for some time, finally, I gave up and left the scene emotionally agitated. Since I felt concerned and insecure how to react to these accusations, I avoided meeting Kojo and Kwabena for some time. After two weeks, I went to Kwabena who had rented a small shop in the same neighbourhood as Kojo's wife. When I came in, he greeted me in a friendly way and without any obvious reason started to talk about how he had achieved a permanent legal status in Germany. I listened quietly to his narration because it felt inappropriate to me to ask any questions. During one of my next visits of Comfort's shop, Kojo did the same. Both men explained to me that they had married German women, whom they divorced after some years. Obviously, they had developed their own idea about what my research would be about, which they had consciously ignored for some months. Therefore, their narrations represented a kind of compensation for accusing me of being a policeman.

After Kwabena had told me his story, he placed his behaviour in the context of the exploitation and colonisation of Africa: "First, the white people came to my country. It was them who took the gold, the diamonds and my grandfather. I thought when I was in Ghana, why shouldn't I go there, where they brought them to and look what had happened to them. And when they asked me in Germany to marry a German lady to stay in this country—man, I was educated by the British; you don't have to tell me twice".

Being in a similar situation, Kojo presented me with a different type of narrative. He expressed his sorrow that he did not have any contact to his ex-wife anymore and explained to me that his ex-wife was an alcoholic. The relationship, therefore, was very difficult. He added: "We are obliged to this woman. It's because of her that we all [referring to his family and relatives in Germany; B.N.] are here."
(Field Protocols, 26 July 2002, 10 August 2002, 16 August 2002, Berlin)

It appears that the initial gesture of accusing me of being a spy was connected to the narrative evocation of feelings of loss of status and disrespect which Kojo and Kwabena experienced as African labour migrants in Germany. The intensity of the feelings was related to the fact that both men had an educational degree above the Ghanaian average and originated from well-respected families. Moreover, the narratives about their marriages indicated that the loss of status was not only connected to socio-economic factors, but also to the ascription of a legal status and the migrants' adaptation to it. To some extent, the legal motivations involved in the marriages were a potentially shameful aspect for Kojo and Kwabena. It contradicted their image of mature, resourceful and independent men, conveyed on other occasions, to admit their dependency on a German woman, who in Kojo's case had a low social status herself.

As a legitimation of their practice, both men engaged in a moral discourse. Kwabena combined a narrative of resistance against colonial oppression ('the white people ... took the gold, the diamonds and my grandfather') with a macho narrative ('I was educated by the British, you don't have to tell me twice') as a means to reconstruct himself as a resourceful and independent person. In contrast to this, Kojo Yeboah formally acknowledged his gratefulness about what his ex-wife had done for him and his family. Thereby, he placed the marriage in the context of patronage. By recognising the patron's good deeds and admitting his dependency, Kojo expressed his commitment to the underlying moral discourse. The fact that he had to represent himself as somebody who had been patronised by a German woman with an alcohol problem in front of me, a younger German man, challenged Kojo's gender and age identity. However, he did not discursively reverse the power relations, as Kwabena did, but admitted his inferior position as a former dependant.

As was mentioned before, in Germany Ghanaian migrants faced the problem that their educational degrees and language skills were not convertible on the German labour market and that racialisation contributed significantly to a general experience of personal devaluation. Although there are different experiences of and opinions on migration to Germany among Ghanaian migrants, many describe their situation as a lack of general respect. Kwame Boateng, a migrant from Sunyani with a secondary school degree, who worked as an unskilled worker in the kitchens of hotels and restaurants, summarised the situation in Germany as follows: 'As an African you will never be ... respected in this country and that hurts'.[6]

Although transcontinental migration appears to be a strategy of overcoming status inconsistency in the country of origin, most migrants to Germany lose status in the receiving countries. However, the described global inequalities in wages and buying power (cf. Chapter 4) provide them with an opportunity structure to gain status in Ghana by transferring resources acquired through their work in Germany. The visibility of the *Burgers*' houses, consumer goods, dependants and money in Ghana causes irritations and envy, in particular among those who feel illegitimately overtaken. Nevertheless, the actuality of the *Burgers*' material success is undeniable. Both admiration for their success and moral condemnation for the means by which it was achieved can be observed in Ghana.

Analogous to the difference between asylum seekers and students (cf. Chapter 3), the distinction between migrants or returnees with academic education and *Burgers* marks a class difference among migrants (Martin 2005: 11–15; Jach 2005: 208). The answer of a Ghanaian engineer, who had returned from Germany to Ghana some years ago and who owned a small consultancy company, illustrated this distinction:

B: Are you a *Burger*?
Y: [laughs; B.N.] No, *Burgers* are those who worked. They have a certain feature; they wear their trousers like this [he stands up from his chair, pulls his trousers up around the waist and laughs; B.N.]. You can recognise them immediately.
(Interview, Yao Dotse, 13 December 2001, Accra)

Yao refused the label of being a *Burger* and highlighted its working-class implications. Although he also worked in Germany to finance his studies, he defined his status identity by his academic background. Thereby, he distinguished himself from the labour migrants. Yaw's laughter about my question and the way he described the *Burger*-style of wearing their trousers expressed that the stereotype of the *Burger* has funny connotations from the perspective of a person with a higher degree of formal education.

The cliché of the *Burgers* with pulled-up trousers is a mythicising narrative (cf. Chapter 3) about their status inconsistency. It implies that they might have the money to claim a middle-class status but their status inferiority is still easily recognisable by their behaviour. Moreover, their supposed urge to dress differently in order to distinguish them from other parts of the population alludes to the point that their status appears to be more dependent on assertive performances and symbolic representations than that of persons, like Yao, with a more consistent status.

Peggy, a Ghanaian physician in Berlin, mentioned another constitutive aspect of being a *Burger*:

The 'asylum people', when they manage one day to get their papers, they are the same ones who will go back and become *Burgers* in Ghana ... They want now to show the people, "I have been to Europe, I have the money. So, who are you to tell me anything with your education?" ... I have problem with those people who have come here [to Germany; B.N.] and they know how hard they struggled and that they go back, they do not tell their people the truth of what they went through to become what they are.
(Interview, Peggy Antwi, 2 November 2002, Berlin)

Peggy highlighted the point that the *Burgers* have a stigmatised status identity because of their strategic adaptation to the procedure of asylum seeking. Nevertheless, they keep silent about these aspects of their migration trajectory in order to create a positive and boastful image of themselves as successful migrants in Ghana. By silencing their stigma and spending money they challenge and provoke those who have acquired their status by legitimate means ('who are you to tell me anything with your education').

In her narrative, Peggy distinguished analytically between asylum seekers and *Burgers*. Only by returning to Ghana and achieving a high status can asylum seekers 'become *Burgers*'. According to Peggy, being a *Burger* in Ghana means to stress the rewards of migration and the positive sides of their status identity. At the same time, the migrants have to manage these pieces of information that contradict the image they want to convey in Ghana ('the truth of what they went through to become what they are'). In this sense, being a *Burger* depends not only on the migrants' performances, as Yao highlighted, but also, as Peggy emphasised, on their economic resources and careful strategies of information management.

In the latter context, Erving Goffman's concepts of *impression* and *stigma management* are analytically useful to develop a better understanding of the relationship between the transnational status paradox of migration, the performativity of being a *Burger* and strategies of information management. Goffman (1990 [1959]: 1–16) argued that much of the information that actors acquire about others, like their intentions, their life trajectories, or their social status, are not directly accessible. They rely on the verbal and non-verbal information, which they perceive in the course of interaction. This means that social actors, in order to get an idea about how they have to position themselves in relation to other persons, constantly make inferences from what the others makes accessible as information to information that is not accessible in a given situation. In order to limit the communication of unintended information, individuals make efforts to discipline their behaviour. Goffman used the metaphor of *performance* to conceptualise the looseness of the link between intentions and actions that he considers fundamental to social practice. In this sense, performativity means neither pretension nor deceit but is a condition of interaction itself. Even impressions of sincerity and true commitment rely on performative means if actors want others to recognise their intentions as such. At the same time, the fragile relationship between intentions and performances creates a large range of possibilities of communicative failures, wrong inferences and deceit.

According to Goffman, performances necessarily go along with idealisations. In order to control the impressions an actor wants to convey, he or she has to accentuate certain aspects and to conceal others (Goffman 1990 [1959]: 65). Moreover, above the level of singular communicative acts, persons have also to take interactional care of the *expressive coherence* of the overall impression they leave, which means: they have to be concerned with limiting unintended irritations that could potentially discredit or contradict the impressions they created by earlier performances. In his work on stigma, Goffman (1986 [1963]) applied these general thoughts on impression management on the special case of stigmatised or 'spoiled' identities. According to Goffman, stigmas present information about a person that constitutes a difference between an aspired virtual identity, which refers to social standards of 'normal personhood', and the actual identity, which is interactively manifest (ibid: 19). Depending on the type of stigma—for instance whether it is observable, as in the case of paralysed persons, or not, as in case of ex-prisoners—actors develop different strategies of managing it. The point of Goffman's argument (ibid: 128) is that there is so much potentially relevant information about a person and so many possible criteria according to which a person can be evaluated that almost everybody has, at least from time to time, to engage in *stigma management*. In this sense stigmas are nothing else than the shadows of a normative, idealised and performative reality in which actors tend to over-emphasise positive information about themselves and under-emphasise or hide these pieces of information that could disturb aspired impressions.

Goffman's argument about stigma can easily be applied to the *Burgers'* problem of status inconsistency. It draws attention to the normativity of modern social imaginaries of social status. Like Goffman's idea of virtual identity as a point of reference in relation to which stigmas are identified, modern imaginaries of social status constitute a standard for the evaluation of the consistency of an individual's status identity. In this sense, modern imaginaries of social status constitute rather a normative frame than a realistic representation of patterns of socio-economic stratification. Their normativity explains why the *Burgers'* status is more vulnerable to stigmatisation than those status identities that better conform with modern imaginaries of social status. *Burgers'* status therefore relies more strongly on assertive performative strategies and careful information management.

It does not surprise that *Burgers*[7] perceived themselves differently from how academic (re)migrants represented them. In interviews they stressed obligations towards and the expectations of their relevant others in Ghana as a main reason for practices of material redistribution and status performance during their home visits. Samuel Badu, for instance, explained his practices of *conspicuous consumption* (Veblen 2004 [1899]) to me:

> I visited Samuel in his room some weeks before he left Germany. The small room was full of consumer goods; among them a Dolby surround system, a DVD player, a large second-hand Sony television, new Nike sneakers and a pair of Levi's jeans . . . He explained to me that as a Christian he personally perceived consumption not as an important value in his life but that people in Ghana expected him to bring money and consumer goods from Europe. If he rejected to act up to the others' expectations, people would believe that he is a wicked person who wants to hide his money or they would doubt that he had been to Europe at all.
> (Field Protocol, 22 June 2001, Leipzig)

Samuel argued that only if he is able to adequately perform his gain of status, which is related to his stay in Europe, will it render him respectable. Not being able to give material evidence of having been to Europe is shameful. According to him, people in Ghana could question his moral integrity if he refused to perform his migrant's status, or might even doubt he had physically been to Europe. Independently of whether or not Samuel over-emphasised the others' expectations as a reason for his practices of conspicuous consumption, and undercommunicated his own interest in the symbolic gains, his comments highlight that there is a close linkage between gaining status through migration, relevant others' expectations and performing status in Ghana.

Jacob Seneadza, a migrant who originated from a poor village in the Eastern Region, ascribed the status gain he experienced on home visits primarily to the perception of the people in his home village:

B: Are you seen as one of the 'big sons' of the village?
J: Yes, if not the biggest. But I do not notice it . . . When I go home, I do not see myself as an extraordinary person. From what they do . . . well, I would say, yes, they look at me that way. But it is not my way of life. I just mix with them in the same way I did when I was in the village.
    (Interview, Jacob Seneadza, 27 July 2002, Berlin)

Jacob raised an important point that was already addressed by Samuel. Status identities depend not only on the migrants' performances but also on the expectations and perceptions of their interaction partners. Even if we take Jacob's representation at face value that he did not intend to represent himself 'as an extraordinary person', the gifts and the money he brought with him to the village, his habitus and the way he was dressed conveyed the impression that he had achieved a socio-economic status by migration which is beyond the reach of the people in the village.

However, Jacob's description of his behaviour remains ambivalent. Although he characterises himself as a modest person who does not want to be treated in a special way, he at the same time pronounced himself one of the 'biggest sons' in the villagers' eyes. In this sense, his strategy of understatement even increased his respectability. His egalitarian attitude became noticeable and appreciable only because the others knew he was not one of them.

The two cited examples indicate that the social reality of the migrants' status gain is self-reinforcing, which means that it is partly independent of their intentions to express it.

Daniel Adamu, a migrant from the Northern Region, accentuated his love and commitment to his family and friends as reasons for his aspired gifting practices:

I miss my family and they like to see me... My thing is—let's say, I am thinking of going but it is like this; if I am going, I must have a gift—I want to give a gift. I have many friends and they know me. I am someone who likes to give and I don't feel easy going with empty arms... In my life, I want to do something.

(Interview, Daniel Adamu, 23 August 2001, Berlin)

Since Daniel was not able to save enough money to meet his own expectations, he postponed his visit repeatedly for years. The material and monetary resources, which would be distributed in the kind of return he imagined, were to function as a big status claim in his peripheral hometown in the north of Ghana. In addition to love and friendship, Daniel stressed the motivation that he wanted to express his social usefulness. Interestingly, 'to do something' in the narrative was limited to the redistribution of resources during his home visit. In this sense, Daniel's wish was not to convey a realistic impression of his socio-economic situation in Germany, which is the reason for the delay of his visit, or to transfer as many resources as possible, but rather to create a temporally limited impression of conducting an individually and collectively successful life during his stay in Ghana. He prefers not going home to failing to convey the aspired impression. Nevertheless, it marks an important difference that Daniel stressed love and moral obligation as motivations for his aspired redistributive practices and not the maximisation of social status.

These cited statements show a multiplicity of interpretations and evaluations. It is contested whether *Burgers* convey an adequate impression of their status or whether they overstate or even understate it, whether their status performances are caused by an urge for distinction or by their relevant others' expectations, and whether they are motivated by the individuals' interest in maximising social recognition or by love for their relevant others. Nevertheless, all different voices and opinions fundamentally agree on the fact that *Burgers* experience a significant gain of social status in Ghana and that this is connected to practices of redistribution of resources.

Moreover, the *Burgers*' statements showed that the migrants are entangled in a net of expectations of others, which they can only ignore by risking a shameful loss of social status in Ghana. Therefore, if *Burgers* over-emphasise their material and social success, as Yao and Peggy suggested, they do it in relation to others who 'over-expect' it. As in Daniel's case, it creates the situation for many migrants—preferring not to go home to going home and not being able to meet the standard.

The pressure on the side of the family is very high. It drives people crazy and they think, instead of going and being perceived as a failure, "I will stay abroad and send every month €50 or €100 home"... This is the reason why many have stayed abroad.

(Interview, Yao Dotse, 13 December 2001, Accra)

During my field stay in Dormaa Ahenkro in 2003, I paid special attention to the question of how *Burgers* were perceived in the public space and asked local friends and informants to explain to me how they could distinguish them from the local population. In this respect consumer goods, like clothes, shoes or jewellery, which were either unavailable in local markets or very expensive by local standards, were of special importance. A younger migrant might, for instance, be dressed in Afro-American types of clothes, wearing a pair of Nike sneakers, baggy jeans, a sports shirt and a baseball cap. Older men were more likely to dress more reputably by using elements of a European business dress code. Status markers for men of all age grades were gold chains, exclusive mobile phones and cars. Woman also used jewellery, West African-style dresses and impressive hairstyles as body-related status markers. One female migrant wore a pair of glasses with a golden frame, which was introduced to me as a *Burger*'s way of distinction.

Moreover, *Burgers* created attention in the framework of public donations. Church services, for instance, provided them with a public stage on which they could act out their status claims. In the context of the offering, they became noticeable by positioning themselves among the upper segment of donators. Similar opportunities of distinction were provided by funerals, in which the money donated to the family was publicly announced by a speaker.

Houses are, as mentioned before, of special importance as status symbols. On walking through the town and asking people about the owners of building sites of large houses in Dormaa Ahenkro, I found that most prestigious newly-built houses were financed with money from abroad and that, in the view of the local population, there is a clear link between building large houses and migration.

What is more, *Burgers* added to their own relevance through the generous sponsoring of celebrations of life-cycle rites, in particular funerals. Mazzucato and her colleagues showed for the Ashanti Region that families with migrants among them organised more elaborate and expensive funerals than families without migrants (Mazzucato, Kabki and Smith 2006: 1054). I could observe the same in Dormaa Ahenkro in the case of funerals and wedding ceremonies.

One incident, which demonstrated a young man's way of performing a *Burger* status, was that of a migrant to Italy whom I met in Dormaa Ahenkro on his first home visit after being abroad for four years.

> I first met Kwaku when Stephen, a friend of mine, and I were sitting in a bar. To treat somebody to a drink or a meal is a status sensitive practice in southern Ghana. Normally, the person who presents the status highest among a party has to pay for the people accompanying him. As a 'white' male foreigner (*oburoni*), I was normally expected to settle the bill. Stephen knew the *Burger* and they had a short chat.

Later, the migrant offered to pay my friend's drinks although I obviously was responsible for him. By offering to pay for Stephen, Kwaku contested my status position in this situation. However, my friend remained loyal, refused the invitation politely and explained that he was with me. Some days later, Stephen and I stood in front of a kiosk and I examined different kinds of candies, which were offered in big glasses. The *Burger*, who was passing by, bought 20 pieces of candy and distributed them among me and my friend. Afterwards he left the place without speaking to me. Obviously, his generosity towards me was not so much a way to make friends with me but was a call for recognition of his status claims. He communicated that he had achieved something abroad, deserved respect and did not have to acknowledge others (presumed) status superiority.

(Field Protocols, 25 August 2003, 1 September 2003, Dormaa Ahenkro)

A particular problem that *Burgers* face is that their mode of accumulating capital is not socially embedded in Ghana. Therefore, they depend on other ways of achieving legitimate recognition. While within the *Burgers'* families they are often treated with special respect as long as they do not fail according to the reciprocity standards, formally educated Ghanaians, like Peggy and Yao, often reject their status claims. Dr. Sarpong, a returnee who had studied in Hungary during the 1960s and early 1970s, explained the typical structures and pitfalls of the status paradox derogatively but very clearly:

In Europe, they sweep the gutter. Then, they buy a car and a nice house in Ghana. Are they supposed to come back and sweep the gutter in Ghana? No, they won't do that.

(Interview, Dr. Sarpong, 13 September 2003, Dormaa Ahenkro)

Generally, the knowledge which Dr. Sarpong and others have about the *Burgers'* status in the receiving country adds a complication to the recognition of their status in Ghana. As stated before, its vulnerability entails practices of information management. Their efficacy is indicated by the fact that migrants' families in Ghana often know very little about the lives and sources of income generation of their relatives in Europe and North America. In the case study of Bonokrom, migrants' relatives were normally able to tell which job their relatives in the large cities in Ghana worked, but they normally did not know how transcontinental migrants earned their money. This pattern of ignorance among relatives about the migrants' living conditions in the receiving countries was also observed by Kabki and her colleagues (2004) in the Ashanti Region, by Miescher and Ashbaugh (1999: 63) in the Kwahu Region and by Jach (2005: 210) among her interviewees in different parts of Ghana. The Ghanaian novelist Amma Darko (cited in Roos 1996: 218), who had been a migrant to Germany herself, highlighted the reciprocity of the silence: 'He [the *Burger*; B.N.] comes and he dresses differently, more attractively, he is riding a car . . . he doesn't tell you how he got the things. You don't ask him.'

Darko points out that it is not only the *Burgers* who do not address issues that might discredit their status identity in Ghana, but also their relevant others, who take preventive measures by not asking. Thereby, silence signifies not the absence of communication but it is itself a form of communication. It is a social act of moving the *Burgers*' status inconsistency to the 'backstage' of social interaction. In this sense, the silence is a collaborative form of stigma management that in the case of the *Burgers* is often embedded in social relationships of patronage. To address the migrants' status inconsistency would endanger the necessary asymmetry in the social relationship between patron and patronised, from which both parts profit. Therefore, the social reality of the status gain in Ghana does not rely on being successful to prevent the relevant others from any information about the migrants' status reality abroad but is created by social norms not to address the status inconsistency too openly.

If this interpretation is correct and silence relies on complementary decisions not to address potentially embarrassing or discrediting issues, it presumes knowledge about the subjects to be excluded from discourse. The quoted statements of the university graduates, who stressed the illegitimacy of the *Burgers*' status, demonstrate that they know about the *Burgers*' status inconsistency. Moreover, the regions where most of the transcontinental migrants come from have a long tradition of immigration themselves. Consequently, the people in these regions have an idea of what it means to be a labour migrant, from which they can make inferences about the status of Ghanaian migrants in Western Europe:

> I asked Stephen, a man in his twenties who has never left Ghana, about the origin of some workers who loaded a lorry with sacks of rice. He explained to me that they were migrants from the north and added, "They are our slaves, like the Ghana people in Europe are your slaves".
> (Field Protocol, 17 September 2003, Dormaa Ahenkro)

The link between migration, status and collaborative silence was also observable on obituary posters in the Dormaa District, which due to the social importance of funerals are a popular genre of public announcement in Ghana. If the status of an individual contributes to the family's prestige, the name on the poster of the respective mourner is supplemented by a reference to his or her distinguishing status features. In particular, three aspects were considered noteworthy in this respect: first, traditional office holders, second, modern sector employees and, third, transnational migrants who were identified by the name of their country of residence. The absence of mentioned occupations was often salient among transnational migrants. For instance, out of 28 persons classified as 'children'[8] on the obituary poster of Mr A.K. Owusu, ten were migrants, in twelve cases the profession was mentioned (traders, teachers and a university student), but only one migrant, a teacher in South Africa, was listed with her profession. Although the country names contributed to the family's prestige, the *Burgers*' occupations obviously did not. However, their omission only makes sense if we assume some knowledge about the potential prestige of the *Burgers*' economic activities.

A field in which the negative aspects of migration became public in Ghana is the case of unsuccessful returnees, in particular deported migrants. During my fieldwork I recurrently encountered migrants who had to leave Europe without being able to accumulate enough capital to have a good and carefree life. Their life histories tell of the dark sides of being a migrant, like the power of legal restrictions, imprisonment, exploitation and expropriation. The particular social disaster about deportation is the fact that the returnees often cannot take pre-emptive face-saving measures. They lose their 'backstage' opportunity to edit and manage their status performances in Ghana.

Although unsuccessful returnees are a significant group, they remain relatively marginal in everyday discourses on transcontinental migration in Ghana. There are at least two reasons for it. First, the deportees I met in Dormaa Ahenkro were able to reintegrate themselves and became socially invisible. Therefore, they had less influence on migrants' public image than the *Burgers*' 'noisy' performances. Second, failure was not seen as a systematic outcome of the risky process of migration itself but was attributed to the individual performance of a particular migrant:

> Yaw Asante visited a friend on his bicycle. When he recognised that I was from Germany, he started to speak German with me. The surrounding persons were surprised. Although they had known Yaw for some time, they did not know that he had been in Germany in the 1990s. After he had left Kofi, one of the surrounding young men, commented disdainfully to me: "What is this? A *Burger* with a bicycle! If he has been to Europe, he should at least have a car".
> (Field Protocol, 10 August 2003, Dormaa Ahenkro)

The bicycle, which is a common transport vehicle in Dormaa Ahenkro, where only very few persons own private cars, became a personal stigma by the mere fact that it was owned by a returnee from Europe. When it became obvious in the situation that Yaw Asante had been a transcontinental migrant in the past, the scheme according to which his self-representation was evaluated changed and his deviance from the expected modern middle-class status was interpreted as personal deficiency.

In 1989, the Lumba Brothers, two singers who were *Burgers* themselves, produced two songs about the sufferings of transcontinental migrants. In their song *Yee ye aka akwantuom* ('We got stuck on our journey')[9], the Lumba Brothers cited insightful mocking names for migrants, which ironically reflected the loss of prestige and respect connected to an unsuccessful return:

> *Burger me-neema-emmaye* ('*Burger* my-things-have-not-arrived'). This expression refers to the excuse a *Burger* gives who is asked by friends or relatives for gifts. He claims that his or her things are still in a container on the way to Ghana. The use of irony in the song indicates that the container will never arrive.

> *Burger ma-hunu-wo* ('*Burger* I-have-seen-you'). "I have seen you" refers to the relative or friend who had not been visited by the migrant or had not been informed about his or her arrival but has seen him or her on the street. It reflects the problem that *Burgers* who cannot be generous have to hide in order to not have to admit it publicly.

> *Burger a-ye-mmere* ('*Burger* who-has-become-weak'). The *Burger*'s weakness relates to money as a source of his or her power. A *Burger* without money becomes weak and has to endure disdain and mockery in Ghana.

These mocking names indicate that a *Burger* without further attributes would be a successful and resourceful person who supports his relatives and friends and reciprocally receives their respect. By lacking the resources to act out this role, *Burgers* 'become weak' and forfeit the symbolic rewards of migration. In the same song, the Lumba Brothers also present a reason why migrants cannot easily ignore these expectations: 'I will not go home and receive shame. Shame does not fit me, Kwadwo. I have seen people who have received shame.'

The shamefulness of not meeting expectations refers to the normative structure of the dominant discourse on transcontinental migration in Ghana, which defines success as normality and failure as a personal insufficiency.

The migrants' sadness and suffering was the central aspect in the Lumba Brothers' song *Aban nsa aka wo* ('The state has caught you') from the same album:

> Our journey is full of sadness (. . .)
> If we travel home and come to meet you, (. . .) try to take us as we are.
> There is nobody who does not like to succeed.

This song addressed, on the one hand, the audience of the *Burgers* who might identify with the representation of migration and, on the other hand, non-migrants in Ghana, who were appealed to be more empathetic with the former. By singing about poverty, homesickness and desperation, the song highlighted the hardships of migration. One of the conditions of its explicitness was that, despite its personalised rhetoric, it factually remains an impersonal speech act. Because the listeners normally do not know Daddy Lumba and Nana Akyeampong personally, it did not endanger the definition of their personal relationships. However, the publicity of the song supports the point that the observable ignorance of relatives about the status of migrants' activities in the receiving areas is primarily due to the personalised principle of tact and not due to the general inaccessibility of information. Tact is in this context an important means to maintain the asymmetric definition of social relationships between migrants and relevant others in Ghana, within which resources are redistributed. This means that the silence has social reasons. At the same time, it implies that those *Burgers* who are unable to maintain the impression of a status increase by redistributing resources become vulnerable or 'weak', as the Lumba Brothers formulated it.

An unintended consequence of the collaborative silence which protects the *Burgers*' status is that it stimulates social fantasies. The uncertainty about how migrants earned their money encouraged speculation about the 'dark side' of the accumulation of wealth. When I asked a Ghanaian student for advice for my field research at the beginning of my project, he instructed me never to ask non-academic Ghanaian migrants in Germany about their sources of income. The suspicion he raised, and which turned out to be a strong exaggeration of the situation, was that people were extensively engaged in criminal activities.[10] In the case of women it is often speculated that they are involved in prostitution although it is much more likely that they work as cleaners or cloakroom attendants in Western Europe.

Both effects—the tactful personalised silence and the fantasies about the means of accumulation of wealth—are linked to the legitimation problem of the migrants' status gain. Since it is neither backed by educational degrees, as modern imaginaries of social status suggests, or by descent, as in the case of traditional Akan imaginaries of social status, it relies on a discourse of performance and smartness to circumvent the formal logic of status attainment. The migrants' status gain that results from producing evidence of material success in Ghana to some extent legitimates itself in a circular way: the migrants deserve it because they were able to achieve it. However, this way of legitimation becomes a burden in cases of failure. If success is perceived as personal achievement, somebody who fails, consequently, was less willing or less able to do it.

Of course, this self-legitimisation of success is highly problematic. Not the least, the rigidification of European border regimes and the increase of social inequality within the economically powerful countries have made migration more dangerous and risky during the last decades. Yaw Asante (the *Burger* with the bicycle), for example, has not only lost prestige by his unsuccessful return but also most of the money he had saved during ten years of work in the Côte d'Ivoire and seven years in Germany.[11] These aspects of passivity and victimhood do not fit into the discourse of daring individual achievement from which the successful *Burgers* profit. A Ghanaian student in Berlin explained to me that in Ghanaian English the term 'suffer guy' was used to refer to a migrant who goes through harsh conditions in the receiving country and fails to overcome them. 'And,' he added, referring to the perception by others, 'nobody wants to be a suffer guy'.[12]

The following newspaper article from 2003 exemplifies that migration not only includes the risk of losing face, but, in times of increasingly restrictive border regimes for a large number of non-privileged migrants, also the danger of losing their lives. At the same time, the article shows how strong the urge to succeed becomes through the self-reinforcing sets of mutual expectations that were described above:

> *200 Ghanaians Die Crossing Libyan Desert*
> About 200 Ghanaians have died in Libya, from January to the first week of June, this year, in their desperate attempt to cross the 3000 km Libyan Desert to Europe in search of economic fortunes. They were reported to have died as a result of extreme dehydration and general fatigue precipitated by the harsh weather conditions on the desert. Conservative estimates indicate that about 10 per cent of those who attempt to cross the desert perish on the way. In an interview in Tripoli on Monday on the general conditions of Ghanaians resident in Libya, Mr George Kumi, Ghana's Ambassador to Libya, said . . . it is usually a pathetic and horrific scene to find some of these persons dehydrated, weak and helpless and on the verge of death after trekking for more 300 kilometres on the desert. He said the unfortunate and frustrating aspect of the operation is that those rescued refuse to come back to Ghana because of their inordinate ambition to go to Europe, irrespective of the consequences.
>
> (*Daily Graphic*, 19 June 2003, Accra)

THE STATUS PARADOX OF MIGRATION

In this chapter, I have shown how a variation of the modern imaginary of social status became institutionalised in what is Ghana today. Within this context, school education in particular as a legitimation of status attainment has gained significance over the last two hundred years. The meritocratic triad, on which modern imaginaries of social status are based, implies that educational degrees should be the key to functionally important, well-paid and prestigious jobs in the modern segment of the labour market. During the economic crises in Ghana of the 1970s and 1980s, the assumption of the co-variation of central status variables became increasingly problematic. Unemployment among the highly and moderately educated and the devaluation of wages by inflation made status inconsistency a mass phenomenon.

Transcontinental migration seemed to offer a way to overcome the experienced status inconsistency and material deprivation. Because in many cases migrants had to accept a significant loss of status in the receiving countries, it turned out to be an inappropriate means of solving their status inconsistency. As a result, many transcontinental migrants are caught in a transnational status paradox of migration as their status gain in the country of origin relies on a simultaneous loss of status in the receiving country.

The exit options out of this status paradox of migration are risky. On the one hand, the savings of the migrants are often not substantial enough to guarantee the maintenance of the achieved status position in Ghana after a permanent return and, on the other hand, cutting off connections to Ghana (even if it would be emotionally feasible) would endanger the success of the whole migration project in terms of status achievement. Therefore, for many Ghanaian migrants in Western Europe the status paradox of migration becomes a relatively stable aspect of their life. Empirically, I focussed on the social figure of the *Burger* and demonstrated how this group's status inconsistency was managed practically. In this respect, I highlighted the collaborative character of the construction of the *Burger* status.

Formally educated middle-class Ghanaians often discursively reject the *Burgers'* status claims because they perceive them as pretentious and illegitimate. Nevertheless, the *Burgers'* money and their material achievements produce evidence of middle-class status independently of its normative legitimacy. In this respect, the intensity of some Ghanaian university graduates' reaction to the *Burgers'* status performances only confirms their success in challenging existing status hierarchies.

In the case of interaction between *Burgers'* and their relevant others in Ghana, I argued that the problem of status inconsistency was often moved to the backstage of social interaction because of tact and because both sides have an interest in the maintenance of an interactive fiction of the *Burgers'* status consistency. On the one hand, *Burgers* themselves are interested in increasing their status in Ghana because it is part of the rewards of migration. On the other hand, the migrants' reference group in Ghana has an interest in maintaining an asymmetric relationship to the migrants because they profit from the involved redistributive practices. Beyond the particular case of the *Burger*, it is a common feature of asymmetric relationships (e.g. bosses and employees or parents and children) that they involve typical silences that protect the definition of the respective relationship.

Conclusion

The changes in the migratory patterns of Ghanaians are part and parcel of the failures and successes of the postcolonial development state. On the one hand, the increase in emigration from Ghana was a reaction to the economic and social crisis and the state's incapacity to keep the promises of development and prosperity, which were made in the course of decolonisation. On the other hand, the growing number of transcontinental migrants was also a result of the successful expansion of mass education in Ghana. It was not the poorest and most marginal who migrated to Europe, but often those who by their education felt entitled to middle-class membership but did not see the opportunity to achieve it in Ghana. As I showed for the case of Bonokrom (cf. Chapter 2), transcontinental migrants from the Dormaa District were likely to have a level of education above the regional average. They were particularly concentrated among those with moderate education. It was argued that this class of people suffered more than any others from the saturation of the formal labour market in Ghana and the devaluation of educational degrees and incomes. Nevertheless, since modern imaginaries that social status can and should be attained through education are essential for the legitimation of modern statehood, they cannot simply be adapted to changed societal conditions.

During the 1970s and 1980s, the geographical focus of migration from Ghana gradually was extended towards Europe and North America. This tendency was reinforced by economic crises in Nigeria and the Côte d'Ivoire, which had both previously absorbed many migrants. A new class of rather economically successful transcontinental migrants emerged, who proved to a broader public that a living standard that was not attainable by the great majority in Ghana could be achieved abroad.

In the course of this development, the imaginary of modernity changed from being a temporal vision of the Ghanaian nation-state to a geographical elsewhere. Although the Ghanaian economy is recovering, the general level of wealth is still comparatively low, and migration continues to provide many of those who find a possibility to enter a country of the global north with the chance to achieve a status gain in Ghana. At the same time, the opportunities for upward mobility are limited for many Ghanaian non-elite migrants in the destination countries. Often migrants' cultural capital is devalued and they are forced to work as unskilled labourers in the low-wage sector.

The transnationalisation of the migrants' life-worlds is connected to broader economic processes. Double economic polarisation between and within nation-states creates an incentive structure for transnational forms of inclusion. It offers migrants an opportunity to achieve a middle-class living standard in Ghana and secure their old age by transferring resources earned in working-class jobs from the receiving country to the country of origin. However, transcontinental migration cannot solve the problems of status inconsistency, as it appears from the Ghanaian perspective, but creates a new form of transnational status inconsistency. The migrants' double inclusion shifts the problem from the national arena to a transnational social field. Above all, it creates two problems: On the one hand, being involved in social relations that are not suited to solve the original status problems leaves migrants with feelings of being despised and underestimated in the context of the receiving country. On the other hand, by creating models for status mobility in the countries of origin they challenge local middle classes and conventional modern legitimations of social status. The transnational status inconsistency, which emerges through the simultaneous process of gaining status in the country of origin by losing it in the receiving country, is called the status paradox of migration.

THE LIMITS OF THE PARADOX

The status paradox of migration and the *Burger* are ideal types. They provide a conceptual frame to describe and interpret the experiences and practices of a class of migrants that emerged in Ghana since the 1970s. As Weber (1985 [1904]: 190–213) argued, ideal types are analytical means to select and accentuate certain aspects of reality. They are not realistic representations of how the world is, but rather yardsticks by which empirical specificity and variance of phenomena can be observed and determined (Weber 1985 [1904]: 194). In this sense, they have to be evaluated based on their functionality in facilitating empirical descriptions and theorisations. Nevertheless, the explanatory strength at the constructed centre of an ideal type corresponds to a decreasing explanatory value at its margins.

In particular, two assumptions form the core of the status paradox of migration:

First, the status paradox of migration accentuated simultaneous inclusion in different nation-states as the normal condition of transnational migrants' ways of being.

Second, I depicted status inconsistency between the two involved main status identities, referring to the receiving country and to the country of origin, as standard for the description of transnational Ghanaian migrants.

This decision was related to characteristic patterns of labour migration from the global south to the global north in general and the case of Ghanaians in Germany in particular. In cases in which the share of elite migrants who do not experience a status loss comparable to the *Burgers* is higher, or in cases in which the differences in wealth and buying power are less developed than in the case of West Africa and Western Europe and, therefore, do not facilitate a comparable status gain in the country of origin, the status paradox does not apply.

Still, in the case of Ghanaian migrants in Germany there were cases that deviated from the standards of the status paradox of migration. For instance, the status of some professionals in Germany, such as medical doctors, scientists, engineers or successful entrepreneurs, is not as downgraded in the receiving country as it was described as characteristic for the case of *Burgers*. Nevertheless, among professionals experiences of racism and of limitations in the extent of upward mobility also sometimes contributed to a rather negative evaluation of their situation in the receiving country.

Other migrants who deviated from the norm of the status paradox were those who did not have the economic resources to support their families in Ghana, to create evidence of a middle-class status and to travel to Ghana. These persons did not experience the gain of status in the country of origin, which the status paradox of migration implied. Nevertheless, by aspiring to achieve material success and to permanently return to Ghana at an unspecified future, even these migrants were able to imagine a virtual social status in Ghana against which they could perceive their concrete living conditions in the receiving country as deviating and unsatisfactory.

Moreover, German-born children of Ghanaian migrants tended to deviate from the standards of the status paradox. Although they often maintained some kind of transnational relationship with relatives and friends in Ghana, they were less interested in a status identity in Ghana. Although their relationship to their parents' country of origin might change over time, the paradox of status was not experienced by them to the same extent as by their parents.[1]

Generally, the ideal type of the *Burger*, which relies on differentials in wealth and buying power between different nation-states, is to some degree 'threatened' by the economic stabilisation of the Ghanaian economy. Although the country still ranks among the low income countries in terms of average income, a new urban middle class has emerged that has profited from liberalisation and the growth of the economy. The increasing buying power of the new urban middle class reduced the *Burgers*' possible status gains. Rita Mends, a Fante woman in her 30s, who had lived in Halle in Germany and in London for some years, wrote me the following email:

> Before, if someone was abroad, it was like big respect and special treatment. But now people just fly to Europe and back ... so it is not a big

deal anymore. It is still the dream of those who are not highly educated that they want to go abroad and hope to have a better future. The educated ones rather go abroad to do their masters, work there for some time to pay for the money spent on their master education and come back. Before, there were less companies in Ghana but now more and more are coming up and some people come together as partners to start a business . . . Before, people back home respected people coming from abroad that much, because of the clothes they wore, cars they drove, and houses they built. But now you get all those clothes, houses and cars back home.

(Email Correspondence, Rita Mends, 1 July 2005)

Although Rita's account was biased by a wish to distinguish herself as an educated migrant from the *Burgers,* which was one of her recurring narratives, the social processes she described are observable in the urban centres of Ghana, particularly in Accra. In fact, a new middle class has emerged, and the larger the number of people who can achieve middle-class status in Ghana by legitimate means, according to the modern imaginary of social status, the lower the *Burgers'* potential profits become who compete with them in the same local status arena. Nevertheless, the economic and social incentives for migration, especially for those with only modest degrees of education, are still stronger than Rita's description might indicate. This is particularly true for medium-scale and small cities, like Dormaa Ahenkro. Therefore, the status paradox still provides a concept to describe and analyse the situations of Ghanaian and other labour migrants from the global south who live and work under comparable conditions.

TRANSMIGRANTS AND IMMIGRANTS

In migration studies, different ideal types were developed to characterise migrants and their relationship to the receiving areas and the areas of origin. The term transmigrant, for instance, was used by students of transnational migration (Glick Schiller, Basch and Szanton Blanc 1995; Goldring 1996; Morawska 2001) to highlight mobility, multiple affiliations across national borders and weak inclusion in the nation-state of the receiving country. In a sense, the term is an adaptation of the concept of 'circular migrant' that was employed in rural–urban migration studies in Africa (Mitchell 1961; Epstein 1967: 279; Hart 1971), to the conditions of transnational mobility. Transmigrants and circular migrants were considered different from permanent immigrants, as conceptualised by the assimilation and integration paradigm of migration studies, who were supposed to undergo an irreversible and permanent process of accommodation, integration and assimilation in the receiving areas (cf. Pries 2005).

The main target group of Ghanaian migrants in Berlin resembled both types of migrants in some respects, but differed from them in others. Like transmigrants, most of them remained included in their country of origin and invested resources in the maintenance of these relationships. Nevertheless, the frequency of cross-border mobility of the majority of Ghanaian migrants in Berlin was too low to characterise their occasional home visits as circulation. After some years of often increased mobility within Western Europe, a significant group of migrants had settled in Berlin rather permanently. This localisation process resembled in some respects the accommodation process, which was described by the assimilation approach. Nevertheless, since the localisation did not empirically contradict the maintenance of transnational forms of inclusion but paralleled it, Ghanaians in Berlin also differed from the ideal type of the immigrant.

It appears that the classification of migrants refers much more to the methodological perspectives employed than to the myriad of overlapping similarities among and gradual differences between them. Therefore, some caution is necessary not to essentialise the labels that are applied to migrants and to naively affirm the underlying societal epistemologies. In this respect it has to be taken into consideration that national and transnational forms of inclusion are often entangled in complex and non-linear ways. They can vary both in the course of the life of an individual and between different migrants (Levitt and Glick Schiller 2004; Smith 2006; Grillo and Mazzucato 2008; Nieswand 2008a). In many cases, it is decided only in a late phase of a life which inclusion is considered more permanent and which more transitory. During longer periods of many migrants' lives, it either remains undecided or decisions remain preliminary and reversible.

RURAL–URBAN MIGRATION AND TRANSCONTINENTAL MIGRATION

The mobility of significant numbers of Ghanaians to Europe is part of a successive expansion of the geographical scope of labour migration from Ghana. In several respects, transcontinental migration to Germany does not differ fundamentally from the rural–urban migration of the late colonial period. The support of the migrants' families in the sending areas, the migrants' house-building activities, the significance of consumer goods for the representation of the migrants' status as well as the imaginary of a successful return and a respectable old age 'at home' had already been documented by students of rural–urban migration in the 1950s and 1960s.

Nevertheless, there were also some significant differences between rural–urban migration and transcontinental migration. The most obvious is that the large majority of the transcontinental migrants come not from the sending areas of rural–urban migration but from the receiving areas. In this sense, the recent developments are not an extension of the geographical scope of migration in a simple and linear way but also reflect significant changes.

Moreover, since wealthier nation-states protect themselves from migration from poorer parts of the world by restrictive border regimes, inequalities can increase between these geographically separated and nationally bounded territories more than within regions that lack strongly institutionalised borders, as was the case in West Africa during the late colonial period (Beck 2008; Stichweh 2000).

What is more, in the case of the transcontinental migration of Ghanaians to Europe, the difficult conditions of legal entry and re-entry and the comparatively high travelling costs are obstructions to circular forms of migration. Nevertheless, it is misleading to take the frequency of mobility between receiving areas and areas of origin as a strong indicator for the relevance of simultaneous forms of social inclusion (Salih 2003: 158). In the case of long-distance migration from the global south to the global north, physical mobility often plays a secondary role in regard to the reproduction of transnational relationships (Vertovec 2004; Levitt and Jaworsky 2007).

The geographical distance involved also matters in terms of information and stigma management. Large geographical distances provide migrants with better opportunities to control what their relatives in Ghana get to know and what not. The link between geographical distance, information management and the status paradox was underlined by Akyeampong who made the remark that Ghanaians preferably migrate to a 'country where one's efforts are not witnessed or supervised by one's kin' (Akyeampong 2000: 186).

Altogether, the geographical distance involved in transcontinental migration matters in three respects: it allows for the existence of higher differentials of wealth and buying power, it normally decreases the frequency of mobility between receiving and sending area and, despite the existence of telecommunication facilities, the empirical data indicates that it improves the opportunities for information management.

In a certain respect, the changes in migration patterns to and from Ghana were also a background to perceive the specificity of the late colonial migration system. The often violent colonial pacification, the expansion of the transport infrastructure and the relative absence of immigration restrictions across borders allowed masses of migrants to participate in a system of circular migration (cf. Chapter 2). In contract to this, the nationalisation of Africa in the process of decolonialisation created obstacles to this open system of mobility and recurrently led, as for instance in Ghana in 1969, in Nigeria in 1982 and in the Côte d'Ivoire in 1999, to mass expulsions of non-nationals.[2]

EDUCATION AND MIGRATION

Education and its effect on personal identities has been a central and recurring issue in the study presented here. Highlighting its role in the context of transcontinental migration has shifted attention to an unintended consequence of the expansion of mass education. It was argued that schooling changes the expectations and positionalities of individuals. As a symbolic attribute of a person, an educational degree has a significant impact on his or her self-perception and an individual's aspirations, which are only loosely related to the concrete knowledge that it implies and the opportunity structure of the labour market school leavers meet.

The theoretical reconstruction of the link between status, education and the imaginary of modernity aimed to explain why status inconsistency emerges as a problem in the first place. In this context, it was argued that the idea of individual and collective progress through education is a core element of imaginaries of modern statehood that can, therefore, not simply be revised in cases in which the empirical reality deviates from it. Modern nation-states seem not to have a serious alternative to propagating the confidance in the individual and collective benefit of formal education. To renounce it would also mean to give up the idea that nation-states should and can develop according to the standards inscribed in social imaginaries of modernity. Discourses on the individual and collective rewards of education in their scope are not limited to state institutions but have in a long and unsteady history become a self-evident part of the everyday knowledge of local populations in Ghana and other parts of the world. Feelings of loss and exclusion from an imagined global modernity can even increase the desirability of the promises of education. The links between the expansion of mass education, social inequality between world regions and transcontinental migration are important for understanding more recent trends towards a globalisation of migratory movements. It contributes to the understanding of why a significant segment of transcontinental south–north labour migration, in contrast to some refugee movements or forceful displacements, is often education-selective and not an unmediated expression of absolute poverty (Portes and Rumbaut 2006: 15–16, 68–76). At the same time, it was also shown that non-recognition of educational degrees in the receiving areas of the global north has a significant impact on migrants' opportunity structures and their conceptualisations of themselves.

SOCIAL STATUS AND THE MODERN SELF

For the case of the *Burgers* it was highlighted that they and their relevant others take efforts to produce relative status consistency under the social conditions of relative status inconsistency. Since questions of the consistency or inconsistency of the self were a central issue in the debate on identity of the 1980s and 1990s (Hall 1990; Gilroy 1996; Brah 1998: 115–27; Butler 1999 [1990]), the empirical description of the *Burgers* and how they managed the status paradox of migration can be read as an empirical comment on this theoretical discussion.

Deconstructivist authors emphasised that identity is an ongoing social process of signification and reinterpretation that leads beyond the classical philosophical idea of the self as a fixed, coherent and stable entity (Brah 1998: 123–27; Butler 1999 [1990]: 22–32). Difference, contingency, fluidity, processuality, relationality, situationality, hybridity and, of course, constructedness of identities became key words around which these discourses gravitated. Accordingly, Brubaker and Cooper (2000) argued for a replacement of the term 'identity' by the term 'identification' because it better accentuated its processual and situational character instead of reifying it as an essence of personhood. Foucault (1983) attacked the idea that developing a reflexive and rational self-consciousness as an individual—in modern terms: an identity—is the condition and driving force of societal progress and political emancipation—an idea that was most fundamentally argued by Hegel (2006 [1807]) and can be found in enlightenment philosophy, in liberal state theory as well as in liberal economic theory. According to Foucault, identitarian self-awareness is not the emphatic point of origin of modern society but a mere effect of modern regimes of power. It is the power of definition, of disciplining and of excluding otherness under which persons are subjected that creates the modern Western subject and not an inherent essence located in the individual that allows for emancipating itself from 'self-incurred immaturity' (Kant 2000 [1784).[3] In this sense, Foucault and those who followed him turned the classical enlightenment argument around. Emancipation is not achieved through the self-realisation of the modern subject but rather through the deconstruction of the modern Western notion of the self and the related categories of identification, like gender, sexual orientation, sanity/insanity, nationality, race and culture (Butler 1999 [1990]: 181–90).

In some sense, this study takes up the questions of consistency, power and modern subjectivity, which were at the core of this criticism, but has a different take on them.[4] At the centre of attention here is not the question of whether the *Burgers*' status identities are consistent—which they are not—or whether modern imaginaries of social status are a means of domination or emancipation, but why and how the migrants themselves and their relevant others actively engage in the (re)production of pseudo-consistent identities which conflict with the complex reality of their transnational ways of living. Mutual interests and politeness norms, like tact, were identified as motivations to maintain a social image of which the actors knew that it was incomplete. In terms of its power structure, the relation between the migrants' status performance and modern imaginaries of social status remained ambivalent. On the one hand, the *Burgers*' gain in social status relied on both an affirmation of a modern imaginary and the possibility to render these aspects marginal that contradict its consistency standards. By practically referring to the latter, the interactive construction of the migrants' status in Ghana contributed to the reinforcement of dominant state-oriented discourses on social status. However, migrants and their relevant others referred to standards inherent in modern imaginaries of social status not in order to reproduce them but because those who were in position to redistribute economic resources and those who received them profited from it socially and economically. It allowed for the conversion of economic resources into social status and for the translation of the irritating ambiguities that are implied in the status paradox into more consistent categories.

On the other hand, knowledge of the fact that migrants circumvented the legitimate logic of status attainment and the visibility of their economic success offered a prominent alternative to the pathways of social mobility that was suggested by the meritocratic triad of education, occupation and income. However, the contestation of this discourse normally was not the migrants' goal but an unintended consequence of their transnational ways of living. In this sense it is neither appropriate to depict their activities as a power-driven and passive reproduction of a hegemonic discourse nor as a counter-hegemonic act of resistance. It cuts across the major lines of the sketched debate about identity. Instead of allowing us to give a clear answer to the philosophical problem of the relation between the power of subjectivity to create discourses and the power of the discourse to create subjectivity, the case study indicates that these two types of powers both enable and limit each other at the same time. The constitution and processing of the *Burgers'* paradox can be best described in terms of an entanglement of subjectivities and discourses, which opens actors (with sufficient resources) spaces for creating back-stages for strategic manoeuvring, rather than as unambiguous and linear power relations.

Above all, the case of the *Burgers* points to the empirical complexities and ambiguities of autonomy and heteronomy that transnational agency creates in a social world in which many identity discourses are heavily influenced by the political form of the nation-state and its corresponding imaginaries and ideologies.

THE TRANSNATIONALISATION OF SOCIAL INEQUALITY

As argued before, research on social inequality in particular was long dominated by methodological nationalism. This meant that conventionally social inequality was considered either as internal or external to the nation-state. External social inequality concerned differences in wealth and living standards between different countries, while internal social inequality referred to the distribution of resources within a particular nation-state (Hoffmann-Nowotny 1973). In both forms, the nation-state was the central unit according to which what is internal and what is external is defined.

The *Burgers*, on the one hand, exploit economic differences between nation-states and, on the other hand, depend on the conversion of their economic capital into social status in the country of origin. By relying on the simultaneous inclusion in two nation-states and the transfers between them, the *Burgers* engage in a transnational form of status production, which challenges simplistic internal/external differentiations and the underlying model of national segmentation of social inequality. The migrants' economic activities rely on nation-states but are not determined by them. The transnational field of manoeuvring across national borders opens up a third space in which the *Burgers* can manage their multiple inclusions and try to 'hedge their bets'. Therefore, the description of the *Burgers*' way of status production contributes to an anthropology of the transnationalisation of social inequalities (cf. Goldring 1998; Glick Schiller and Fouron 2001b; Newell 2005). It fills an abstract discourse with lived experience and helps to understand and to explore the local consequences of these processes.

Globally, private remittances are the second largest source of external funding for developing countries (Ratha 2003). The statistically reported remittances amounted to U.S. $221 billion in 2008 and were twice as high as the official assistance developing countries received (Gupta, Pattillo and Wagh 2009: 104). This well-documented global increase in migrants' remittances (Ratha 2003; Munzele Maimbo and Ratha 2005; Vertovec 2009: 103–19) supports the hypothesis that is suggested by this study, namely, that migrants' extensive engagement in transnational forms of resource management, which is most closely interlinked with modes of status production (cf. Chapter 4), has become a structurally relevant factor in the making of world society. Although 'migrant' is an utterly diverse category, which includes such different types of persons as technical experts, sportspersons, agricultural workers, refugees, sex labourers and domestic servants, many of them share the experience that the receiving countries are not the only relevant sites for the ascription and production of their social status. In this respect the status paradox is not a marginal experience of a handful of Ghanaian migrants but—although it exists in different local variations—characteristic for a whole class of labour migrants.[5]

Transnational migrants and their transfers of resources have a particular impact on local status systems in the sending areas. They offer role models for the local youth, create new standards for consumption, are attractive marriage partners, increase the local prices for land and houses by their demand and, last but not least, present an irritation to the meritocratic triad. A field of study that promises to increase the understanding of transnational status economies is the functioning of formal and informal regimes of convertibility (and non-convertibility) of resources between nation-states and localities (Weiß 2002). It appears that there are two complementary global processes taking place at the same time, which influence migrants' opportunity structure.

On the one hand, a global tendency towards standardisation of educational degrees, the development of few global languages of communication and the successive opening of several Western European and North American labour markets for highly qualified migrants have decreased the opportunity costs of migration for those who control some of these highly convertible resources. On the other hand, those who are excluded from these resources are exposed to a process of marginalisation, which presents the shady side of the institutionalisation of global regimes of convertibility. Not being in possession of an internationally recognised school or university degree, speaking languages of local relevance and owning a passport of a poor country, which are just the consequences of growing up in a place with very limited or no access to convertible social resources, are important dimensions of global inequality. In this sense 'control of migration and differential treatment of migrants' and persons who might become migrants 'have become the basis for a new type of class structure' (Castles and Miller 2009: 57) which is not to a small extent based on the differential degrees of convertibility of personal resources.

These forms of inequality go beyond mere economic inequality and, therefore, have to be differentiated from it, although economic inequality is both as condition and as consequence closely linked to them. Since formal and informal regimes, mechanisms and rates of converting social and economic resources between different politically defined territories influence patterns of social inequality, they deserve a higher degree of academic attention.

Although inequality also divides national populations, countries that lack infrastructure and resources, such as globally recognised universities, passports with which persons can freely travel to high wage countries or effective language training in global languages, are affected more negatively than others.

Despite ongoing globalisation processes nation-states and national markets remain important units for the determination of the value of resources as well as for their rates of conversion. For instance, in the case of education, nation-states can recognise degrees from educational institutions of some countries and refuse it in other cases. Thereby, they achieve a huge impact on the value of migrants' cultural capital. Even money, which appears to be a particular convertible and generalised resource, is in practice more discontinuous and contextual than it might appear at first glance. A certain amount of money in dollars, euros or cedis does not say much about its value in terms of local buying power or in terms of the corresponding living standard. Having one dollar in Ghana or Bangladesh is not the same as having one dollar in the United States or Switzerland. Moreover, individuals face, as I highlighted in Chapter 5, particular problems if they want to convert money earned in one context into 'social goods' like recognition, status or the ancestors' benevolence in another one. In this way, the described status paradox links up to a social and moral problem that is caused by the quality of money as being a generalised medium of exchange. It is a basic feature of market economies that money is used to exchange goods and services of different quality against each other. This feature of money raises at one point or the other the question of how far reaching this exchangeability should be. Especially, the exchangeability of those 'goods' or aspects of social life that are connected to honour, salvation or the integrity of the human body, often face legal or moral restrictions. Shipton (1997) described, for the example of the East African Luo, that they distinguish different forms of acquiring money and believe that the moral value of how the money is earned leaves an imprint on the quality of the money. They call money that is gained by unfair or unjust activities *bitter* and try to keep it away from those social spheres that are concerned with permanent lineage wealth and welfare. As Shipton argued, the discourse of *bitter money* provides the Luo with a general interpretative frame in which they can negotiate and determine the moral implications of the accumulation of wealth and property.

Although in Western-type nation-states ideas about the moral differentiations between types of money are less developed than among the Luo, there are legal and moral restrictions to its exchangeability. For instance, it is prohibited to trade in political offices, academic degrees, organs, human beings or illicit drugs. As the case of the *Burger* indicates, the conversion of money into the 'social good' of legitimate social status also faces specific difficulties. On the one hand, monetary wealth plays an important role for the ascription of social status, the intergenerational reproduction of social inequality and the purchase of status symbols that are provided by a vast global consumer industry. On the other hand, modern imaginaries of social status rely on the idea that wealth requires legitimation. Wealth acquired by morally dubious or criminal activities, wealth without or with insufficient legitimation by other status variables, as in the case of the *Burgers,* or wealth that does not go along with a certain degree of morally appreciated forms of redistribution, such as adequate tax-paying or philanthropic activities, easily becomes suspicious.

For the case of the Ashanti Region during the nineteenth century, I demonstrated how an ascending class of merchants explored certain opportunities to convert their economic capital into legitimate prestige. The *Burgers* have a problem similar to the merchants. They are also, relative to the historical context in which they are situated, a challenge to dominant ideas of status attainment and have to look for opportunities to convert their primarily economic capital into social recognition. The redistribution of resources, the fulfilment of kinship obligation and the purchase of socially recognised status symbols, particularly houses, are most important in this respect. The crucial role of redistribution for legitimating status claims became obvious in cases in which *Burgers* 'became weak' and had no resources left to distribute.

THE POLITICS OF TRANSNATIONALISM

This study has highlighted that politicised and popular representations of migrants from the global south in Western Europe as well as in the countries of origin are often incomplete. The widespread perception in Ghana that migration is a way to achieve wealth and upward mobility, is distorting because it does not sufficiently reflect the loss of status and agency, which many migrants experience by being exposed to insecure migration routes, rigid immigration regimes, economic marginalisation and racialisation. At the same time, the distorted descriptions of migrants from the global south as either wicked defrauders or victims of global and national regimes of power is also based on an incomplete representation. I tried to demonstrate that Ghanaian migrants gain and lose agency at the same time in different spheres of their lives. However, those who are able to accommodate themselves in Western Europe or North America *economically* perform better than many of their compatriots who stay in Ghana.

The status paradox aimed to include both aspects, the gains and the losses, in the representation of migration and highlighted their relatedness. By relativising the discourse on victimhood and economic marginalisation of migrants from a methodologically transnationalist perspective, the status paradox in some sense became an irritation to conventional pro-migration discourses. Although there are general sympathies among the liberal and left parts of the political spectrum for a moderate de-centring of the nation-state, there are resentments against it when it comes to questions of social inequality. Redistribution of wealth within nation-states traditionally is a social democratic key concern. It appears that in the past students of transnational migration were more reluctant to criticise this form of methodological nationalism than that of the conservative and right end of the political spectrum.

Against this background, those elements of the status paradox that stress the success of Ghanaian migrants can be misunderstood as an apology for anti-immigration politics and sentiments (cf. Crumbely 2006). Therefore, I would like to add a few comments: The status paradox of migration is a theorem that was developed from a case study. Of course, it has to be carefully scrutinized whether it applies to other cases or not. Nevertheless, the described forms of migration and resource management reveal a weak point of the political debate on migration. As long as different migration and integration policies rely on representing migrants either as wicked perpetrators or as poor victims, empirical complexities and relativisations of these representations, like the status paradox, have to be depicted either as empirical misrepresentations and/or as ideological statements (ibid).

Instead of banalising the problems of social inequality, in my opinion, the present study demonstrated that questions of global inequality are even more pressing than ever before. The extension of migration routes and the migrants' partly successful attempts to circumvent restrictive migration regimes made global inequality in many respects an internal issue of the countries of the global north. The only sustainable political strategy, in my opinion, is to integrate transnational and global perspectives into the national debates on migration and social inequality. This requires critically and partially painful revisions of conventional perspectives on the triadic relation between society, social inequality and migration, and a search for adequate entry points for bringing alternative perspectives into the debates. The recent policy debate on migration and development in which the individual or collective contributions of migrants to the development of their home countries are discussed (Hunger 2000; Faist and Reisenauer 2009; Laschet 2009: 255–68) might offer such an entry point. In this context, it appears most important to me that it represents a discourse in the receiving countries that refers to migrants' transnational activities in an affirmative or at least neutral way. If migrants' forms of transnational inclusion are recognised by national or local authorities as legitimate and appreciable activities of migrants as citizens of the receiving countries (and not as citizens of their countries of origin), it implies a movement towards the enlargement of the political horizon that overcomes conventional national inside-outside distinctions and challenges expectations of exclusive loyalty which has, in particular in Germany, dominated the political sphere for a long time. Potentially, this change in the perspective on migrants' development activities might also offer opportunities to open up the national political horizon of perception in other respects. However, this process is not very developed. A core question that this study has brought up is how Western countries will deal with the class of migrants at the centre of this study that does not fit in the conventional schemes of migration policies: persons who are neither highly qualified nor absolutely poor or politically persecuted but who become mobile to follow the promises of modern statehood and education in the countries of the global north. By reconstructing the context for this type of migration and the power-loaded entanglement of European and African history, I tried to show that it is not adequate for Western countries to deny the legitimacy of and a political responsibility for these forms of mobility. I highlighted these political issues because they emerge from this study and I wanted to make them explicit and transparent. However, I will leave them at this preliminary point because a thorough discussion of the political consequences of the suggested change in perspectives goes beyond what I consider the scope and the goal of this study.

METHODOLOGICAL TRANSNATIONALISM

In Chapter 1 methodological transnationalism was identified as the analytical framework of this case study. It was argued that methodological transnationalism not only changes the perspective on migration but also the notion employed of society. Society was not perceived as a bounded and *normatively* integrated national whole, but as a *practically* integrated global system in which heterogeneous and complex forms of sociality interact and coexist. The move from national to world society was not meant to deny the relevance of nation-states as political actors but to make it an object of empirical study within a broader analytical frame of reference.

Despite being affected by it, society is not identical with polity (Stichweh 2000: 48–65; Glick Schiller 2003: 125). It was not least social anthropology that has demonstrated (cf. Fortes and Evans-Pritchard 1940; Sigrist 1979 [1967]; Schlee 2001a) that states were never and still are not the only form of integration of larger social systems—an insight that has regained relevance in the debates on globalisation and transnationalisation. Nevertheless, both migration studies and research on social inequality maintained reception barriers for a long time that hindered them from integrating this knowledge into their research agendas (Kreckel 2008).

On the most general level, the empirical case of the *Burgers* and the status paradox of migration was to demonstrate the analytical usefulness of methodological transnationalism. The importance of the involved nation-states for shaping migrants' lives was stressed in the cases of the economic crisis in Ghana, the global differentials in wealth between nation-states, the role of border regimes and the significance of national labour markets. At the same time, the impact of transnational forms of sociality was described for the issues of migrants' remittances, systems of family reciprocity and transnational modes of status production.

Methodological transnationalism functioned as the meta-frame in which the actors' switches between different socio-spatial contexts of reference could be described. In this sense, the case study argued that the most important contribution of transnationalism to the broader field of migration studies is not the empirical description of transnational phenomena in itself but the broadening of the analytical frame of observation.[6] Methodological transnationalism presents a world societal alternative to the classical integration and assimilation paradigm of migration studies. Since it refers to a methodological perspective, and not an empirical object, it does not exclude the research questions of the assimilation and integration paradigm, but only points to their analytical limitations. Empirically, methodological transnationalism can even contribute to a differentiation of assimilation hypotheses. If one takes into consideration that the majority of first generation migrants are simultaneously included in the receiving country (e.g. their place of work and of residence) and the country of origin (e.g. by friendship and kinship relationships), multiple and simultaneous incorporations of migrants within and across state borders are the normal case. Even if a cross-generational tendency towards exclusive inclusion of migrants' descendants in the receiving country is observable, it would be important to explore how transnational pathways of inclusion, non-inclusion and exclusion affect the pathways of national inclusion. There is empirical evidence that the latter is not independent of the former. For instance, the political constellations of the two world wars and the emergence of authoritarian and fascistic regimes in Europe during the 1920s and 1930s have reinforced assimilative tendencies among descendants of European migrants in the United States (Waldinger and Fitzgerald 2004: 1188–89). In contrast to this, the political developments after the end of the Cold War, the improved technical infrastructure of transnational inclusion and the active diaspora policy of many emigration countries have contributed to an intensification and extension of migrants' transnational relationships during the last decades.

If the relationship between transnational and national inclusions and exclusions was taken into consideration, a more differentiated understanding of the processes of national integration of migrants could be achieved. It would allow for describing integration as a contingent and partial process, which takes place in the interaction of different socio-spatial units of reference instead of reducing it exclusively to the pull-forces of the immigration country.

Apart from the differentiation of assimilation hypotheses, methodological transnationalism provides a framework to study the heterogeneity of forms of transnational involvement which is part and parcel of the diversification processes of migrant populations (Vertovec 2007). Since the relevance of transnational forms of inclusion for migration-related phenomena can only be determined empirically, a methodological framework is required which allows for an observation and differentiation of different types of social inclusion within and across national borders and their specific interaction. In this respect, the present study has aimed to spell out the analytical framework of methodological transnationalism and to demonstrate its usefulness for the description and analysis of migration-related phenomena.

Notes

NOTES TO THE INTRODUCTION

1. The general increase in transcontinental mobility does not contradict the fact that the largest number of migrants remain within the global south.
2. Beyond the field of migration studies, also in the field of religious studies an intensified interest in African migrants is noticeable (e.g. Adogame and Weißköppel 2005). Since the early 1980s, West and Central African migrants established churches and church congregations in Western Europe. In this framework, migrants from Ghana (Appiah 1985; Ter Haar 1998a, 1998b; Jach 2005; Koning 2009; Nieswand 2010a), Nigeria (Becken 1982; Adogame 1997, 2000a; Ludwig 2005; Ukah 2005; Knibbe 2009) and Congo (Simon 2001, 2003) were most active. An important theme in this literature is in how far religion facilitates or impedes local integration (Ekué 1998; Gerloff 1999; Jach 2005: 326–32; Simon 2005; Ter Haar 1998a, 1998b). Other authors highlighted the transnational dimension of Pentecostal forms of Christianity practised by African migrants in Europe (van Dijk 1997, Glick Schiller, et al. 2005).
3. The colonial name Gold Coast was changed into Ghana in 1957.
4. An exception is the legal and even encouraged migration of formally qualified migrants. A well-documented example is the case of Ghanaian physicians and nurses to Great Britain (Grillo and Mazzucato 2008).
5. The 15 months is a conservative estimate. In fact, it is difficult to determine the temporal extension of the research because it continued occasionally even after it had formally ended.

NOTES TO CHAPTER 1

1. The original German quotation was translated into English.
2. In contrast to this, for Luhmann society consists of communication and human beings are only part of the environment of society (Luhmann 1998: 106–108).
3. The original German quotation has been translated into English.
4. Although the race relation circle became one of Park's most prominent contributions to the social sciences, it is more of a theoretical sketch than a fully developed theory (Park 1950 [1926]: 150).
5. Besides assimilation, a caste system in which one group was ruled by another and the maintenance of a minority group status without clear-cut power relations were depicted as possible outcomes of interethnic group relations.

6. Altogether Gordon differentiated seven variables: 1. acculturation, 2. structural assimilation, 3. marital assimilation, 4. identificational assimilation, 5. attitude receptional assimilation (absence of prejudice in the core society), 6. behaviour receptional assimilation (absence of discrimination in the core society) and 7. civic assimilation (absence of value and power conflict between immigrants and the core society).
7. Habermas (1996: 237–76) and Kymlicka (2003 [1995]: 45–48) objected that Taylor's opposition between multiculturalism and liberalism is based on a too simplistic understanding of the latter.
8. Over the last decades multiculturalism experienced different waves of criticism. An important criticism was that collective minority rights might contribute to reproduce or even to reinforce inequalities within a given minority; for instance, those between men and women (Okin, Cohen, Howard and Nussbaum 1999). As a reaction, Anne Phillips (2007) proposed a 'multiculturalism without culture'. Its goal is to provide a model which allows for context-sensitive switches between repertoires of individualistic and collective rights. More recently the notion of multiculturalism experienced a profound political backlash. Despite the continuity of multicultural policies, political actors often represent it as an outdated and unsuccessful approach to cultural diversity (Vertovec and Wessendorf 2010).
9. Multiculturalism does not only deal with migration-related forms of diversity. Kymlicka (2003 [1995]: 10–33) distinguished between a pluralism based on multi-nationality and a pluralism based on multiethnicity. While multi-nationality refers to problems of the coexistence of culturally distinct groups who have competing historical land claims within the same state, multiethnicity refers to a pluralism caused by a rather recent immigration, which is normally not connected to claims of territorial autonomy.
10. Instead of 'racialisation' the term *Ethnisierung* (ethnicisation) is preferred in German-speaking countries (Bukow and Llaryora 1988; Bukow 1992). The historical experience of Nazism discredited the concept of race to such an extent in Germany and Austria that even constructivist reformulations sound dubious to native German speakers.
11. Outside migration research, some authors applied views on racialisation. Balibar and Wallerstein (1990: 87–130), for instance, analysed the link between racism, colonialism and the development of the capitalist world system.
12. The distinction between 'modern' and 'feudal' refers to the relevance of ascriptive (i.e. age, gender, birth rights) or performative features, respectively, for the allocation of resources in society. Modernisation theory understood the dominance of ascriptive criteria in determining the status of a person as a characteristic of premodern or, as Hoffmann-Nowotny called it, feudal societies. Since he argued that in 'the context of the Swiss immigration and citizenship politics' ethnicity was re-introduced as a criterion of status ascription, in his view it was a re-feudalisation of modern society.
13. In contrast, conflict theoreticians (Gluckman 1966; Dahrendorf 1959; Schlee 2001b) argued that integration should not be understood in opposition to conflict, but conflict may even be a possible means to achieve societal integration.
14. In this context, Alba and Nee (2003) argued that cross-generationally a tendency of adaptation to the mainstream is observable but that the mainstream to which migrants adapt is not static and migrants themselves also contribute to the 'remaking of the mainstream'.
15. Most of the academic literature on migration in West Africa is about rural–urban migration. It is noteworthy that urban–urban migration, although being

quantitatively relevant (Caldwell 1969), was more or less neglected by the migration researchers of that time. Migrants who migrated within what was considered modern society did not fit into the dominant schemes of attention. Much less relevant but at least covered to some extent was rural-rural migration in the context of cash crop economy (e.g. Hill 1963; Stucki 1992).
16. Epstein (1967: 276) refined Gluckman's original argument by acknowledging that different degrees of commitment to urban life and the extent of socialisation in the urban sphere may constitute significant differences for the enactment of the respective roles.
17. European imaginaries of society as an organic whole go, according to Luhmann (2005 [1971]), as far back as antiquity.
18. Sociological globalisms built on earlier globalisms like the classical Greek idea of *cosmopolitanism*, the Christian idea of *ecumenism*, the *universalism* of Enlightenment philosophy and the *internationalism* of the workers' movement.
19. In the field of media studies, Appadurai's terminology turned out to be empiraclly more productive than in other fields (e.g. Cunningham and Jacka 1996; Çaglar 2004).
20. Some authors highlighted that transnationalism's entanglement with the idea of the nation is an analytical limitation. This has Thomas Faist (2000) motivated to speak of trans-state spaces instead of transnational spaces.
21. Since imaginaries of relatively exclusive and permanent integration of persons into one territorialised society appear to be the product of the underlying methodological framework, it does not surprise that multiple and situational forms of inclusion, which cut across dominant political entities, are not recent globalisation phenomena. Günther Schlee (1989), for instance, showed in his work on northern Kenya that they can also be found in so-called traditional non-Western societies.
22. Khagram and Levitt's notion of methodological transnationalism refers to a corpus of concrete methods that can reveal the transnational dimension of social life while the notion that is proposed in this study puts a stronger accent on the underlying societal epistemology of migration studies. Ulrich Beck's alternative notion of methodological cosmopolitanism (Beck 2007) has a comparable epistemological orientation but is part of his larger theory of reflexive modernisation to which this study maintains a sceptical distance.

NOTES TO CHAPTER 2

1. The Gold Coast was one of few colonies in Africa at that time where no poll tax was levied (Berg 1964: 403).
2. Mechanical gold mining spread in the Gold Coast in the late 1870s. In 1950, it was estimated that gold made up 6 per cent of the total GDP (Rimmer 1992: 34).
3. Only after the resistance against the British colonial regime was finally broken in 1906, did the north become a labour reservoir for the south (Lentz and Erlmann 1989: 74).
4. The boundary between seasonal and permanent migration is difficult to draw. Factually, these terms have to be thought of as end points of a continuum that covers a large variety of mobility patterns.
5. Marcus Garvey (1887–1940) was a Jamaica-born Afro-American political leader whose work was essential for the foundation of the pan-Africanist movement.
6. Joseph Ephraim Casely Hayford (1866–1930) was a pan-Africanist from the Gold Coast.

7. Cedi has been the name of the Ghanaian currency since 1965.
8. Presumably, the neologism *kalabule* derives from the Hausa expression *kere kabure*, which means 'keep quiet about it' (Siebold 1988: 162).
9. During the 1960s the average black market rate of the Cedi was 1.7 times higher than the official rate, during the 1970s it was 3.5 times, and between 1981 and 1985 it was more than twelve times higher (Rimmer 1992: 209).
10. In the framework of an announced 'war on hoarders' the large Makola market in the centre of Accra was destroyed in August 1979 and acts of violence against market women in Accra and Kumasi were reported (Robertson 1983: 469).
11. World Bank (2010). If not indicated otherwise the quoted World Bank data was accessed from an online data base (http://data.worldbank.org/indicator).
12. In 1992, the first presidential elections since 1979, and in 1996 J. J. Rawlings was elected as president.
13. World Bank (2010).
14. As in the case of Ghana, the expulsion of foreigners from Nigeria turned out to be politically and economically unsuccessful. Shagari was overthrown by a military coup in the very same year.
15. Because of differences in the naturalisation practices and citizenship laws of the various European countries, different proportions of undocumented migrants and differences in the way migrants are counted, national statistics are difficult to compare. Nevertheless, these numbers at least give a superficial impression of the relative distribution of Ghanaians in Europe.
16. In consideration of concerns of the villagers, I have changed the name of the village.
17. Interview, Kojo Yeboah, 20 July 2003, Berlin.
18. With less than 1,000 inhabitants, Bonokrom is an average Ghanaian village with respect to its size (Twum-Baah, Nabila and Aryee 1995a: 3). The data of the village census was collected by a research team including John Appiah Kubi, Stephen Kofi Owusu and me. Concretely, we asked the heads of the households in the village about their parents and all the persons who descended from them.
19. Interview, Elders Bonokrom, 21 September 2003, Bonokrom.
20. According to UN figures, 7 per cent of the returnees from Nigeria to Ghana in 1983 came from the Brong Ahafo Region (cited in Brydon 1985: 570).
21. The case of Kojo Yeboah and his family will be discussed in Chapter 4 (pp. 105–10).
22. Morocco and Libya were integrated in this sample on transcontinental migration because the migrants themselves consider these countries not as migration destinations but as transit countries on the way to Europe.
23. Presumably, in regions of Ghana where the opportunities for capital accumulation by female traders, as in Kumasi, are better, the proportion of female migrants is higher.
24. There were two cases but we could not obtain sufficient data to evaluate them.

NOTES TO CHAPTER 3

1. Statistisches Bundesamt Deutschland (2010). The data originates from the database of the Statistisches Bundesamt and was provided to me by email in the indicated year.
2. The largest group of immigrants after the stop of labour recruitment in 1973 were ethnic Germans, so-called *Aussiedler* or *Spätaussiedler*, from the countries of the former Eastern bloc. They came in large numbers in the late

1980s and 1990s. As ethnic Germans they fit into another scheme of immigration and are not included in this brief overview.
3. According to Nuscheler (1995), two thirds of all asylum seekers in the EU came to Germany between 1972 and 1993.
4. Statistisches Bundesamt Deutschland (2001). Cf. endnote 1.
5. Statistisches Bundesamt Deutschland (2006). Until 1990 the statistical data refers exclusively to West Germany. After 1990 it includes East Germany.
6. The system of registration of foreigners in Germany produces a methodical problem: Any non-German with a legal residence in Germany is registered by a local *Ausländerbehörde* (foreigner department). If a person leaves the country without giving notice to the local administration, he or she still appears in the statistics. Therefore, periodically the statistic has to be corrected.
7. Between 1989 and 2000, 0.26 per cent of the Ghanaian asylum applicants were granted asylum (Bundesamt für die Anerkennung ausländischer Flüchtlinge 2002). The data originates from the database of the Bundesamt für die Anerkennung ausländischer Flüchtlinge and was provided to me by email.
8. The other seven countries were Bulgaria, Poland, Romania, Senegal, the Slovakian Republic, the Czech Republic and Hungary.
9. The decrease in 2005 was caused by a correction of the official statistic.
10. Statistisches Bundesamt Deutschland (2009). Cf. endnote 1.
11. The migration pattern from the Dormaa District where men are the majority of migrants is different from the patterns which the statistics show for Germany. One hypothesis to explain this difference is that emigration from the Dormaa District started later than in other parts of southern Ghana and that, therefore, the gender ratio is falling behind the general trend.
12. Statistisches Bundesamt Deutschland, cited after Martin (2005: 313).
13. Statistisches Bundesamt Deutschland (2006).
14. Statistisches Bundesamt Deutschland (2006).
15. Statistisches Bundesamt Deutschland (2006).
16. All of the 10 cities that accommodate the largest number of Ghanaian migrants have over 500,000 inhabitants; 58 per cent of the Ghanaian, but only 13 per cent of the German population live in the 10 listed cities. The data originates from the data bases of the institutions indicated in Table 3.1 and was provided to me by email.
17. Report of the *Direktorat für Ausländerstudium*, 19 April 1966/ 25 April 1966; Interview, Mary Amponsah, 19 October 2001, Accra.
18. Report of the *Direktorat für Ausländerstudium*, 24 November 1966.
19. Interview, Raphael Darkoh, 10 October 2001, Accra.
20. Interview, John Ofori, 8 July 2001, Mülheim.
21. Statistisches Bundesamt Deutschland (2010). Cf. endnote 1.
22. Berliner Landesamt für Statistik (2010). The data originates from the database of the Berliner Landesamt für Statistik and was provided to me by email.
23. Berliner Landesamt für Statistik (2005).
24. Berliner Landesamt für Statistik (2006). Until 1990 the statistical data refers only to West Berlin. After 1990 the data also includes East Berlin.
25. Some of my informants went to London where the labour market situation was better than in Berlin in the early 2000s.
26. Interview, George Sarpong, 24 June 2002, Berlin.
27. I gave a more detailed description of the history of some of the churches elsewhere (Nieswand 2010b).
28. Since racialisation of Ghanaians in Germany remains a topic throughout the study and also within some of the depicted identity discourses, I have

not written a separate paragraph on it but, in this framework, have selected identity discourses that were more interesting in regard to the dynamic of localisation and transnationalisation.
29. In the 1980s, the Ghana Union was supposed to be the representative body of the 'asylum seekers', while the Ghana Student Union was expected to represent the interests of students.
30. Interview, Henry Oppong, 3 May 2002, Berlin.
31. The Ghana Community is the successor organisation of the Ghana Union (cf. Nieswand 2008b).
32. Interview, Yaa Serwaa and Leticia Badu, 11 April 2002, Berlin.
33. Interview, Daniel Adamu, 14 July 2002, Berlin.
34. Interview, Moses Lartey, 16 April 2002, Berlin.
35. The terms 'charismatic' and 'neo-Pentecostal' are used synonymously.
36. Interview, President, Ghana Community, 25 June 2008, Berlin.
37. This was for instance the case when Kojo granted a migrant from Dormaa the opportunity to sell drinks in the back room of his wife's afro shop.
38. These paragraphs are descriptive of a setting made up largely by persons with migration backgrounds. They are not meant to imply a denial of the fact that discrimination in other contexts is practised by Germans.
39. Field Protocol, 2 August 2002, Berlin.
40. cf. endnote 23.
41. cf. endnote 23.
42. cf. endnote 23.
43. The controversial question to what extent this is an appropriate representation or an exaggeration will not be discussed in this context.
44. *Ossi* is a colloquial term for East Germans. The corresponding term for West Germans is *Wessi*.
45. In the GDR, Russian is privileged as a foreign language.

NOTES TO CHAPTER 4

1. After the change of government in 2009, the term 'Diasporian Relations' was taken out of the name of the ministry again. By the time this book was completed, it was not clear whether this symbolic gesture indicates a more general change of the policy.
2. World Development Report (2001).
3. World Bank (2006). cf. endnote 11 Chapter 2.
4. In Twi, the word *nua* (sibling) is also used to refer to matrilineal and patrilineal cousins. Presumably, Kofi used in this passage the English expression 'brothers and sisters' in the broader meaning of the Twi-word *nua*.
5. In Ghana, it is common to pay rent for one or more years in advance.
6. I observed the incident when I stayed with the part of the family that lives in Dormaa Ahenkro in 2003.
7. It is difficult to assess whether the representation that the German police confiscated Kwaku's money is correct or whether it is a defensive manoeuvre to give his relatives an explanation for his 'failure'. Legally, the German state can confiscate money which is found with an undocumented migrant to defray the costs of their imprisonment and deportation. This can go up to several thousands of Euros.
8. The Twi proverb *nsa ko nsa ba* literally means 'a hand goes, a hand comes'. It can be translated as 'you scratch my back and I will scratch yours.'
9. Field Protocol, 29 September 2003, Dormaa Ahenkro.
10. Field Protocol, 9 October 2003, Dormaa Ahenkro.

11. For the relevance of kinship relations in the context of transnational migration see also: Bryceson and Vuorella 2002; Baldassar, Baldock and Wilding 2007; Grillo 2008; Drotbohm 2009 and Kastner 2010.

NOTES TO CHAPTER 5

1. Altogether, the research on status inconsistency was empirically not very successful because the results were too ambiguous and contradictory (cf. Kreckel 1985: 29–30; Meulemann 1985: 461–62).
2. The stool is the Akan symbol of chieftaincy. The power of the state and the office is, according to Akan belief, incorporated in it.
3. Before, there had been the so-called 'castle schools'. They were mainly attended by a small number of the descendants of Europeans and local persons and did not have a great social impact.
4. The emphases in the text were done by Daniel himself.
5. There are terms referring to comparable types of migrants in other countries and languages. In the neighbouring Ivory Coast, a similar type of migrant is called *Bengiste* (Newell 2005: 164), in Senegal *modou modou* (Riccio 2001) and in Turkey *Almanya beyi* (Elwert 1984: 67).
6 Interview, Yaw Asare, 18 July 2002, Berlin.
7. Although the term *Burger* is more ambiguous than clearly negative, my informants did not normally use it as a form of self-description.
8. The Twi category of children includes own children as well as brothers' children.
9. The songs were translated by John Appiah Kubi, Stephen Kofi Owusu and me.
10. According to the official criminal statistics Ghanaians in Germany are not particularly conspicuous (Bundeskriminalamt 2002). This information was provided to me by email.
11. Interview, Yaw Asante, 3 September 2003, Dormaa Ahenkro.
12. Interview, Thomas Akyeampong, 8 June 2002, Berlin.

NOTES TO THE CONCLUSION

1. Discrimination on the labour market, experiences of racialisation, having children of one's own or political developments in the sending or the receiving country can lead to unexpected changes in attitude towards the parents' country of origin (Levitt and Glick Schiller 2004: 1018; Smith 2002).
2. This is not meant as an idealisation of colonialism. It is just an exemplification of the general point that—methodologically and politically—nationalism has a strong impact on the perception and management of cross-border migration.
3. In the context of the argument presented above, the philosophical dissent between Hegel and Kant about the foundation of subjectivity is not relevant. It is sufficient to recognise that both authors consider the critical and self-reflexive subject a major driving force of emancipation and progress.
4. This perspective is not innovative but builds on earlier works of Goffman (1986 [1963]) and Krappmann (1969).
5. It is the frequent pattern of recent forms of labour migration that many of those who are marginalised according to standards of the receiving countries of the global north still have an educational level above the average in their regions of origin. Portes and Rumbaut (2006: 16) argued for the case of the United States that 'even those from the most modest origins—for instance undocumented

migrants from Mexico and Central America—tend to have educational levels that are higher on average than their respective sending populations.'
6. Not differentiating between methodological and empirical transnationalism, Bommes (2003: 105), for instance, concluded that transnational migration studies were a mere 'supplementary programme with more or less no effects for the established integration and inequality paradigm of migration studies.'

References

Achanfuo-Yeboah, D. (1993) 'Grounding a Theory of African Migration in Recent Data on Ghana', *International Sociology,* 8(2): 215–26.
Adepoju, A. (1986) 'Expulsion of Illegals from Nigeria: Round Two', *Migration World,* 14(5): 21–24.
Adogame, A. and Weißköppel, C. (eds) (2005) *Religion in the Context of African Migration,* Bayreuth: Thielman & Breitinger.
Adomako-Sarfoh, J. (1974) 'The Effects of the Expulsion of Migrant Workers on Ghana's Economy, with Particular Reference to Cocoa Industry', in S. Amin (ed.) *Modern Migration in Western Africa,* London: Oxford University Press.
Akyeampong, E. (2000) 'The Africans in the Diaspora', *African Affairs,* 99(395): 183–215.
Alba, R. and Nee, V. (2003) *Remaking the American Mainstream: Assimilation and Contemporary Immigration,* Cambridge (Mass.) and London: Harvard University Press.
Alderson, A. and Nielsen, F. (2002) 'Globalization and the Great U-Turn: Income Inequality Trends in 16 OECD Countries', *American Journal of Sociology,* 107: 1244–99.
Anderson, B. R. (1983) *Imagined Communities: Reflections on the Origin and Spread of Nationalism,* London: Verso.
Anthias, F. (1998) 'Evaluating "Diaspora": Beyond Ethnicity?', *Sociology,* 32: 557–80.
Appadurai, A. (1996) *Modernity at Large: Cultural Dimensions of Globalization,* Minneapolis: University of Minnesota Press.
———. (1998) "Globale ethnische Räume: Bemerkungen und Fragen zur Entwicklung einer transnationalen Anthropologie", in U. Beck (ed.) *Perspektiven der Weltgesellschaft,* Frankfurt am Main: Suhrkamp.
———. (1999) "Globalization and the Research Imagination", *International Social Science Journal,* 51(2): 229–38.
Appiah, J. J. (1985) "Die Musama Disco Church in London", *Zeitschrift für Mission,* 11(1): 35–38.
Arhin, K. (1979) "Introduction: The Brong", in K. Arhin (ed.) *Brong Kyempin. Essays on the Society, History and Politics of the Brong People,* Accra: Afram Publications.
———. (1983) 'Rank and Class among the Asante and Fante in the Nineteenth Century', *Africa,* 53(1): 2–22.
Arthur, J. A. (1991) 'International Labor Migration Patterns in West Africa', *African Studies Review,* 34(3): 65–87.
Asiedu, A. (2005) 'Some Benefits of Migrants' Return Visits to Ghana', *Population, Space and Place,* 11: 1–11.

References

Assal, M. (2004) *Sticky Labels or Rich Ambiguities: Diaspora and Challenges of Homemaking for Somalis and Sudanese in Norway*, Bergen: Bric.
Bade, K. (1994) *Ausländer, Aussiedler, Asyl: Eine Bestandsaufnahme*, München: Beck.
Bade, K. and Oltmer, J. (2004) *Normalfall Migration: Deutschland im 20. und frühen 21. Jahrhundert*, Bonn: Bundeszentrale für politische Bildung.
Baldassar, L., Baldock, C. V. and Wilding, R. (2007) *Families Caring Across Borders: Migration, Ageing and Transnational Caregiving*, Basingstoke: Palgrave MacMillan.
Balibar, E. (1990) 'Rassismus und Nationalismus', in E. Balibar and I. M. Wallerstein (eds) *Rasse, Klasse, Nation: Ambivalente Identitäten*, Hamburg: Argument Verlag.
Balibar, E. and Wallerstein, I. M. (eds) (1990) *Rasse, Klasse, Nation: Ambivalente Identitäten*, Hamburg: Argument Verlag.
Baraulina, T., Kreienbrink, A. and Riester, A. (2011) 'Potenziale der Migration Zwischen Afrika und Deutschland', Nürnberg: Bundesamt für Migration und Flushlinge.
Barot, R. and Bird, J. (2001) 'Racialization: The Genealogy and Critique of a Concept', *Ethnic and Racial Studies*, 24(4): 601–18.
Barthes, R. (1964 [1957]) *Mythen des Alltags*, Frankfurt am Main: Suhrkamp.
Basch, L., Glick Schiller, N. and Szanton Blanc, C. (1994) *Nations Unbound: Transnational Projects, Postcolonial Predicaments and Deterritorialized Nation-States*, Amsterdam: Gordon and Breach.
Bata, M. and Bergesen, A. J. (2002) 'Global Inequality: An Introduction', *Journal of World-Systems Research*, 8(1): 2–6.
Bauman, Z. (1990) 'Modernity and Ambivalence', *Theory, Culture and Society*, 7: 143–69.
Beck, U. (1986) *Risikogesellschaft: Auf dem Weg in eine andere Moderne*, Frankfurt am Main: Suhrkamp.
———. (2007) *Die Weltrisikogesellschaft: Auf der Suche nach der verlorenen Sicherheit*, Frankfurt am Main: Suhrkamp.
———. (2008) 'Risikogesellschaft und die Transnationalisierung sozialer Ungleichheiten', in P. A. Berger and K. Weiß, (eds) *Transnationalisierung sozialer Ungleichheit*, Wiesbaden: VS Verlag für Sozialwissenschaften.
Becken, H.-J. (1982) 'Die himmlische Kirche Christi: Eine Afrikanische Unabhängige Kirche in Mitteleuropa', *Zeitschrift für Mission*, 8(2): 98–103.
Benneh, G. (1988) 'The Land Tenure and Agrarian System in the New Cocoa Frontier of Ghana: Wassa Akropong Case Study', in W. Manshard and W. B. Morgan (eds) *Agricultural Expansion and Pioneer Settlements in the Humid Tropics*, Tokyo: United Nations University.
Berg, E. J. (1964) 'The Development of a Labour Force in Sub-Saharan Africa', *Economic Development and Cultural Change*, 13(4): 394–412.
———. (1965) 'The Economics of the Migrant Labor System', in H. Kuper (ed.) *Urbanization and Migration in West Africa*, Berkeley: University of California Press.
Black, R., King R. and Tiemoko, R. (2003) 'Migration, Return and Small Enterprises Development in Ghana? A Route out of Poverty?', Paper presented at International Workshop on Migration and Poverty in West Africa, Sussex, March 2003.
Bommes, M. (2003) 'Der Mythos des transnationalen Raumes: Oder: Worin besteht die Herausforderung des Transnationalismus für die Migrationsforschung?', in D. Thränhardt and U. Hunger (eds) *Migration im Spannungsfeld von Globalisierung und Nationalstaat*, Opladen: Westdeutscher Verlag.
Bornschier, V. and Trezzini, B. (1997) 'Social Stratification and Mobility in the World System: Different Approaches and Recent Research', *International Sociology*, 12(4): 429–55.

Bourdieu, P. (1979) *Distinction: A Social Critique of the Judgment of Taste*, Cambridge: Harvard University Press.
Brah, A. (1998) *Cartographies of Diaspora: Contesting Identities*, London: Routledge.
Braudel, F. (2002 [1979]) *Civilization and Capitalism*, Vols. I-III, London: Phoenix Press.
Brentjes, B. (1976) *Anton Wilhelm Amo: Der schwarze Philosoph in Halle*, Leipzig: Koehler & Amelang.
Bronschier, V. (2002) 'Changing Income Inequalities in the Second Half of the 20th Century: Preliminary Findings and Propositions for Explanations', *Journal of World System Research*, 8(1): 100–127.
Brubaker, R. (2005) 'The "Diaspora" Diaspora', *Ethnic and Racial Studies*, 28(1): 1–20.
Brubaker, R. and Cooper, F. (2000) 'Beyond Identity', *Theory and Society*, 29(1): 1–47.
Bryceson, D. and Vuorella, U. (eds) (2002) *The Transnational Family: New European Frontiers and Global Networks*, Oxford: Berg.
Brydon, L. (1985) 'Ghanaian Responses to the Nigerian Expulsions of 1983', *African Affairs*, 84(337): 561–86.
Bukow, W.-D. (1992) 'Ethnisierung und nationale Identität', in Institut für Migrations und Rassismusforschung (ed.) *Rassismus und Migration in Europa*, Hamburg: Argument Verlag.
Bukow, W.-D. and Llaryora, R. (1988) *Mitbürger aus der Fremde: Soziogenese ethnischer Gruppen*, Opladen: Westdeutscher Verlag.
Bump, M. (2006) 'Ghana: Searching for Opportunities at Home and Abroad', *Migration Information Source*, Washington, Migration Policy Institute, Online Available, HTTP: <http://www.migrationinformation.org/feature/display.cfm?ID=381> (accessed 17 March 2007).
Butler, J. (1999 [1990]) *Gender Troubles: Feminism and the Subversion of Identity*, New York: Routledge.
Çaglar, A. (2004) 'Mediascapes, Advertisement Industries and Cosmopolitan Transformations: German Turks in Germany', *New German Critique*, 92: 39–61.
Caldwell, J. C. (1967) 'Migration and Urbanization', in W. B. Birmingham, I. Neustadt and E. N. Omaboe (eds) *A Study of Contemporary Ghana: Some Aspects of Social Structure*, Vol. II, London: George Allen and Unwin.
———. (1969) *African Rural-Urban Migration: the Movement to Ghana's Towns*, New York: Columbia University Press.
Carter, D. M. (1995 [1992]) *Invisible Cities: Touba Turin, Senegalese Transnational Migrants in Northern Italy*, Minneapolis: University of Minnesota Press.
———. (1997) *States of Grace: Senegalese in Italy and the New European Immigration*, Minneapolis: University of Minnesota Press.
Castells, M. (1996) *The Rise of the Network Society*, Oxford: Blackwell.
Castles, S. and Miller, M. J. (2009) *The Age of Migration. International Population Movements in the Modern World*, 4th edition, Basingstoke: Palgrave Macmillan.
Census Office Accra. (1962) *Population Census of Ghana: Tribes in Ghana*, Special Report 'E', Accra.
Chazan, N. (1982) 'Ethnicity and Politics in Ghana', *Political Science Quarterly*, 97(3): 461–85.
Chicago Cultural Studies Group. (1992) 'Critical Multiculturalism', *Critical Inquiry*, 18(3): 530–55.
Clifford, J. (1994) 'Diasporas', *Cultural Anthropology*, 9(3): 302–38.
Cohen, R. (1996) 'Diasporas and the Nation-State: From Victims to Challengers', *International Affairs*, 72(3): 507–20.

References

———. (1997) *Global Diasporas: An Introduction*, Seattle: University of Washington Press.
Cohn-Bendit, D. and Schmid, T. (1992) *Heimat Babylon: Das Wagnis der multikulturellen Demokratie*, Hamburg: Hoffman und Campe.
Conrad, B. (2005) 'From Revolution to Religion? Politics of Religion in the Eritrean Diaspora', in A. Adogame and C. Weißköppel (eds) *Religion in the Context of African Migration*, Bayreuth: Eckhard Breitinger.
Cox, O. C. (1948) *Class, Caste and Race: A Study in Social Dynamics*, New York: Doubleday.
Crumbely, D. (2006) 'Review: Adogame, Afe and Cordula Weissköppel (eds). Religion in the Context of African Migration', *Journal of Religion in Africa*, 36(2): 230–35.
Cunningham, S. and Jacka, E. (1996) *Australian Television and International Mediascapes*, Cambridge: Cambridge University Press.
Dahrendorf, R. (1959) *Class and Class Conflict in Industrial Society*, Stanford: Stanford University Press.
Darkwa, A. and Kwabena, J. (2009) 'Pentecostal and Charismatic Churches in Ghana and the African Culture: Confrontation or Compromise', *Journal of Pentecostal Theology*, 18: 123–40.
Davis, K. and Moore, W. E. (1945) 'Some Principles of Stratification', *American Sociological Review*, 10(2): 242–49.
Decker, K. (2005) 'Fighting Poverty in Ghana: Central Government Strategies and Performance', *Nord-Süd aktuell*, 19(3/4): 296–305.
Dettmar, E. (1989) *Rassismus, Vorurteile, Kommunikation: Afrikanisch-Europäische Begegnungen in Hamburg*, Berlin: Reimer.
van Dijk, R. A. (1997) 'From Camp to Encompassment: Discourses of Transsubjectivity in the Ghanaian Pentecostal Diaspora', *Journal of Religion in Africa*, 27(2): 135–59.
Diko, J. and Tipple, A. G. (1992) 'Migrants Build at Home: Long Distance Housing Development by Ghanaians in London', *Cities* 9(4): 288–94.
Dormaa District Assembly. (2003) 'Medium-Term Development Plan (2002–2004)', Dormaa Ahenkro: District Planning Coordinating Unit, Dormaa District Assembly.
Drotbohm, H. (2009) 'Horizons of Long-distance Intimacies: Reciprocity, Contribution and Disjuncture in Cape Verde', *History of the Family*, 14: 132–49.
Dumett, R. E. (1981) 'Pressure Groups, Bureaucracy and the Decision-Making Process: Slavery Abolition and Colonial Expansion in the Gold Coast, 1874', *Journal of Imperial and Commonwealth History*, 9: 193–215.
———. (1998) *El Dorado in West Africa: The Gold-Mining Frontier, African Labor, and Colonial Capitalism in the Gold Coast, 1875–1900*, Athens: Ohio University Press.
Duncan, H. G. (1933) *Immigration and Assimilation*, Boston: Heath.
Durkheim, E. (2002 [1897]) *Suicide: A Study in Sociology*, London: Routledge.
Eades, J. S. (1987) 'Prelude to an Exodus: Chain Migration, Trade, and the Yoruba in Ghana', in J. S. Eades (ed.) *Migrants, Workers, and the Social Order*, New York: Tavistock.
Ekué, A. A. A. (1998) 'And How Can I Sing the Lord's Song in a Strange Land? A Reinterpretation of the Religious Experience of Women of the African Diaspora in Europe with Special Reference to Germany', in G. Ter Haar (ed.) *Strangers and Sojourners: Religious Communities in the Diaspora*, Leuven: Peters.
Elwert, G. (1984) 'Die Angst vor dem Ghetto: Binnenintegration als erster Schritt zur Integration', in A. Bayaz, M. Damolin and H. Ernst (eds) *Integration: Anpassung an die Deutschen?*, Weinheim: Beltz.

——. (2002) 'Unternehmerische Illegale: Ziele und Organisationen eines unterschätzen Typs illegaler Einwanderung', *IMIS-Beiträge*, 19: 7–20.
Englert, A. (1995) *Die Liebe kommt mit der Zeit: Interkulturelles Zusammenleben am Beispiel deutsch-ghanaischer Ehen in der BRD*, Münster: Lit.
Englund, H. and Leach, J. (2000) 'Ethnography and the Meta-Narratives of Modernity', *Current Anthropology*, 41(2): 225–48.
Epstein, A. L. (1967) 'Urbanization and Social Change in Africa', *Current Anthropology*, 8(4): 275–95.
Eschenhagen, W. (1990) 'Kakaoernte bei Adwoa Addae', in E. Schmidt-Kallert (ed.) *Zum Beispiel Kakao*, Göttingen: Lamuv Verlag.
Esman, M. J. (1977) *Ethnic Conflict in the Western World*, Ithaca: Cornell University Press.
——. (1986) 'Diasporas and International Relations', in G. Sheffer (ed.) *Modern Diasporas in International Politics*, New York: St. Martin's Press.
Esser, H. (1999) 'Inklusion, Integration und ethnische Schichtung', *Journal für Konflikt- und Gewaltforschung*, 1(1): 5–34.
——. (2001) 'Kulturelle Pluralisierung und strukturelle Assimilation: Das Problem der ethnischen Schichtung', *Swiss Political Science Review*, 7(2): 95–130.
Faist, T. (2000) 'Grenzen überschreiten: Das Konzept Transstaatliche Räume und seine Anwendungen', in T. Faist (ed.) *Grenzen überschreiten: Das Konzept Transstaatliche Räume und seine Anwendungen*, Bielefeld: Transcript.
Faist, T. and Reisenauer, E. (2009) 'Introduction: Migration and Developments: Transformations of Paradigms. Organisations, and Gender Orders', *Sociologus*, 59: 1–15.
Featherstone, M. (1990) 'Global Culture: an Introduction', in M. Featherstone (ed.) *Global Culture: Nationalism, Globalization and Modernity*, London: Sage.
——. (ed.) (1999) *Global Culture: Nationalism, Globalization and Modernity: a Theory*, London: Sage.
Ferguson, J. (1999) *Expectations of Modernity: Myths and Meanings of Urban Life on the Zambian Copperbelt*, Berkeley: University of California Press.
——. (2001) 'Global Disconnect: Abjection and the Aftermath of Modernism', in J. X. Inda and R. Rosaldo (eds) *The Anthropology of Globalization*, Malden: Blackwell.
Fitzgerald, D. (2009) *A Nation of Emigrants: How Mexico Manages its Migration*. Berkeley, University of California Press.
Fleischer, A. (2007) 'Family, Obligations, and Migration: the Role of Kinship in Cameroon', *Demographic Research*, 16: 413–40.
Foner, N. (1997) 'What's New About Transnationalism? New York Immigrants Today and at the Turn of the Century', *Diaspora*, 6: 355–76.
Fortes, M. (1936) 'Culture Contact as a Dynamic Process: An Investigation in the Northern Territories of the Gold Coast', *Africa*, 9(1): 24–55.
——. (1950) 'Kinship and Marriage among the Ashanti', in A. R. Radcliffe-Brown and D. Forde (eds) *African Systems of Kinship and Marriage*, London: Oxford University Press.
——. (1971) 'Some Aspects of Migration and Mobility in Ghana', *Journal of Asian and African Studies*, 6(1): 1–20.
Fortes, M. and Evans-Pritchard, E. E. (eds) (1940) *African Political Systems*, London: Oxford University Press.
Foster, P. (1965) *Education and Social Change in Ghana*, Chicago: University of Chicago Press.
——. (1980) 'Education and Social Inequality in Sub-Saharan Africa', *Journal of Modern African Studies*, 18(2): 201–36.
Foucault, M. (1983) 'The Subject and Power', in H. L. Dreyfus and P. Rabinow (eds) *Beyond Structuralism and Hermeneutics*, Chicago: University of Chicago Press.

Frank, A. G. (1967) *Capitalism and Underdevelopment in Latin America: Historical Studies of Chile and Brazil*, New York: Monthly Review Press.
Friedman, J. (2004) 'Globalization, Transnationalization, and Migration: Ideologies and Realities of Global Transformation', in J. Friedman and S. Randeria (eds) *Worlds on the Move: Globalization, Immigration, and Cultural Security*, London: I. B. Tauris.
Fuchs, M. and Berg, E. (1993) 'Phänomenologie der Differenz', in M. Fuchs and E. Berg (eds) *Die Krise der ethnographischen Repräsentation*, Frankfurt am Main: Suhrkamp.
Fuchs-Heinritz, W., Lautmann, R., Rammstedt, O. and Wienold, H. (eds) (1994) *Lexikon zur Soziologie*, Opladen: Westdeutscher Verlag.
Gabaccia, D. R. (1999) 'Is Everywhere Nowhere? Nomads, Nations, and the Immigrant Paradigm of United States History', *Journal of American History*, 86: 1115–34.
Gabriel, J. and Ben-Tovim, G. (1978) 'Marxism and the Concept of Racism', *Economy and Society*, 7(2): 118–54.
Galitzi, C. A. (1929) *A Study of Assimilation among Romanians in the United States*, New York: Columbia University.
Galtung, J. (1972 [1971]) 'Eine strukturelle Theorie des Imperialismus', in D. Senghaas (ed.) *Imperialismus und strukturelle Gewalt: Analysen über abhängige Reproduktion*, Frankfurt am Main: Suhrkamp.
Gans, H. J. (1979) 'Symbolic Ethnicity: Future of Ethnic Groups and Cultures in America', *Ethnic and Racial Studies*, 2(1): 1–20.
van der Geest, S. (1997) 'Money and Respect: The Changing Value of Old Age in Rural Ghana', *Africa*, 67(4): 534–59.
——. (1998) 'Yebisa Wo Fie: Growing Old and Building a House in the Akan Culture of Ghana', *Journal of Cross-Cultural Gerontology*, 13(4): 333–59.
——. (2000) 'Funerals for the Living: Conversations with Elderly People in Kwahu, Ghana', *African Studies Review*, 43(3): 103–29.
Gerloff, R. (1999) 'Pentecostals in the African Diaspora', in A. H. Anderson and W. J. Hollenweger (eds) *Pentecostals After a Century: Global Perspectives on a Movement in Transition*, Sheffield: Sheffield Academic Press.
Gerold-Scheepers, T. J. and van Binsbergen, W. M. (1978) 'Marxist and Non-Marxist Approaches to Migration in Tropical Africa', in W. M. van Binsbergen and H. A. Meilink (eds) *Migration and the Transformation of Modern African Society. African Perspectives*, Leiden: Afrika-Studiecentrum.
Geschwender, J. A. (1967) 'Continuities in Theories of Status Consistency and Cognitive Dissonance', *Social Forces*, 46(2): 160–71.
Gifford, P. (2004) *Ghana's New Christianity: Pentecostalism in a Globalizing African Economy*, Bloomington: Indiana University Press.
Gilroy, P. (1993) *The Black Atlantic: Modernity and Double Consciousness*, Cambridge (Mass.): Harvard University Press.
——. (1994) 'Diaspora', *Paragraph*, 17(3): 209–12.
——. (1996) 'British Cultural Studies and the Pitfalls of Identity', in H. A. Baker, M. Diawara and R. H. Lindeborg (eds) *Black British Cultural Studies: A Reader*, Chicago: University of Chicago Press.
——. (1997) 'Diaspora and the Detours of Identity', in K. Woodward (ed.) *Identity and Difference*, Thousand Oaks: Sage.
Glazer, N. and Moynihan, D. P. (1963) *Beyond the Melting Pot: The Negroes, Puerto Ricans, Jews and Irish of New York*, Oxford: MIT Press.
Glick Schiller, N. (2003) 'The Centrality of Ethnography in the Study of Transnational Migration: Seeing the Wetlands Instead of the Swamp', in N. Foner (ed.) *American Arrivals: Anthropology Engages the New Immigration*, Oxford: James Currey.

——. (2004) 'Transnationality', in D. Nugent and J. Vincent (eds) *A Companion to the Anthropology of Politics*, Malden: Blackwell.
Glick Schiller, N., Basch, L. and Szanton Blanc, C. (eds) (1992) *Towards a Transnational Perspective on Migration: Race, Class, Ethnicity, and Nationalism Reconsidered*, New York: New York Academy of Sciences.
——. (1995) 'From Immigrant to Transmigrant: Theorising Transnational Migration', *Anthropological Quarterly*, 68(1): 48–63.
Glick Schiller, N. and Fouron, G. E. (1999) 'Terrains of Blood and Nation: Haitian Transnational Social Fields', *Ethnic and Racial Studies*, 22(2): 340–66.
——. (2001a) *Georges Woke Up Laughing: Long-Distance Nationalism and the Search For Home*, Durham: Duke University Press.
——. († 2001b) '"I Am Not a Problem without a Solution", Poverty and Transnational Migration', in J. Goode and J. Maskovsky (eds) *The New Poverty Studies: The Ethnography of Power, Politics and Impoverished People in the United States*, New York: New York University Press.
Glick Schiller, N., Nieswand, B., Schlee, G., Darieva, T., Yalcin-Heckmann, L., and Fosztó, L. (2005) 'Pathways of Migrant Incorporation in Germany', *Transit*, (1)1, Online Available, HTTP: <http://repositories.cdlib.org/ucbgerman/transit/vol1/iss1/art50911> [accessed 10 August 2010].
Gluckman, M. (1961) 'Anthropological Problems Arising from the African Industrial Revolution', in A. Southall (ed.) *Social Change in Modern Africa*, New York: Oxford University Press.
——. (1966) *Custom and Conflict in Africa*, Oxford: Blackwell.
Goffman, E. (1986 [1963]) *Stigma: Notes on the Management of Spoiled Identity*, New York: Simon & Schuster.
——. (1990 [1959]) *The Presentation of Self in Everyday Life*, London: Penguin.
Goldring, L. (1996) 'Blurring Borders: Constructing Transnational Community in the Process of Mexico–U.S. Migration', *Research in Community Sociology*, 6: 69–104.
——. (1998) 'The Power of Status in Transnational Social Fields', in M. P. Smith and L. E. Guarnizo (eds) *Transnationalism From Below*, New Brunswick: Transaction Publishers.
Goldthorpe, J. (2002) 'Globalisation and Social Class', *West European Politics*, 25: 1–28.
Goody, J. (2003) '"Kalabule" and the Death of African Socialism', in F. Kröger and B. Meier (eds) *Ghana's North: Research on Culture, Religion, and Politics of Societies in Transition*, Frankfurt am Main: Peter Lang.
Gordon, M. M. (1964) *Assimilation in American Life: The Role of Race, Religion and National Origins*, New York: Oxford University Press.
——. (1975) 'Toward a General Theory of Racial and Ethnic Group Relations', in N. Glazer and D. P. Moynihan (eds) *Ethnicity: Theory and Experience*, Cambridge (Mass.): Harvard University Press.
Gould, W. T. (1985) 'International Migration of Skilled Labour within Africa: A Bibliographical Review', *International Migration*, 23(1): 5–27.
Greenstreet, M. (1972) 'Labour Conditions in the Gold Coast During the 1930s, With Particular Reference to Migrant Labour and the Mines', *Economic Bulletin of Ghana*, 2: 32–46.
Gregory, J. W. and Piché, V. (1978) 'African Migration and Peripheral Capitalism', in W. M. van Binsbergen and H. A. Meilink (eds) *Migration and the Transformation of Modern African Society: African Perspectives*, Leiden: Afrika-Studiecentrum.
Grillo, R. (2008) *The Family in Question: Immigrant and Ethnic Minorities in Multicultural Europe*, Amsterdam: Amsterdam University Press.

Grillo, R. and Mazzucato, V. (2008) 'Africa <> Europe: A Double Engagement', *Journal of Ethnic and Migration Studies*, 34: 175–98.
Grillo, R. and Riccio, B. (2004) 'Translocal Development: Italy–Senegal', *Population, Space and Place*, 10(2): 99–111.
Guarnizo, L. E. (2003) 'The Economics of Transnational Living', *International Migration Review*, 37(3): 666–99.
Guarnizo, L. E. and Smith, M. P. (1998a) 'The Locations of Transnationalism', in L. E. Guarnizo and M. P. Smith (eds) *Transnationalism From Below*, New Brunswick: Transactions Publishers.
——. (eds) (1998b) *Transnationalism From Below*, New Brunswick: Transactions Publishers.
Gupta, Sanjeev, Pattillo, Catherine A. and Wagh, Smita (2009) 'Effect of Remittances on Poverty and Financial Development in Sub-Saharan Africa', *World Development*, 37(1): 104–15.
Habermas, J. (1996) *Die Einbeziehung der Anderen: Studien zur politischen Theorie*, Frankfurt am Main: Suhrkamp.
Haferkamp, R. (1989) *Afrikaner in der Fremde: Lehrjahre zwischen Wunsch und Wirklichkeit*, München: Trickster.
Hahn, A. (1997) '"Partizipative" Identitäten', in H. Münkler (ed.) *Furcht und Faszination: Facetten der Fremdheit*, Berlin: Akademie Verlag.
Hahn, H. P. (2004) 'Zirkuläre Arbeitsmigration in Westafrika und die "Kultur" der Migration', *Africa Spectrum*, 39(3): 381–404.
Hall, S. (1990) 'Cultural Identity and Diaspora', in J. Rutherford (ed.) *Identity: Community, Culture, Difference*, London: Lawrence and Wishart.
——. (1996 [1980]) 'Race, Articulation and Societies Structured in Dominance', in H. A. Baker, M. Diawara and R. H. Lindeberg (eds) *Black British Cultural Studies Reader*, Chicago: University of Chicago Press.
Hankel, W. (2001) 'Entwicklung braucht Regeln: Ein monetäres Völkerrecht', in R. E. Thiel (ed.) *Neue Ansätze zur Entwicklungstheorie*, Bonn: Informationszentrum Entwicklungspolitik.
Hannerz, U. (1974) 'Ethnicity and Opportunity in Urban America', in A. Cohen (ed.) *Urban Ethnicity*, London: Tavistock.
——. (1996) *Transnational Connections: Culture, People, Places*, London: Routledge.
Hart, K. (1971) 'Migration and Tribal Identity among the Frafras of Ghana', *Journal of Asian and African Studies*, 6(1): 21–36.
——. (1987) 'Rural Urban Migration in West Africa', in J. S. Eades (ed.) *Migrants, Workers, and the Social Order*, London: Tavistock.
Harvey, D. (1989) *The Condition of Postmodernity: An Enquiry Into the Origins of Cultural Change*, Oxford: Blackwell.
Häußermann, H. (2001) 'Marginalisierung als Folge sozialräumlichen Wandels in der Großstadt', in F. Gesemann (ed.) *Migration und Integration in Berlin: Wissenschaftliche Analysen und politische Perspektiven*, Opladen: Leske & Budrich.
Heckmann, F. (2005) 'Integration or Assimilation', in H.-J. Aretz and C. Lahusen (eds) *Die Ordnung der Gesellschaft: Festschrift zum 60. Geburtstag von Richard Münch*, Frankfurt am Main: Peter Lang.
Hegel, G. W. F. (2006 [1807]) *Phänomenologie des Geistes*, Teddington: Echo Library.
Heidenreich, M. (2003) 'Regional Inequalities in the Enlarged Europe', *Journal of European Social Policy*, 13(4): 313–33.
Heinz, B., Münch, R. and Tyrell, H. (eds) (2005) *Weltgesellschaft: Theoretische Zugänge und empirische Problemlagen*, Stuttgart: Lucius & Lucius.
Herberg, W. (1956) *Protestant, Catholic, Jew: An Essay in American Religious Sociology*, Garden City: Anchor Books.

Hill, P. (1963) *The Migrant Cocoa-Farmers of Southern Ghana: A Study in Rural Capitalism*, Cambridge: Cambridge University Press.

——. (1970) *Studies in Rural Capitalism in West Africa*, Cambridge: Cambridge University Press.

Hitti, P. K. (1924) *The Syrians in America*, New York: Doran.

Hoffmann-Nowotny, H.-J. (1973) *Soziologie des Fremdarbeiterproblems: Eine theoretische und empirische Analyse am Beispiel der Schweiz*, Stuttgart: Enke.

Hofmann, E. (1994) *Moderne Migrationsstrukturen in Kumasi/Ghana: Eine empirische Studie über den Zusammenhang zwischen Wanderungsverhalten und Zugang zu städtischen Ressourcen*, Düsseldorf: Geographisches Institut, Heinrich-Heine-Universität.

Hopkins, A. G. (1973) *An Economic History of West Africa*, London: Longman.

Hornung, C. A. (1977) 'Social Status, Status Inconsistency and Psychological Stress', *American Sociological Review*, 42(4): 623–38.

House, J. S. (1975) 'Why and When Is Status Inconsistency Stressful?', *American Journal of Sociology*, 81(2): 395–412.

Hunger, Uwe (2000) '"Vom Brain-Drain" zum "Brain Gain". Migration, Netzwerkbildung und sozio-ökonomische Entwicklung. Das Beispiel der indischen "Software-Migranten"', *IMIS-Beiträge*, 16: 7–21.

IMF (International Monetary Fund). (2005) 'Ghana: 2005 Article IV Consultation. Third Review Under the Poverty Reduction and Growth Facility, and Request for Waiver of Nonobservance of Performance Criteria and Extension of the Arrangement', *IMF Country Report*, 5/292, Washington: International Monetary Fund.

ISSER (Institute of Statistical Social and Economic Research). (2003) *The State of the Ghanaian Economy in 2002*, Accra: ISSER, University of Ghana.

Jach, R. (2005) *Migration, Religion und Raum: Ghanaische Kirchen in Accra, Kumasi und Hamburg in Prozessen von Kontinuität und Kulturwandel*, Münster: Lit Verlag.

Jackson, E. F. (1962) 'Status Consistency and Symptoms of Stress', *American Sociological Review*, 27(4): 469–80.

Jenkins, R. (1985) 'Gold Coasters Overseas, 1880–1919: With Specific Reference to Their Activities in Britain', *Immigrants and Minorities*, 4(3): 5–52.

Kabki, M., Mazzucato, V. and Appiah, E. (2004) 'Wo benane a eye bebree: The Economic Impact of Remittances of Netherlands-based Ghanaian Migrants on Rural Ashanti', *Population, Space and Place*, 10: 85–97.

Kant, I. (2000 [1784]) 'What is Enlightenment', in B. Gupta and J. N. Mohanty (eds) *Philosophical Questions: East and West*, Oxford: Rowman and Littlefield.

Kastner, K. (2010) 'Moving Relationships: Family Ties of Nigerian Migrants on Their Way to Europe', *African and Black Diaspora*, 3: 17–34.

Kearney, M. (1995) 'The Local and the Global: The Anthropology of Globalization and Transnationalism', *Annual Review of Anthropology*, 24(1): 547–65.

Kennedy, R. J. (1944) 'Single or Triple Melting Pot? Intermarriage Trends in New Haven, 1870–1940', *American Journal of Sociology*, 49(4): 331–39.

——. (1952) 'Single or Triple Melting Pot? Intermarriage Trends in New Haven, 1870–1950', *American Journal of Sociology*, 58(1): 56–59.

Khagram, S. and Levitt, P. (2008) 'Constructing Transnational Studies', in L. Pries (ed.) *Rethinking Transnationalism: The Meso-Link of Organisations*, London: Routledge.

Killick, T. (1978) *Development Economics in Action: A Study of Economic Policies in Ghana*, London: Heinemann.

Kleist, N. (2008) 'In the Name of Diaspora; Between Struggles for Recognition and Political Aspirations', *Journal of Ethnic and Migration Studies*, 34: 1127–43.

Knibbe, K. (2009) 'We Did Not Come Here as Tenants, but as Landlords: Nigerian Pentecostals and the Power of Maps', *African Diaspora*, 2: 133–58.
Konadu-Agyemang, K. (1999) 'Travel Patterns and Coping Strategies of Ghanaian Immigrants in Toronto', *Ghana Studies*, 2: 13–34.
Koning, D. (2009) 'Place, Space, and Authority: The Mission and Reversed Mission of the Ghanaian Seventh-day Adventist Church in Amsterdam', *African Diaspora*, 2: 203–26.
Korboe, D. and Tipple, A. G. (1995) 'City Profile: Kumasi', *Cities*, 12(4): 267–74.
Koser, K. (2003) *New African Diasporas*, London: Routledge.
Krappmann, L. (1969) *Soziologische Dimensionen der Identität*, Stuttgart: Klett-Cotta.
Kreckel, R. (1982) 'Class, Status and Power? Begriffliche Grundlagen für eine politische Soziologie der sozialen Ungleichheit', *Kölner Zeitschrift für Soziologie und Sozialpsychologie*, 34: 617–48.
———. (1985) 'Statusinkonsistenz und Statusdefizienz in gesellschaftstheoretischer Perspektive', in S. Hradil (ed.) *Sozialstruktur im Umbruch: Karl Martin Bolte zum 60. Geburtstag*, Opladen: Leske & Budrich.
———. (1992) *Politische Soziologie der sozialen Ungleichheit*, Frankfurt am Main: Campus-Verlag.
———. (2008) 'Soziologie der sozialen Ungleichheit im globalen Kontext', in B. Michael, G. Mordt, S. Terpe and M. Winter (eds) *Transnationale Ungleichheitsforschung: Eine neue Herausforderung für die Soziologie*, Frankfurt am Main: Campus-Verlag.
Kymlicka, W. (2003 [1995]) *Multicultural Citizenship: A Liberal Theory of Minority Rights*, Oxford: Clarendon Press.
Laschet, A. (2009) *Die Aufsteiger Republik: Zuwanderung als Chance*, Köln: Kiepenheuer & Witsch.
Lenski, G. E. (1954) 'Status Crystallization: A Non-Vertical Dimension of Social Status', *American Sociological Review*, 19(4): 405–13.
Lentz, C. (2003) 'Afrikaner in Frankfurt: Migration, Netzwerke, Identitätspolitik. Ergebnisse einer Lehrforschung', *Sociologus*, 53: 43–80.
Lentz, C. and Erlmann, V. (1989) 'A Working Class in Formation? Economic Crises and Strategies of Survival Among Dagara Mine Workers in Ghana', *Cahiers d'Études Africaines*, 29(113): 69–111.
Levitt, P. (2001) *The Transnational Villagers*, Berkeley: University of California Press.
Levitt, P. and Glick Schiller, N. (2004) 'Conceptualizing Simultaneity: A Transnational Social Field Perspective on Society', *International Migration Review*, 38(3): 1002–39.
Levitt, P. and Jaworsky, N. (2007) 'Transnational Migration Studies: Past Developments and Future Trends', *Annual Review of Sociology*, 33: 129–56.
Lewis, W. A. (1953) *Report on Industrialisation and the Gold Coast*, Accra: Government Printing Department.
Little, K. (1973) 'Urbanization and Regional Association', in A. Southall (ed.) *Urban Anthropology: Cross-Cultural Studies of Urbanization*, New York: Oxford University Press.
Loeffelholz von Collberg, D. (1987) 'Migranten aus Ghana in der Bundesrepublik', Diplomarbeit. Fachbereich Philosophie und Sozialwissenschaften, Berlin: Freie Universität Berlin.
Ludwig, F. (2005) 'The Proliferation of Cherubim & Seraphim Congregations in Great Britain', in A. Adogame and C. Weißköppel (eds) *Religion in the Context of African Migration*, Bayreuth: Breitinger.
Luhmann, N. (1987 [1984]) *Soziale Systeme: Grundriß einer allgemeinen Theorie*, Frankfurt am Main: Suhrkamp.

——. (1993) 'Die Paradoxie des Entscheidens', *Zeitschrift für Verwaltungsrecht und Verwaltungspolitik*, 84(3): 287–310.
——. (1998) *Die Gesellschaft der Gesellschaft*, Frankfurt am Main: Suhrkamp.
——. (2005 [1971]) 'Die Weltgesellschaft', in N. Luhmann (ed.) *Soziologische Aufklärung: Aufsätze zur Theorie der Gesellschaft*, Opladen: Westdeutscher Verlag.
MacGaffey, J. and Bazenguissa-Ganga, R. (2000) *Congo–Paris: Transnational Traders on the Margins of the Law*, Bloomington: Indiana University Press.
Manchuelle, F. (1997) *Willing Migrants: Soninke Labour Diasporas*, Athens: University of Ohio Press.
Marcus, G. E. (1995) 'Ethnography in/of the World System: The Emergence of Multi-Sited Ethnography', *Annual Review of Anthropology*, 24: 95–117.
Martin, J. (2005) *'Been-To', 'Burger', 'Transmigranten': Zur Bildungsmigration von Ghanaern und ihrer Rückkehr aus der Bundesrepublik Deutschland*, Münster: Lit.
Mazzucato, V. (2006) 'Migrant Transnationalism: Two-way Flows, Changing Institutions and Community Development Between Ghana and the Netherlands', *Economic Sociology. The European Electronic Newsletter*, 7: 8–16.
——. (2007) 'The Role of Transnational Networks and Legal Status in Securing a Living: Ghanaian Migrants in the Netherlands', *ESRC Centre on Migration, Policy and Society Working Paper*, 7/43, Oxford: University of Oxford.
Mazzucato, V., van den Boom, B. and Nsowah-Nuamah, N. N. N. (2008) 'Remittances in Ghana: Origin, Destination and Issues of Measurement', *International Migration*, 46: 103–22.
Mazzucato, V., Kabki, M. and Smith, L. (2006) 'Transnational Migration and the Economy of Funerals: Changing Practices in Ghana', *Development and Change*, 37(5): 1047–72.
McCaskie, T. C. (1983) 'Accumulation, Wealth and Belief in Asante History (I): To the Close of the Nineteenth Century', *Africa*, 53(1): 23–43.
Meulemann, H. (1985) 'Statusinkonsistenz und Sozialbiographie: Eine Forschungsperspektive für die Analyse der Mehrdimensionalität moderner Sozialstrukturen', *Kölner Zeitschrift für Soziologie und Sozialpsychologie*, 37(3): 461–77.
Meyer, B. (1998) '"Make a complete break with the past": Memory and Post-Colonial Modernity in Ghanaian Pentecostalist Discourse', *Journal of Religion in Africa*, 27(3): 316–49.
Meyer, J. W. (1980) 'Background: A Perspective on the Curriculum and Curricular Research', in J. W. Meyer, D. H. Kamens and A. Benavot (eds.) *School Knowledge for the Masses: World Models and Primary Curricular Categories in the Twentieth Century*, London: Falmer Press.
Meyer, J. W., Boli, J., Thomas, G. M. and Ramirez, F. O. (1997) 'World Society and the Nation-State', *American Journal of Sociology*, 103(1): 144–81.
Meyer, J. W. and Kamens, D. H. (1992) 'Conclusion: Accounting for a World Curriculum', in J. W. Meyer, D. H. Kamens and A. Benavot (eds) *School Knowledge for the Masses: World Models and Primary Curricular Categories in the Twentieth Century*, London: Falmer Press.
Meyer, J. W., Kamens, D. H. and Benavot, A. (eds) (1992) *School Knowledge for the Masses: World Models and Primary Curricular Categories in the Twentieth Century*, London: Falmer Press.
Miescher, S. F. and Ashbaugh, L. (1999) 'Been-To Visions: Transnational Linkages among a Ghanaian Dispersed Community in the Twentieth Century', *Ghana Studies*, 2: 57–76.
Miles, R. (1993a) 'The Articulation of Racism and Nationalism: Reflections on European History', in J. Wrench and J. Solomos (eds) *Racism and Migration in Western Europe*, Oxford: Berg.

———. (1993b) *Racism after 'Race Relations'*, London: Routledge.

———. (1998) 'Rassismus und Nationalismus in Großbritannien und Nordirland: Ein Blick aus der Peripherie', in C. Flatz, M. Kröll and S. Riedmann (eds) *Rassismus im virtuellen Raum*, Hamburg: Argument Verlag.

Mitchell, J. C. (1959) 'Labour Migration in Africa South of the Sahara: The Causes of Labour Migration', *Bulletin Inter-African Labour Institute*, 6(1): 12–46.

———. (1959 [1956]) 'The Kalela Dance: Aspects of Social Relationships among Urban Africans in Northern Rhodesia', *The Rhodes-Livingstone Papers*, 27, Manchester: Manchester University Press.

———. (1961) 'Wage Labour and African Population Movements in Central Africa', in K. M. Barbour and R. M. Prothero (eds) *Essays on African Population*, London: Routledge and Kegan Paul.

———. (1969) 'Structural Plurality, Urbanisation and Labour Circulation in Southern Rhodesia', in J. A. Jackson (ed.) *Migration*, Cambridge: Cambridge University Press.

Mohan, G. (2006) 'Embedded Cosmopolitanism and the Politics of Obligation: The Ghanaian Diaspora and Development', *Environment and Planning A*, 38: 867–83.

Mohan, G. and Zack-Williams, A. B. (2002) 'Globalisation From Below: Conceptualising the Role of the African Diasporas in Africa's Development', *Review of African Political Economy* 29(92): 211–36.

Morawska, E. (2001) 'Immigrants, Transnationalism, and Ethnicization: A Comparison of this Great Wave and the Last', in G. Gerstle and J. Mollenkopf (eds) *E Pluribus Unum? Contemporary and Historical Perspectives on Immigrant Political Incorporation*, New York: Sage.

Müller-Mahn, D. (2005) 'Transnational Spaces and Migrant Networks: A Case Study of Egyptians in Paris', *Nord-Süd aktuell*, 19(1): 29–33.

Munzele Maimbo, S. and Ratha, D. (2005) *Remittances: Development Impact and Future Prospects*. Washington: The World Bank.

Newell, S. (2005) 'Migratory Modernity and the Cosmology of Consumption in Côte d'Ivoire', in L. Trager (ed.) *Migration and Economy: Global and Local Dynamics*, Walnut Creek: AltaMira Press.

Nieswand, B. (2008a) 'Wege aus dem Dilemma zwischen Transnationalismus und Integrationsansatz: Simultane Inklusion von migranten-initiierten charismatischen Gemeinden in Berlin', in A. Lauser and C. Weißköppel (eds) *Migration und religiöse Dynamik: Ethnologische Religionsforschung im transnationalen Kontext*, Bielefeld: Transcript.

———. (2008b) Ghanain Migrants in Germany and the Social Construct of a Diaspora, *African Diaspora*, 1:28:52.

———. (2009) 'Development and Diaspora: Ghana and its Migrants', *Sociologus*, 59: 17–31.

———. (2011) 'Der Migrations-Entwicklungs-Nexus in Afrika: Diskurswandel und Diasporaformation' in A. Riester and T. Baraulina (eds) *Potenziale der Migration zwischen afrikanischen Ländern und Deutschland*, Nürnberg: Bundesamt für Migration und Flüchtlinge.

———. (2010a) 'Enacted Destiny: West African Charismatic Christians in Berlin and the Immanence of God', *Journal of Religion in Africa*, 40: 1–27.

———. (2010b) 'Nationalist Rituals and Diaspora: Ghana@50 in Berlin', *MPI MMG Working Paper*, 10–09, Göttingen: Max Planck Institute for the Study of Religious and Ethnic Diversity.

Nieswand, B. and Vogel, U. (2000) 'Dimensionen der Fremdheit: Eine empirische Analyse anhand qualitativer Interviews mit Angehörigen einer Migrantengruppen', *Soziale Probleme*, 11(1/2): 140–76.

Nkrumah, K. (1961) *I Speak of Freedom: A Statement of African Ideology*, New York: Praeger.

Nuscheler, F. (1995) *Internationale Migration: Flucht und Asyl*, Opladen: Leske & Budrich.
Nyamnjoh, F. B. (2005) 'Images of Nyongo amongst Bamenda Grassfielders in Whiteman Kontri', *Citizenship Studies*, 9(3): 241–69.
Okin, S., Cohen, J., Howard, M. and Nussbaum, M. C. (1999) *Is Multiculturalism Bad for Women?*, Princeton: Princeton University Press.
Okwuasa, A. O. 1975. *Consequences of the Cash-Crop Economy for the Family Structure of Selected Societies of West Africa*, Freiburg: Johannes Krause.
Omenyo, C. N. (2002) *Pentecost Outside Pentecostalism: A Study of the Development of Charismatic Renewal in the Mainline Churches in Ghana*, Zoetermeer: Boekencentrum.
Overseas Development Institute. (1996) 'Adjustment in Africa: Lessons from Ghana', *Overseas Development Institute. Briefing Papers*, Online Available, HTTP: <http://www.odi.org.uk/publications/briefing/3_96.html> (accessed 12 October 2003).
Owusu, T. Y. (2003) 'Transnationalism among African Immigrants in North America: The Case of Ghanaians in Canada', *Journal of International Migration and Integration*, 4(3): 395–415.
Park, R. E. (1950) (ed.) *Race and Culture: The Collected Papers of Robert Ezra Park*, Vol. 1, Glencoe: Free Press.
——. (1950 [1926]) 'Our Racial Frontier on the Pacific', in R. E. Park (ed.) *Race and Culture: The Collected Papers of Robert Ezra Park, Vol. 1*, Glencoe: Free Press.
——. (1950 [1937]) 'The Race Relations Cycle in Hawaii', in R. E. Park (ed.) *Race and Culture: The Collected Papers of Robert Ezra Park, Vol. 1*, Glencoe: Free Press.
Park, R. E. and Burgess, E. W. (1969 [1921]) *Introduction to the Science of Sociology: Including the Original Index of Basic Sociological Concepts*, Chicago: University of Chicago Press.
Parkin, F. (1971) *Class Inequality and Political Order: Social Stratification in Capitalist and Communist Societies*, London: MacGibbon & Kee.
Parsons, T. (1954 [1940]) 'An Analytical Approach to the Theory of Social Stratification', in T. Parsons (ed.) *Essays in Sociological Theory*, Glencoe: Free Press.
——. (1966) 'Full Citizenship for the Negro American? A Sociological Problem', in T. Parsons and K. B. Clark (eds) *The Negro American*, Boston: Houghton Mifflin.
Parsons, T. and Shils, E. (2001 [1951]) *Toward a General Theory of Action*, New Brunswick: Transactions Publishers.
Pasura, D. (2008) 'Gendering the Diaspora: Zimbabwean Migrants in Britain', *African Diaspora*, 1: 86–109.
Peil, M. (1971) 'The Expulsion of West African Aliens', *Journal of Modern African Studies*, 9(2): 205–29.
——. (1974) 'Ghana's Aliens', *International Migration Review*, 8(3): 367–81.
——. (1995) 'Ghanaians Abroad', *African Affairs*, 94(376): 345–67.
Phillips, A. (2007) *Multiculturalism without Culture*, Princeton: Princeton University Press.
Plange, N. K. (1979) '"Opportunity Cost" and Labour Migration: a Misinterpretation of Proletarianisation in Northern Ghana', *Journal of Modern African Studies*, 17(4): 655–76.
Portes, A., Fernández-Kelly, P. and Haller, W. (2005) 'Segmented Assimilation on the Ground: The New Second Generation in Early Adulthood', *Ethnic and Racial Studies*, 28(6): 1000–1040.
Portes, A., Guarnizo, L. E. and Haller, W. (2002) 'Transnational Entrepreneurs: An Alternative Form of Immigrant Economic Adaptation', *American Sociological Review*, 67(2): 278–98.

Portes, A. and Manning, R. (1986) 'The Immigrant Enclave: Theory and Empirical Examples', in S. Olzak and J. Nagel (eds) *Competitive Ethnic Relations*, Orlando: Academic Press.

Portes, A. and Rumbaut, R. G. (2006) *Immigrant America. A Portrait*, 3rd edition, Berkeley: University of California Press.

Portes, A. and Zhou, M. (1993) 'The New Second Generation: Segmented Assimilation and its Variants Among Post-1965 Immigrant Youth', *Annals of the American Academy of Political and Social Science*, 530: 74–96.

Pries, L. (1996) 'Transnationale soziale Räume: Theoretisch-empirische Skizze am Beispiel der Arbeitswanderungen Mexiko–USA', *Zeitschrift für Soziologie*, 25(6): 456–72.

———. (1997) *Transnationale Migration*, Baden-Baden: Nomos.

———. (1998) 'Transnationale soziale Räume', in U. Beck (ed.) *Perspektiven der Weltgesellschaft*, Frankfurt am Main: Suhrkamp.

———. (2001) 'The Approach of Transnational Spaces: Responding to New Configurations of the Social and the Spatial', in L. Pries (ed.) *New Transnational Social Space: International Migration and Transnational Companies in the Early Twenty-First Century*, London: Routledge.

———. (2005) 'Transnational Migration as a Chance for Spanning the North–South-Gap', *Nord-Süd aktuell*, 19(1): 5–18.

———. (2008) *Rethinking Transnationalism: The Meso-Link of Organisations*, London: Routledge.

Rado, E. (1986) 'Notes Towards a Political Economy of Ghana Today', *African Affairs*, 85(341): 563–72.

Ratha, D. (2003) 'Workers' Remittances: An Important and Stable Source of External Development Finance', in T. W. Bank (ed.) *Global Development Finance 2003*, Washington: The World Bank.

Rawls, J. (1987) 'The Idea of an Overlapping Consensus', *Oxford Journal of Legal Studies*, 7: 1–25.

Rex, J. (1961) *Key Problems of Sociological Theory*, London: Routledge & Kegan Paul.

———. (1970) *Race Relations in Sociological Theory*, London: Weidenfeld & Nicolson.

Rex, J. and Mason, D. (eds) (1994 [1986]) *Theories of Race and Ethnic Relations*, Cambridge: Cambridge University Press.

Rhoda, R. (1980) 'Migration and Employment of Educated Youth in Ghana', *International Migration Review*, 14(1): 53–76.

Riccio, B. (2001) 'From "Ethnic Group" to "Transnational Community"? Senegalese Migrants' Ambivalent Experiences and Multiple Trajectories', *Journal of Ethnic and Migration Studies*, 27(4): 583–99.

———. (2008) 'West African Transnationalisms Compared: Ghanaians and Senegalese in Italy', *Journal of Ethnic and Migration Studies*, 34: 217–34.

Rimmer, D. (1992) *Staying Poor: Ghana's Political Economy, 1950–1990*, Oxford: Pergamon Press for the World Bank.

Robertson, C. (1983) 'The Death of Makola and Other Tragedies', *Canadian Journal of African Studies*, 17(3): 469–95.

Robertson, R. (1990) 'Mapping the Global: Globalization as the Central Concept', in M. Featherstone (ed.) *Global Culture: Nationalism, Globalization and Modernity: A Theory*, London: Sage.

———. (1992) *Globalization: Social Theory and Global Culture*, London: Sage.

Rocksloh-Papendieck, B. (1990) *Afrikaner in Berlin: Untersuchung zur Ausbildungs-, Arbeits- Lebenssituation von Ghanaern sowie zu ihren Zukunftsplänen*, Berlin: Friedrich-Ebert-Stiftung.

Roos, C. (1996) '"No Visa". Remigration aus Deutschland: Migrationsprozesse von ehemaligen Asylbewerbern und irregulären MigrantInnen aus Ghana', in G.

Zdunnek (ed.) *Modell Ghana? Arbeiten aus dem Lehrforschungsprojekt Ghana 1994*, Arbeitspapiere Wirtschaft, Gesellschaft und Politik in Entwicklungsländern, Berlin: Schwerpunkt Entwicklungssoziologie, Institut für Soziologie der freien Universität Berlin.

Rottenburg, R. (2001) 'Marginalität und der Blick aus der Ferne', in H. Behrend (ed.) *Geist, Bild und Narr: Zu einer Ethnologie kultureller Konversion*, Berlin: Philo.

Rouch, J. (1956) *Migrations au Ghana (Gold Coast): Enquête 1953–1955*, Paris: Société des Africanistes Musée de l'Homme.

Rouse, R. (1991) 'Mexican Migration and the Social Space of Postmodernism', *Diaspora*, 1(1): 8–23.

——. (1992) 'Making Sense of Settlement: Class Transformation, Class Struggle, and Transnationalism among Mexican Migrants in the United States', in N. Glick Schiller, L. Basch and C. Szanton Blanc (eds) *Towards a Transnational Perspective on Migration: Race, Class, Ethnicity, and Nationalism Reconsidered*, New York: New York Academy of Sciences.

Safran, W. (1991) 'Diasporas in Modern Societies: Myth of Homeland and Return', *Diaspora*, 1(1): 83–99.

Salih, R. (2003) *Gender in Transnationalism: Home, Longing and Belonging among Moroccan Migrant Women*, London: Routledge.

Salzbrunn, M. (2001) 'Transnationale Räume und multidimensionale Referenzsysteme westafrikanischer MigrantInnen in der Pariser Region', in A. Horstmann and G. Schlee (eds) *Integration durch Verschiedenheit*, Bielefeld: Transcript.

Sassen, S. (1991) *The Global City: New York, London, Tokyo*, Princeton: Princeton University Press.

——. (1994) *Cities in a World Economy*, Thousand Oaks: Pine Forge Press.

Schaaf, T. (1988) 'Ländliche Pioniersiedlungen in der Brong-Ahafo Region Ghanas unter besonderer Berücksichtigung des Kakaoanbaus', in R. Mäckel (ed.) *Natürliche Ressourcen und ländliche Entwicklungsprobleme der Tropen*, Stuttgart: Steiner.

Schildkrout, E. (1970) 'Strangers and Local Government in Kumasi', *Journal of Modern African Studies*, 8(2): 251–69.

——. (1974) 'Ethnicity and Generational Differences among Urban Immigrants in Ghana', in A. Cohen (ed.) *Urban Ethnicity*, London: Tavistock.

Schlee, G. (1989) *Identities on the Move: Clanship and Pastoralism in Northern Kenya*, Manchester: Manchester University Press.

——. (2001a) 'Einleitung', in G. Schlee and A. Horstmann (eds) *Integration durch Verschiedenheit: Lokale und globale Formen interkultureller Kommunikation*, Bielefeld: Transcript.

——. (2001b) *Globalisierung von unten: Strategien und mentale Landkarten von afrikanischen Migranten*, Online Available, HTTP: <http://www.eth.mpg.de/people/schlee/project01.pdf> (accessed 16 May 2004).

——. (2004a) 'Somalia und die Somali Diaspora vor und nach dem 11. September' in H. Lehmann (ed.) *Koexistenz und Konflikt von Religionen im vereinten Europa*, Göttingen: Wallstein.

——. (2004b) 'Taking Sides and Constructing Identities: Reflections on Conflict Theory', *Journal of the Royal Anthropological Institute*, 10(1): 135–56.

Schlee, G. and Werner, K. (1996) 'Inklusion und Exklusion: Die Dynamik von Grenzziehungen im Spannungsfeld von Markt, Staat und Ethnizität', in G. Schlee and K. Werner (eds) *Inklusion und Exklusion: Die Dynamik von Grenzziehungen im Spannungsfeld von Markt, Staat und Ethnizität*, Köln: Rüdiger Köppe.

Schmelz, A. (2009) *Die ghanaische Diaspora in Deutschland: Ihr Beitrag zur Entwicklung Ghanas*, Gesellschaft für technische Zusammenarbeit (GTZ), Eschborn.

Schmidt-Kallert, E. (1994) *Ghana: 44 Tabellen*, Gotha: Perthes.

Schröder, G. (1992) 'Eritreer in der BRD: Materialen zu einer Soziographie', *Arbeitsheft Berliner Institut für eine vergleichende Sozialforschung*, Berlin: Edition Parabolis.
Sennett, R. (2002) *Respekt im Zeitalter der Ungleichheit*, Berlin: Berlin-Verlag.
Sheffer, G. (1986) 'A New Field of Study: Modern Diasporas in International Politics', in G. Sheffer (ed.) *Modern Diasporas in International Politics*, New York: St. Martin's Press.
——. (1995) 'The Emergence of New Ethno-National Diasporas', *Migration*, 28: 5–28.
Shipton, P. (1997) 'Bitter Money: Forbidden Exchange in East Africa', in R. R. Grinker and C. B. Steiner (eds) *Perspectives on Africa: A Reader in Culture, History, and Representation*, Oxford: Blackwell.
Siebold, T. (1988) *Ghana 1957–1987: Entwicklung und Rückentwicklung, Verschuldung und IWF-Intervention*, Vol. 31, Hamburg: Institut für Afrikakunde.
Sieveking, N., Fauser, M. and Faist T. (2008) 'Gutachten zum entwicklungspolitischen Engagement der in NRW lebenden MigrantInnen afrikanischer Herkunft', *COMCAD Working Paper*, 38/08, Bielefeld: Center on Migration, Citizenship and Development, University of Bielefeld.
Sigrist, C. (1979 [1967]) *Regulierte Anarchie: Untersuchungen zum Fehlen und zur Entstehung politischer Herrschaft in segmentären Gesellschaften Afrikas*, Frankfurt am Main: Syndikat.
Simon, B. (2001) '"Damit sie alle eins seien": Afrikanische Pfingstler und Ökumene: Das Beispiel der Church of the Lord Aladura (Worldwide)', in C. Dahling-Sander, K. M. Funkschmidt and V. Mielke (eds) *Pfingstkirchen und Ökumene in Bewegung (Beiheft zur Ökumenischen Rundschau 71)*, Frankfurt am Main: Lembeck.
——. (2003) *Afrikanische Kirchen in Deutschland*, Frankfurt am Main: Lembeck.
——. (2005) 'Preaching as a Source of Religious Identity: African Initiated Churches in the Diaspora', in A. Adogame and C. Weißköppel (eds) *Religion in the Context of African Migration*, Bayreuth: Eckhard Breitinger.
Skinner, E. P. (1960) 'Labour Migration and its Relationship to Socio-Cultural Change in Mossi Society', *Africa: Journal of the International African Institute*, 30(4): 375–401.
——. (1965) 'Labor Migration among the Mossi of the Upper Volta', in H. Kuper (ed.) *Urbanization and Migration in West Africa*, Westport: Greenwood Press.
Smith, R. C. (1998) 'Transnational Localities: Community, Technology and the Politics of Membership within the Context of Mexico–USA Migration', in L. E. Guarnizo and M. P. Smith (eds) *Transnationalism from Below*, New Brunswick: Transactions Publishers.
——. (2002) 'Life Course: Generation and Social Location as Factors Shaping Second-Generation Transnational Social Life', in P. Levitt and M. C. Waters (eds) *The Changing Face of Home: The Transnational Lives of the Second Generation*, New York: Sage.
——. (2006) *Mexican New York: Transnational Lives of New Immigrants*, Berkeley: University of California Press.
Solomos, J. (1994 [1986]) 'Varieties of Marxist Conceptions of "Race", Class and the State: A Critical Analysis', in J. Rex and D. Mason (eds) *Theories of Race and Ethnic Relations*, Cambridge: Cambridge University Press.
Stehr, N. (1971) 'Statuskonsistenz', *Kölner Zeitschrift für Soziologie und Sozialpsychologie*, 23: 34–54.
Stichweh, R. (2000) *Die Weltgesellschaft: Soziologische Analysen*, Frankfurt am Main: Suhrkamp.

Stucki, B. R. (1992) 'The Long Voyage Home: Return Migration among Aging Cocoa Farmers of Ghana', *Journal of Cross-Cultural Gerontology*, 7(4): 363–78.
Swindell, K. (1990) 'International Labour Migration in Nigeria 1976–1986. Employment, Nationality and Ethnicity', *Migration*, 8: 135–55.
Tabatabai, H. (1986) 'Economic Stabilization and Structural Adjustment in Ghana, 1983–86', *Labour and Society*, 11(3): 395–414.
Taylor, C. (1994) 'The Politics of Recognition', in A. Gutmann and Taylor, C. (eds) *Multiculturalism: Examining the Politics of Recognition*, Princeton: Princeton University Press.
——. (2002) 'Modern Social Imaginaries', *Public Culture*, 14(1): 91–124.
Ter Haar, G. (1998a) 'The African Diaspora in the Netherlands', in P. B. Clarke (ed.) *New Trends and Developments in African Religions*, Westport: Greenwood Press.
——. (1998b) *Halfway to Paradise*, Cardiff: Cardiff Academic Press.
Theborn, G. (2001) 'Globalization and Inequality: Issues of Conceptualization and Explanation', *Soziale Welt*, 52(4): 449–76.
Thomas, P. (1998) 'Conspicuous Construction: Houses, Consumption and "Relocalization" in Manambondro, Southeast Madagascar', *Journal of the Royal Anthropological Institute*, 4(3): 425–46.
Thomas, R. G. (1973) 'Forced Labour in British West Africa: The Case of the Northern Territories of the Gold Coast 1906–1927', *Journal of African History*, 14(1): 79–103.
Thornton, R. J. (1988) 'The Rhetoric of Ethnographic Holism', *Cultural Anthropology*, 3(3): 285–303.
Timera, M. (1997) *Les Soninké en France: D'une Histoire à l'Autre*, Paris: Karthala.
Twum-Baah, K. A., Nabila, J. S. and Aryee, A. F. (1995a) *Migration Research Study in Ghana: Internal Migration*, Vol. I, Accra: Ghana Statistical Service.
——. (1995b) *Migration Research Study in Ghana: International Migration*, Vol. II, Accra: Ghana Statistical Service.
Ukah, A. (2005) 'Mobilities, Migration and Multiplication: The Expansion of the Religious Field of the Redeemed Christian Church of God (RCCG), Nigeria', in A. Adogame and C. Weißköppel (eds) *Religion in the Context of African Migration Studies*, Bayreuth: Eckhard Breitinger.
Van Hear, N. (2002) 'Sustaining Societies under Strain: Remittances as a Form of Transnational Exchange in Sri Lanka and Ghana', in N. Al-Ali and K. Koser (eds) *New Approaches to Migration? Transnational Communities and the Transformation of Home*, London: Routledge.
Veblen, T. (2004 [1899]) *The Theory of the Leisure Class*, London: Routledge/Thoemmes.
Velsen, J. V. (1960) 'Labor Migration as a Positive Factor in the Continuity of Tonga Tribal Society', *Economic Development and Cultural Change*, 8(3): 265–78.
Vertovec, S. (1997) 'Three Meanings of Diaspora: Exemplified among South Asian Religions', *Diaspora*, 6: 277–300.
——. (1999) 'Conceiving and Researching Transnationalism', *Ethnic and Racial Studies*, 22(2): 447–62.
——. (2004) 'Cheap Calls: The Social Glue of Migrants' Transnationalism', *Global Networks*, 4: 219–24.
——. (2007) 'Super-Diversity and its Implications', *Ethnic and Racial Studies*, 29(6): 1024–54.
——. (2009) *Transnationalism*, London: Routledge.
Vertovec, S. and Wessendorf, S. (2010) *The Multicultural Backlash: European Discourses, Policies and Practices*, London: Routledge.

Verwiebe, R. (2006) 'Transnationale Mobilität in Europa und soziale Ungleichheit', in M. Heidenreich (ed.) *Die Europäisierung sozialer Ungleichheit: Zur transnationalen Klassen- und Sozialstrukturanalyse*, Frankfurt am Main: Campus.
Vester, M., von Oertzen, P., Geiling, H., Hermann, T. and Müller, D. (2001) *Soziale Milieus im gesellschaftlichen Strukturwandel*, Frankfurt am Main: Suhrkamp.
Waldinger, R. and Fitzgerald, D. (2004) 'Transnationalism in Question', *American Journal of Sociology*, 109(5): 1177–95.
Wallerstein, I. M. (1960) 'Ethnicity and National Integration in West Africa', *Cahiers d'Études Africaines*, 1(3): 129–39.
——. (1965) 'Migration in West Africa: The Political Perspective', in H. Kuper (ed.) *Urbanization and Migration in West Africa*, Berkeley: University of California Press.
——. (1974) *The Modern World-System*, New York: Academic Press.
——. (1975) 'Class-Formation in the Capitalist World-Economy', *Politics and Society*, 5: 367–75.
Warner, W. L., Meeker, M. and Eells, K. (1949) *Social Class in America*, Chicago: Science Research Associates.
Watson, W. (1971 [1958]) *Tribal Cohesion in a Money Economy: A Study of the Mambwe People of Northern Rhodesia*, Manchester: Manchester University Press.
Weber, M. (1985 [1904]) 'Die "Objektivität" sozialwissenschaftlicher und sozialpolitischer Erkenntnis', in M. Weber (ed.) *Gesammelte Aufsätze zur Wissenschaftslehre*, Tübingen: J. C. B. Mohr.
Weiß, A. (2002) 'Raumrelationen als zentraler Aspekt weltweiter Ungleichheiten', *Mittelweg 36*, 11(2): 76–91.
——. (2005) 'The Transnationalization of Social Inequality: Conceptualizing Social Positions on a World Scale', *Current Sociology*, 53(4): 707–28.
——. (2006) 'Vergleichende Forschung zu hochqualifizierten Migrantinnen und Migranten: Lässt sich eine Klassenlage mittels qualitativer Interviews rekonstruieren', *Forum Qualitative Sozialforschung*, 7(3), Online Available, HTTP: <http://www.qualitative-research.net/fgs/> (accessed 9 January 2007).
Weißköppel, C. (2005a) 'Kreuz und Quer: Zur Theorie und Praxis der Multi-Sited-Ethnography', *Zeitschrift für Ethnologie*, 130: 45–68.
——. (2005b) 'Transnationale Qualitäten in Netzwerken von Sudanesen in Deutschland', *Nord-Süd aktuell*, 19(1): 34–44.
Werbner, R. P. (1984) 'The Manchester School in South-Central Africa', *Annual Review of Anthropology*, 13: 157–85.
Wiley, N. F. (1967) 'The Ethnic Mobility Trap and Stratification Theory', *Social Problems*, 15(2): 147–59.
Wilks, I. (1979) 'The Golden Stool and the Elephant Tail: An Essay on Wealth in Asante', in G. Dalton (ed.) *Research in Economic Anthropology*, Vol. 2, Greenwich: JAI Press.
——. (1993) *Forests of Gold: Essays on the Akan and the Kingdom of Asante*, Athens: Ohio University Press.
Wimmer, A. (2002) *Nationalist Exclusion and Ethnic Conflict: Shadows of Modernity*, Cambridge: Cambridge University Press.
——. (2008) 'Elementary Strategies of Ethnic Boundary Making', *Ethnic and Racial Studies*, 31: 1025–55.
Wimmer, A. and Glick Schiller, N. (2002a) 'Methodological Nationalism and Beyond. Nation-State Building, Migration and the Social Sciences', *Global Networks*, 2(4): 301–34.
——. (2002b) 'Methodological Nationalism and the Study of Migration', *Archives Européennes de Sociologie*, 43(2): 217–40.

de Witte, M. (2003) 'Money and Death: Funeral Business in Asante, Ghana', *Africa*, 73(4): 531–59.
Wolf, E. R. (1982) *Europe and the People without History*, Berkeley: University of California Press.
World Bank. (2001) *Global Economics Prospect 2002*, Washington: World Bank.
———. (2001) *World Development Report 2000/2001: Attacking Poverty*. New York: Oxford University Press.
Zarachariah, K. C. and Condé, J. (1981) *Migration in West Africa: Demographic Aspects*, New York: Oxford University Press.
Zimmerman, E. (1980) 'Statusinkonsistenz in der Bundesrepublik: Ein Stiefkind sozialstruktureller Analyse', *Kölner Zeitschrift für Soziologie und Sozialpsychologie*, 32(2): 325–38.
Zinn, D. L. (1994) 'The Senegalese Immigrants in Bari: What Happens When the African Peers Back', in B. Rina and A. Skotnes (eds) *Migration and Identity*, Oxford: Oxford University Press.

Index

Note: Page numbers ending in "f" refer to figures. Page numbers ending in "m" refer to maps. Page numbers ending in "t" refer to tables.

A
Abrefa, Lydia, 92
acculturation, 17–18, 21–22
Acheampong, I. K., 47–49
Adamu, Daniel, 88, 141–142
Adoma, Akosua, 115
African migrants: destinations of, 61–63, 72; ethnicity of, 86; to Europe, 7–10; reversing migration and, 51; studies of, 167n2. *See also* Ghanaians
African migration, 8, 22, 25. *See also* migration
Agyeman, Yaw, 90
Akuffo, Fred W. K., 49
Annan, Thomas, 88, 92–93
anti-immigration policies, 11, 63, 69–70, 163
anti-nationalism, 33
Antwi, Peggy, 80–81, 103–105, 138–139, 142–144
Antwi, Peter, 104–105
Antwi, Steve, 70
Appiah, John, 90
Appiah, Kwasi, 112
Appiah, Sebastian, 82
Asante, Yaw, 146, 148
Asantehene, 129–131
Asare, Yaw, 110–113, 111f, 119, 121
Asiedu, John, 84
Assimilation in American Life, 17
assimilation theory, 16–20, 167n5
assimilationism, 15–22
asylum law, 68–72, 80, 96
asylum seekers: crimes and, 88; political asylum and, 68–75; status of, 100, 135; students and, 80–84, 94, 138–139, 172n29
awunnyade system, 131

B
Badu, Samuel, 140–141
Barthes, Roland, 81
Beyond the Melting Pot, 18
bitter money, 162
Black Atlantic, The, 28
Boadum, Kofi, 102–103
Boakye, Ralph, 75–76, 93, 101, 121
Boateng, Daniel Kwame, 134, 137
Burgers: examples of, 13, 125; status inconsistency of, 135–140, 145, 149–152, 157–158; status paradox of, 125, 135–150, 152–154, 157–162, 165; stigma management of, 139–140, 145; transcontinental migration of, 13, 137, 146–152
Busia, Comfort, 93, 106
Busia, Kofi A., 46–47, 51–52

C
Canada: Ghanaians in, 54–55, 61; immigration to, 73, 115; minority in, 19
capitalism, 20, 25, 27
Catholics, 78–79, 84–85
Christianity, 78–79, 84–85
'circular migrants,' 24, 154
citizenship, 9–10, 21, 96
Class, Caste and Race, 20
class formation, 129–135
colonialism, 37–43
'conspicuous consumption,' 140–141
Cox, Oliver C., 20
cross-border relationships, 1, 32, 35, 95, 101
cultural assimilation, 17–18, 21–22

D
Daily Graphic, 149

Darko, Amma, 144–145
death duty, 131
decolonisation, 23, 52, 151
desert migration, 149
deterritorialisation, 30–31
detribalisation, 22–23
diaspora, 27–29, 96
disconnection, 44–51
Dormaa District: economic development of, 57; education and, 63–64; family unit in, 65–66; migration from, 55–67, 86–87, 151; population of, 56; resources of, 56–57
Dotse, Yao, 82, 138–139, 142, 144

E

East Germany, 70, 73–74, 91–94. *See also* Germany
economic globalisation, 3, 5, 13, 27, 97–99
economic inequalities, 3, 22, 97–99, 122, 131, 161
economic marginalisation, 3, 21, 90, 163
economic stratification, 140
economic transnationalisation, 97–101
education: class formation and, 129–135; formal education, 6–7, 13, 41–42, 57–64, 127–138, 157; labour markets and, 13, 41–42, 113, 151, 157; mass education, 66, 129, 151, 157; migration and, 73–74, 151, 156–157; promises of, 6–7; rural–urban migration and, 41; social inequality and, 157; wage levels and, 41–42
educational status of migrants, 64t. *See also* migrants
empirical transnationalism, 35–36
ethnic differences, 20–21, 28. *See also* ethnicity
ethnic enterprises, 77–78, 94
ethnic stratification, 21
ethnicity: cultural differences and, 17–22; identity and, 85–89; role of, 20–23
ethnography, 4, 8, 11–13, 31, 125
ethnoscape, 26–27, 29–31, 33–34
'everyday myth,' 81

F

Ferguson, James, 43–44, 133

Firi, Afua, 109
'foreigner in nation-state,' 15, 35
formal education, 6–7, 13, 41–42, 57–64, 127–138, 157. *See also* education
Frimpomaa, Akosua, 108

G

Garvey, Marcus, 44
gender: gender ratio, 71, 119; inequality and, 128; migration and, 41–42, 63, 71, 77, 83–84, 119; social status and, 127
German cities, 72t, 74–79, 74f, 76f
Germany, 7–10, 13, 69f, 70–79, 72t, 74f, 76f, 91–94
Ghana: changes in, 39–51; economic development of, 43–51; labour markets in, 60–64; map of, 56m; migrants and, 37–67; population of, 40–41; research region of, 56m; resources of, 39–40; taking over, 50; wage levels of, 41
Ghanaian diaspora, 96
Ghanaians: in Berlin, 70–79, 72t, 74f, 76f, 91–94; in Canada, 54–55, 61; destinations of, 62t; in East Germany, 70, 73–74, 91–94; in German cities, 70–79, 72t, 74f, 76f, 91–94; in Germany, 7–10, 13, 69–79, 69f, 72t, 91–94; identity and, 89–91; in Nigeria, 52–53; by place of residence, 59t; political system of, 9–10, 37–38; in United States, 54–55, 61; in West Germany, 70, 73, 91–94; in Western Europe, 7–10, 54–55, 54t
Glazer, N., 18
global capitalism, 25
global ethnoscape, 29–31
globalisation: debates on, 165; economic globalisation, 3, 5, 13, 27, 97–99; of migratory movements, 157; processes of, 2–8, 15, 26–33, 97–99, 161
Goffman, Erving, 139–140
Gold Coast: changes on, 39–43; labour markets on, 132; labour migration and, 37–43; resources of, 38–40. *See also* Ghana
Gordon, Milton, 17–18

H

Hayford, Casely, 44

Henry, Pastor, 85
Hoffmann-Nowotny, H.-J., 21, 159

I
identity: asylum seekers and, 80–84; configurations of, 79–94; debates on, 157–158; ethnicity and, 85–89; social identity, 79–94, 158
immigrants: assimilation of, 15–22; destinations of, 61–63, 71–72; localisation of, 94; transmigrants and, 154–155
impression management, 139–140
income sources, 98–100, 105, 144, 148
integration process: conceptualisation of, 1; versus conflict, 21; labour markets and, 38, 122, 154; nationalism and, 34–35; theory of, 2–6, 15–17, 21–23, 27, 163–166

K
kalabule system, 48–50, 57
Kennedy, R. J., 18
kinship diagrams, 107f, 111f, 114f
kinship reciprocity, 13, 67, 101–105, 109–123, 165
kinship relationships: Afua Konadu, 113–117, 114f; family unit in, 101–102; Kojo Yeboah, 86–87, 105–110, 107f, 119, 121, 135; obligations in, 13, 66, 101–117, 119, 162; support in, 105–123; transnationalisation of, 101–121; Yaw Asare, 110–113, 111f, 119, 121
Konadu, Afua, 113–117, 114f
Kufuor, J. A., 9, 51, 84, 96
Kumi, Yaw, 105
Kyeremaa, Abenaa, 105
Kyeremeh, Kwame, 112–113

L
labour markets: access to, 5; competition of, 80, 91; education and, 13, 41–42, 113, 151, 157, 160; in Germany, 137; in Ghana, 60–64; on Gold Coast, 132; new hourglass labour market, 122; status of, 3, 38, 71, 99, 106, 149–151, 165
labour migrants: class of, 2–5, 58, 160; destinations for, 9–10, 135; status of, 2–6, 13, 124–154; success of, 3, 82, 106, 135; type of, 13, 41, 125
labour migration, 8–9, 37–43, 51, 73, 90, 153–157
labour recruitment, 68–69
liberalism, 18–19, 46, 50
Liman, Hilla, 49
localisation process, 68–94, 155
Luhmann, Niklas, 14, 26–27, 35
Lumba Brothers, 146–148

M
marginalisation, 3, 21–22, 90–91, 161, 163
Marxist views, 20, 47, 97, 126
mass education, 66, 129, 151, 157
mass migration, 10, 30–32, 38, 42, 51–55, 96. See also migration
melting pot, 16–18
Mends, Rita, 153–154
Mensah, Minister, 47
meritocratic triad, 127, 129, 133–134, 149, 159–160
methodological nationalism, 1, 4, 28, 33–35, 128, 159, 163
methodological transnationalism, 2, 13, 35–36, 164–166, 169n22
Meyer, John, 128–129
migrant investments, 3, 10, 44–45, 65, 100–101, 112, 117
migrant remittances, 3, 9–10, 24–25, 64–65, 95–120, 160, 165
migrants: circular migrants, 24, 154; cross-border relationships of, 1, 32, 35, 95, 101; cultural difference of, 17–22; destinations of, 61–63, 62t; educational status of, 64t; Ghana and, 37–67; transmigrants, 154–155, 160–161. See also African migrants; Ghanaians
migration: African migration, 8, 22, 25; danger of, 149; debates on, 22, 80, 163–164; disconnection from, 44–51; from Dormaa District, 55–67, 86–87, 151; education and, 73–74, 151, 156–157; to Europe, 7–10; financing, 65–66; mass migration, 10, 30–32, 38, 42, 51–55, 96; nation-state and, 15–22, 25–26; patterns of, 9, 13, 55, 65, 151–152, 171n11; postcolonial

migration, 43–54; restrictive measures against, 63, 68–69; reversing, 51–54; society and, 14–36; status paradox of, 2–6, 13, 124–154, 163; transcontinental migration, 7, 13, 54–58, 63–65, 119, 137, 146–152, 155–157
migration studies, 1–6, 14–27, 31–36, 125, 154, 165–166
migratory patterns, 9, 13, 55, 65, 151–152, 171n11
Miles, Robert, 20–21
Mill, J. E. Atta, 51
modern self, 157–159
'modern society,' 15, 18–27, 124, 158, 168n12
modernity: benefits of, 7, 15; expectations of, 133; imaginaries of, 6–7, 13, 29, 43, 151, 157; promises of, 66
Modernity at Large, 30
Moynihan, D. P., 18
multiculturalism, 1, 18–22, 168n8
mythicising narrative, 81, 138

N
nationalism: expulsions and, 52; ideology of, 20, 28; methodological nationalism, 1, 4, 33–35, 128, 159, 163
nation-state: foreigner in, 15, 35; migrant in, 13; migration and, 15–22, 25–26; social fields and, 95–101; society and, 14–15; transnationalism and, 13, 33, 95–123
naturalisation practices, 75, 170n15
Nkrumah, Kwame, 44–47, 51–52, 73

O
Obetsebi-Lamptey, Minister, 96
Oppong, Belinda, 76
Oppong, Henry, 81–82
Our Racial Frontier on the Pacific, 16
Owusu, A. K., 145

P
paradox of migration, 2–6, 13, 124–154, 163
Park, Robert E., 15, 16
patterns of migration, 9, 13, 55, 65, 151–152, 171n11
Pentecostalists, 78–79, 84–85

political asylum, 68–71, 96
political offices, 130, 162
political systems, 9–10
Politics of Recognition, The, 18
postcolonial migration, 43–54
Prempreh, Agyeman, 131
Presbyterians, 78–79

R
race relation circle, 15–16, 167n4
racialisation, 3, 5, 20–22, 89–91, 137, 163, 171n28
Rawlings, J. J., 49–50, 96
reciprocity within families, 13, 67, 101–105, 109–123, 165
religions, 78–79, 84–85
research methods, 11–12
research region, 56m, 59t
resource management, 3, 160, 163
reversing migration, 51–54
Rousseau, Jean-Jacques, 44
rural–urban migration: circular migrant and, 154; context of, 43; destinations for, 58–59; education and, 41; labour migration and, 40; reversing migration, 51; society and, 22–26; transcontinental migration and, 155–157

S
Sarpong, Dr., 144
schools, 59, 131–132, 173n3
Seneadza, Jacob, 141
Serwaa, Yaa, 90, 92
Shagari, Alhaji Shehu, 53
simultaneous incorporation, 1, 5, 33, 122, 165
social fields: kinship relationships and, 117–122; migration and, 26–27, 31–35; nation-states and, 95–101; social status and, 125, 152
social identity, 79–94, 158
social inequality: debates on, 161, 163; education and, 157; increase of, 148; perspectives on, 4–5, 97–98, 124, 128, 163; research on, 165; transnationalisation of, 97–98, 124, 159–162
social sciences, 125–129
social status: explanation of, 125; imaginary of, 125–129, 134–135, 140, 148–149, 151, 154, 158, 162; modern self and, 157–159; in social sciences, 125–129

social stratification, 2, 21, 124–126, 131–132, 140
society: defining, 14; imaginaries of, 15, 25, 34, 124; importance of, 14; migration and, 14–36; modern society, 15, 18–27, 124, 158, 168n12; nation-state and, 14–15; rural–urban migration and, 22–26; traditional society, 15, 22–25. *See also* world society
sociocultural impact, 3, 10–12
socio-economic conditions, 6, 22, 51, 122–125, 134, 137
socio-economic marginalisation, 21, 90
socio-economic status, 90, 99, 140–142
socio-economic stratification, 140
socio-spatial contexts, 33, 36, 79–94, 166
status consistency, 126–128, 150, 157
status inconsistency: of *Burgers*, 135–140, 145, 149–152, 157–158; experiences of, 7, 60, 64–66, 126–128, 135–140, 145, 149–152; forms of, 3, 13, 157
status paradox: of *Burgers*, 125, 135–150, 152–154, 157–162, 165; limits of, 152–154; of migration, 2–6, 13, 124–154, 163
status production, 4, 125, 160, 165
status theory, 2–6
stigma management, 139–140, 145, 156
structural assimilation, 17–18
supertribalisation, 23

T
Taylor, Charles, 18–19, 126
territorialisation, 29–31
'traditional society,' 15, 22–25
traditionalists, 84–85
transcontinental migration: *Burgers* and, 13, 137, 146–152; from Dormaa District, 61–65, 151; education and, 7, 63–64; financing, 65–66; gender and, 119; rural–urban migration and, 155–157; in Western Europe, 54–55. *See also* migration

transmigrants: circular migrants and, 154; immigrants and, 154–155; role of, 160–161
transnational migration studies, 1–27, 31–36, 125, 154, 165–166
transnational social fields: kinship relationships and, 117–122; migration and, 26–27, 31–35; nation-states and, 95–101; social status and, 125, 152
transnationalisation: debates on, 165; economics of, 97–101; of kinship relationships, 101–121; methodological transnationalism, 35–36; nation-state and, 13, 33, 95–123; processes of, 13, 95–123; of social inequality, 97–98, 124, 159–162
transnationalism: empirical transnationalism, 35–36; methodological transnationalism, 2, 13, 35–36, 164–166, 169n22; nation-state and, 33; politics of, 162–164
tribalism, 23–24
'tribesman in the city,' 13, 15, 22, 25, 35
Turkish migrants, 89–91, 94

U
United States: Ghanaians in, 54–55, 61; immigration to, 15–16, 18, 73

W
West Africa, 37–43. *See also* Ghana
West Germany, 68, 70, 73, 91–94. *See also* Germany
Western Europe, 7–10, 54–55, 54t
world society: idea of, 3; migrant in, 13; migration and, 26–35; resource management in, 3, 160, 165. *See also* society

Y
Yeboah, Kojo, 86–87, 105–110, 107f, 119, 121, 135
Yeboah, Kwabena, 106, 120, 135–137